InfoTech Governance, Policy, Ethics & Law

1st Edition

David Tuffley PhD

To my beloved Nation of Four

Concordia Domi – Foris Pax

Effective IT governance ensures strategic alignment,
risk mitigation, and optimal resource utilization
for technological advancement.
- David Tuffley

Published 2023 by Altiora Publications

AltioraPublications.com/

ISBN: 9798858323341

About the Author

David Tuffley is a Senior Lecturer in the School of ICT at Griffith University in Australia. The content of this book is the product of research performed while an employee of Griffith University, principally in relation to the *IT Governance, Policy, Ethics and Law* course.

CONTENTS

Contents

INTRODUCTION

Welcome to this textbook on *IT Governance, Policy, Ethics and Law*. It is the culmination of 30 years of practical experience and academic research to create a practical guide for IT professionals that is based on academic methods.

The text is organised into nine thematically linked chapters:

Chapter 1 explores the different IT governance frameworks that are used to align IT strategy with business goals, manage IT risks and resources, and ensure IT compliance and accountability. We compare the main models, such as COBIT, ITIL, ISO 27000, and NIST.

Chapter 2 focuses on cybersecurity and data protection, two of the most critical challenges for IT today. We learn about the threats and vulnerabilities that affect IT systems and data, and the best practices and standards to prevent and respond to them. We will also discuss the legal and ethical issues related to data privacy and security, such as GDPR, HIPAA, and CCPA.

Chapter 3 examines the benefits and challenges of cloud computing and outsourcing, two of the most popular ways to deliver IT services in the modern world. We will look to the different types of cloud services and models, such as SaaS, PaaS, IaaS, public, private, and hybrid clouds. We also analyse the risks and opportunities of outsourcing IT functions to third parties, such as vendors, contractors, or consultants.

Chapter 4 investigates the topic of digital ethics and responsible AI, two of the most rapidly emerging and controversial areas of IT. We explore the ethical principles and dilemmas that arise from the use of digital technologies and artificial intelligence in various domains, such as health care, education, business, or entertainment. We will also learn about the frameworks and guidelines that aim to ensure that AI is fair, transparent, accountable, and human-centric.

Chapter 5 covers the topic of intellectual property and copyright, two of the most important legal aspects of IT. We learn about the different types of intellectual property rights that apply to IT products and services, such as patents, trademarks, trade secrets, and copyrights. We will also understand the implications and challenges of protecting and enforcing these rights in the digital age.

Chapter 6 discusses e-gov and digital transformation, two of the most significant trends in IT today. We see how governments use IT to improve their efficiency, effectiveness, transparency, and citizen engagement. We will also examine how organizations use IT to transform their processes, products, services, and culture.

Chapter 7 looks at the impact of IT on society, both positive and negative. We evaluate how IT affects various aspects of social life, such as communication, education, work, leisure, culture, democracy, inequality, environment, health, and security. We will also reflect on our own roles and responsibilities as IT users and creators.

Chapter 8 addresses employee IT usage and policies, two of the most relevant issues for IT managers and workers. We learn about the rights and obligations of employees regarding their use of IT resources and devices in the workplace. We will also review the best practices and policies to regulate employee IT behaviour, such as acceptable use policies, social media policies, and BYOD policies.

Chapter 9 examines IoT security and privacy, two urgent problems for IT governance in the era of smart devices and connected things.

We will understand the architecture and applications of IoT systems, such as smart homes, smart cities, smart health, and smart agriculture.

We will also identify the risks and challenges of securing and protecting the data and devices that make up IoT networks.

I trust you will find this this book useful for your personal and professional development.

David Tuffley

CHAPTER 1:
IT GOVERNANCE FRAMEWORKS

CHAPTER SUMMARY

IT governance frameworks are the rules and guidelines that help organizations manage their IT resources and processes effectively. They help align IT goals with business objectives, ensure compliance with laws and regulations, and protect data from unauthorized access or loss. Some examples of IT governance frameworks are COBIT, ITIL, ISO 27001, and NIST.

IT compliance and regulatory standards are the requirements that organizations have to follow to meet the expectations of external stakeholders, such as customers, auditors, or government agencies. They help ensure quality, security, privacy, and accountability of IT services and products. Some examples of IT compliance and regulatory standards are GDPR, HIPAA, PCI DSS, and SOX.

Data retention and deletion are the policies and practices that determine how long and where organizations store their data, and when and how they dispose of it. They help balance the needs of data availability, performance, cost, and risk. Some examples of data retention and deletion factors are legal obligations, business value, storage capacity, and backup frequency.

In this chapter workshop, you will learn how to apply IT governance frameworks to your organization, how to comply with IT standards and regulations, and how to design and implement data retention and deletion policies. You will also learn how to assess the benefits and challenges of IT governance, compliance, and data management in different scenarios.

1.1. IT GOVERNANCE FRAMEWORKS

There are many IT governance frameworks available, each with its own strengths, weaknesses, and applicability. Some of the most common IT governance frameworks are:

- **COBIT**. This is a comprehensive framework that covers 37 IT processes, each with detailed objectives, practices, inputs, outputs, activities, and metrics. COBIT helps organizations achieve effective IT governance and management by linking IT goals to business goals, ensuring IT resources are optimized, and managing IT risks and performance.

- **AS8015-2005**. This is a simple and concise framework developed in Australia that defines six principles for good IT governance: establish clearly understood responsibilities for IT; plan IT to best support the organization; acquire IT validly; ensure that IT performs well; ensure that IT conforms with formal rules; and respect human factors in IT.

- **ISO/IEC 38500**. This is an international standard that provides high-level guidance on the principles, roles, and responsibilities for effective IT governance. ISO/IEC 38500 helps organizations evaluate, direct, and monitor their use of IT to achieve their business objectives and fulfill their legal and ethical obligations.

- **ITIL**. This is a widely adopted framework that focuses on the delivery and management of quality IT services that meet the needs and expectations of customers and stakeholders. ITIL covers the entire service lifecycle from strategy to design, transition, operation, and improvement. ITIL helps organizations improve their service efficiency, effectiveness, reliability, and value.

Choosing the right IT governance framework depends on various factors such as the size, complexity, culture, industry, and maturity of the organization. It is also possible to adopt a hybrid or customized approach that combines elements from different frameworks to suit the specific needs and context of the organization.

IT governance frameworks are not static or one-size-fits-all solutions. They require regular review and adaptation to keep up with the changing business environment and technology landscape. They also require strong leadership commitment, stakeholder involvement, clear communication, and continuous improvement to ensure successful implementation and outcomes.

COBIT ORCHESTRATING CONTROL & ASSURANCE

COBIT is a comprehensive framework for the governance and management of enterprise information and technology (I&T). It helps organizations align their I&T goals with their business objectives, optimize their I&T resources and processes, and ensure effective control and assurance over their I&T activities.

COBIT consists of seven enablers: principles, policies and frameworks; processes; organizational structures; culture, ethics and behaviour; information; services, infrastructure and applications; and people, skills and competencies.

COBIT & IT GOVERNANCE FRAMEWORKS

IT governance frameworks are essential for ensuring that I&T supports the achievement of enterprise goals, delivers value to stakeholders, manages risks and complies with external requirements.

COBIT provides a holistic and integrated approach to IT governance that covers all aspects of I&T from strategy to operations.

COBIT also provides a common language and terminology for I&T governance that can be understood by all stakeholders, including business executives, IT managers, auditors and regulators.

HOW COBIT CONTROLS AND ASSURES

One of the key benefits of COBIT is that it enables organizations to establish and maintain a system of internal control and assurance over their I&T activities.

COBIT defines control as "the means of managing risk to ensure that enterprise objectives will be achieved" and assurance as "the provision of objective evidence that the design and operation of the system of internal control meets the agreed-upon requirements".

COBIT provides guidance on how to design, implement, monitor, evaluate and improve the system of internal control and assurance using the following processes:

MEA01: Managed Performance and Conformance Monitoring.

This process collects, validates, and evaluates enterprise and alignment goals and metrics, monitors that processes and practices are performing against agreed performance and conformance goals and metrics, provides systematic and timely reporting, and provides transparency of performance and conformance and drives achievement of goals.

MEA02: Managed System of Internal Control.

This process continuously monitors and evaluates the control environment, including self-assessments and self-awareness, enables management to identify control deficiencies and inefficiencies and to initiate improvement actions, plans, organizes and maintains standards for internal control assessment and process control effectiveness, obtains transparency for key stakeholders on the adequacy of the system of internal controls.

MEA03: Managed Compliance with External Requirements

This process evaluates that I&T processes and I&T-supported business processes are compliant with laws, regulations and contractual requirements, obtains assurance that the requirements have been identified and complied with; integrates IT compliance with overall enterprise compliance, ensures that the enterprise is compliant with all applicable external requirements.

MEA04: Managed Assurance

This process plans, scopes and executes assurance initiatives to comply with internal requirements, laws, regulations and strategic objectives, enables management to deliver adequate and sustainable assurance in the enterprise by performing independent assurance reviews and activities, enables the organization to design and develop efficient and effective assurance initiatives.

ITIL ELEVATING SERVICE MANAGEMENT

ITIL is a library of best practices used in IT Service Management (ITSM). ITSM is the process of designing, delivering, managing and improving IT services that meet the needs and expectations of customers and stakeholders. ITSM covers a wide range of activities, such as incident management, change management, problem management, service level management, service design, service transition, service operation and continual service improvement.

ITIL provides a comprehensive and consistent framework for ITSM that is aligned with business goals and customer value. ITIL helps organizations to:

- Improve customer satisfaction by delivering reliable and high-quality IT services.
- Enhance IT services delivered using best practice procedures.
- Reduce costs and risks by optimizing the use of resources and avoiding service disruptions.
- Increase agility and innovation by enabling faster and more effective changes to IT services.

- Support digital transformation by integrating ITSM with other frameworks such as DevOps, Agile and SRE.

ELEVATING SERVICE MANAGEMENT WITH ITIL

To elevate service management with ITIL, you need to adopt a holistic and value-driven approach that encompasses the entire service lifecycle. You need to understand the needs and expectations of your customers and stakeholders, and design, deliver, manage, and improve IT services that create value for them. You need to establish clear and measurable service levels, and ensure that they are properly assessed, monitored and managed against these targets.

Collaborate with other teams and departments across the organization, and leverage the capabilities of people, processes, information and technology. You need to foster a culture of continual improvement that seeks feedback, learns from mistakes, identifies opportunities and implements changes.

Here are some practical steps you can take to elevate service management with ITIL:

Assess the current state of your ITSM practices and identify gaps and areas for improvement.

Define a vision and strategy for your ITSM that aligns with your organizational goals and customer value propositions.

Implement the ITIL Service Value System (SVS) that consists of five components: *guiding principles, governance, service value chain, practices, and continual improvement*.

Use the SVS to plan, engage, design, transition, obtain/build, deliver/support and improve your IT services.

Apply the seven guiding principles of ITIL to guide your decisions and actions: focus on value, start where you are, progress iteratively with feedback, collaborate and promote visibility, think and work holistically, keep it simple and practical, optimize and automate.

Establish a Service Management Office (SMO) that provides a central point for consistency and governance in organizational best practice.

Monitor and measure your service performance using relevant metrics and indicators.

Report and communicate your service achievements and challenges to your customers and stakeholders.

Review and evaluate your service outcomes and feedback using various methods such as surveys, audits, reviews, benchmarks etc.

Identify and prioritize improvement initiatives using techniques such as SWOT analysis, gap analysis, root cause analysis etc.

Implement improvement actions using methods such as PDCA cycle (plan-do-check-act), CSI approach (what is the vision? where are we now? where do we want to be? how do we get there? did we get there? how do we keep the momentum going?) etc.

ISO/IEC 38500 THE GOVERNING STANDARD

Advice on ISO/IEC 38500 The Governing Standard

ISO/IEC 38500 is an international standard for the corporate governance of information technology (IT), and provides guidance to those advising, informing or assisting directors on the effective and acceptable use of IT within the organization. It is based on six principles and a model for good governance of IT.

PRINCIPLES

The six principles of ISO/IEC 38500 are:

Responsibility. Assigning roles and responsibilities for the use of IT.

Strategy. Aligning the use of IT with the organizational objectives.

Acquisition. Procuring IT solutions and services to meet the organizational needs.

Performance. Measuring and evaluating the contribution of IT to the organization

Conformance. Ensuring compliance with laws, regulations, and policies.

Human Behaviour. Considering the human aspects of IT use.

MODEL

The model of ISO/IEC 38500 consists of three main elements:

Governing Body. The individual or group of individuals responsible and accountable for the performance and conformance of the organization

Evaluation. The process of assessing the current and future use of IT

Direction. The process of deciding on the objectives and policies for the use of IT

Monitoring. The process of verifying that the use of IT meets the objectives and policies

The governing body should evaluate, direct, and monitor the use of IT in a continuous cycle, considering the six principles and the stakeholders' interests.

BENEFITS

The benefits of applying ISO/IEC 38500 include:

- Improving the alignment of IT with the organizational strategy.
- Enhancing the delivery of value from IT investments.
- Reducing risks related to IT projects and operations.
- Increasing transparency and accountability for IT decisions and outcomes.
- Fostering a culture of trust and collaboration among IT stakeholders.
- Supporting continuous improvement and innovation in IT.

UNIFYING BUSINESS & TECHNOLOGY

IT governance is a process that enables the IT staff to better manage risk and operate at its most efficient to the benefit of the organization. It is part of the corporate governance, which is a collection of processes that are designed to keep the entire corporation effective and efficient.

IT governance aims to:

- Ensure business value is generated by information and technology.
- Oversee the performance of IT managers.
- Assess risks associated with the IT department and mitigate them as needed.

THE SIGNIFICANCE OF IT GOVERNANCE

IT governance is important because it helps the organization to align its IT priorities, decisions and investments with its strategic goals and stakeholder requirements. It also helps the organization to comply with legal, contractual and policy obligations that impact IT. Furthermore, it supports the continuous improvement and optimization of IT services and resources.

IMPLEMENTING IT GOVERNANCE

There are different frameworks and standards that can guide the implementation of IT governance in an organization. Some of the most common ones are:

- **COBIT**. This is a comprehensive framework that covers 37 IT processes, with each process having a set of objectives, inputs, outputs, activities, roles, and responsibilities. It also provides maturity models, performance indicators and best practices for each process.
- **AS8015-2005**. This is a technical standard developed in Australia that defines six principles for good IT governance: establish clearly understood responsibilities for IT; plan IT to best support the organization; acquire IT validly; ensure that IT performs well, whenever required; ensure IT conforms with formal rules; ensure respect for human factors.
- **ISO/IEC 38500**. This is an international standard that provides a high-level framework for effective governance of IT. It defines six principles for good IT governance: responsibility; strategy; acquisition; performance; conformance; human behaviour.

These frameworks and standards can be adapted to suit the specific needs and context of each organization. However, some common steps for implementing IT governance are:

- Define the scope and objectives of IT governance.
- Establish the roles and responsibilities of IT governance stakeholders.
- Identify the key IT processes and activities that need to be governed.
- Define the policies, procedures, guidelines, and standards that govern IT.
- Establish the mechanisms and tools for monitoring, reporting, and evaluating IT performance and compliance.
- Implement continuous improvement initiatives to enhance IT value and maturity.

GUIDELINES FOR DECISION-MAKING

Guidelines for decision-making in IT governance frameworks, based on research and best practice:

- What is IT governance and why is it important?
- What are the key principles of IT governance?
- What are the common IT governance frameworks and how do they support decision-making?
- How to define the roles and responsibilities of decision-makers in IT governance?
- How to ensure transparency, accountability, and compliance in IT governance decisions?

WHAT IS IT GOVERNANCE AND WHY IS IT IMPORTANT?

IT governance is the process of defining the structures and processes that enable the organization to effectively oversee, direct and control its IT resources and processes. It involves evaluating stakeholder requirements, setting direction, prioritizing investments, monitoring performance, and ensuring compliance with legal, contractual and policy requirements that impact IT.

IT governance is important because it helps the organization to:

- Achieve its strategic goals and objectives by aligning IT with the business needs and expectations.
- Optimize the value of IT by delivering benefits to the organization and its stakeholders.
- Manage the risks associated with IT by identifying, assessing, and mitigating them.
- Enhance the performance of IT by improving the quality, efficiency, and effectiveness of IT services.
- Foster a culture of continuous improvement by learning from feedback and best practices.

WHAT ARE THE MAIN IT GOVERNANCE FRAMEWORKS?

There are many IT governance frameworks available in the world, but some of the most popular ones are:

COBIT. This is by far the most popular framework out there. It gives staff a reference of 37 IT processes, with each process having a set of objectives that can be measured using key performance indicators (KPIs).

AS8015-2005. A technical standard developed in Australia and published in 2005, this framework is a 12-page framework that defines six principles for good corporate governance of information technology.

ISO/IEC 38500. An international standard published in 2008, this framework provides a set of six principles for governing bodies to use when evaluating, directing and monitoring the use of information technology within their organizations.

ITIL. A widely adopted framework for managing IT service delivery, this framework defines a set of best practices for designing, implementing, operating and improving IT services that meet customer needs.

Each framework has its own strengths and weaknesses, depending on the context and needs of each organization. Therefore, it is important to select a framework that suits the organization's culture, size, complexity, maturity and objectives.

DEFINING ROLES & RESPONSIBILITIES

One of the key aspects of effective decision-making in IT governance is to clearly define who has the authority to make decisions, who is accountable for those decisions, who needs to be consulted or informed about those decisions, and who is responsible for implementing those decisions.

A common tool for defining the roles and responsibilities of decision-makers in IT governance is the RACI matrix, which stands for Responsible, Accountable, Consulted and Informed. A RACI matrix is a table that maps each IT governance process or activity to the roles or stakeholders involved in that process or activity, and assigns one of the following labels to each role or stakeholder:

Responsible. The role or stakeholder who performs the work or task

Accountable. The role or stakeholder who has the ultimate authority and accountability for the outcome or result

Consulted. The role or stakeholder who provides input or feedback to the decision or action

Informed. The role or stakeholder who needs to be notified or updated about the decision or action

A RACI matrix helps to avoid confusion, duplication, conflict and gaps in IT governance decision-making by clarifying the expectations and responsibilities of each role or stakeholder.

ENSURING COMPLIANCE IN IT GOVERNANCE DECISIONS?

Another key aspect of effective decision-making in IT governance is to ensure that the decisions are transparent, accountable and compliant with the relevant legal, contractual and policy requirements that impact IT.

Some of the ways to ensure transparency, accountability and compliance in IT governance decisions are:

- Documenting and communicating the IT governance framework, including the principles, rules, processes, roles, responsibilities and authorities that guide decision-making.
- Establishing and maintaining a repository of IT governance decisions, including the rationale, criteria, evidence, alternatives and impacts of each decision.
- Implementing and monitoring a set of KPIs and metrics that measure the performance and outcomes of IT governance decisions.
- Conducting regular audits and reviews of IT governance decisions to verify their validity, effectiveness and efficiency.
- Reporting and disclosing IT governance decisions to relevant stakeholders, such as senior management, board of directors, regulators, customers and suppliers
- Establishing and enforcing a mechanism for escalating, resolving and learning from issues, disputes and complaints related to IT governance decisions.

By following these steps, organizations can enhance the trust, confidence and satisfaction of their stakeholders regarding their IT governance decisions.

RISK MANAGEMENT & MITIGATION

Risk management and mitigation is the process of identifying, analysing, evaluating, and treating the potential threats and vulnerabilities that could affect the performance, security, reliability, and compliance of IT systems and processes. It also involves monitoring and reviewing the risk situation and taking corrective actions as needed.

Risk management and mitigation is important because it helps organizations to:

- Protect their assets, data, reputation, and stakeholders from harm or loss.
- Ensure the continuity and availability of their IT services and operations.
- Achieve their strategic objectives and deliver value to their customers.
- Comply with legal, regulatory, contractual, and ethical obligations.
- Enhance their decision-making and innovation capabilities.
- Reduce costs and optimize resources.

Implementing Risk Management & Mitigation?

To implement a successful risk management and mitigation strategy, organizations should follow these steps:

- Establish a risk management framework that defines the scope, objectives, roles, responsibilities, policies, procedures, tools, and metrics for managing and mitigating risks.
- Conduct a risk assessment that identifies and prioritizes the sources and impacts of risks for each IT system and process.
- Develop a risk treatment plan that specifies the actions, resources, timelines, and owners for reducing or eliminating the risks or their consequences.
- Implement the risk treatment plan by executing the actions and allocating the resources as planned.
- Monitor and review the risk situation by measuring the performance, effectiveness, and efficiency of the risk treatment actions and reporting the results and progress.
- Update the risk management framework, assessment, treatment plan, and actions as needed to reflect changes in the internal or external environment or feedback from stakeholders.

ACCOUNTABILITY & TRANSPARENCY

IT governance frameworks are sets of principles, structures and processes that guide and oversee the effective and efficient use of IT resources and services in an organization. They help align IT strategies and investments with the organization's goals and objectives, ensure compliance with legal and regulatory requirements, manage risks and optimize performance and value.

Accountability and transparency are two key elements of good IT governance. Accountability means that IT decision-makers and stakeholders are responsible for the outcomes and impacts of their actions and choices. Transparency means that IT decisions, processes and performance are clear, understandable and accessible to all relevant parties.

Cultivating accountability and transparency in IT governance frameworks can bring many benefits to an organization, such as:

- Enhancing trust and collaboration among IT staff, business units, senior management and external partners
- Improving communication and feedback loops to ensure alignment and responsiveness
- Increasing stakeholder engagement and satisfaction with IT services and solutions
- Reducing complexity, duplication and waste of IT resources
- Strengthening risk management and compliance capabilities
- Fostering a culture of continuous improvement and innovation

CULTIVATING ACCOUNTABILITY & TRANSPARENCY

Based on research and best practice, here are some practical steps to cultivate accountability and transparency in IT governance frameworks:

- **Define clear roles, responsibilities and authorities** for IT governance structures, such as committees, boards, advisory groups and working groups. Ensure that they have adequate representation, diversity, expertise and empowerment to make informed decisions.
- **Establish clear objectives, priorities and criteria** for IT governance decisions, such as strategy, planning, investment, policy, risk and compliance. Ensure that they are aligned with the organization's vision, mission and values.
- **Implement regular reporting and monitoring mechanisms** to track and measure the performance and outcomes of IT governance decisions. Use relevant indicators, metrics and benchmarks to assess the efficiency, effectiveness, quality and value of IT services and solutions.
- **Communicate openly and proactively** with all IT governance stakeholders, such as staff, customers, suppliers, regulators

and auditors. Use appropriate channels, formats and languages to share information, solicit feedback, address issues and celebrate successes.

- **Encourage a learning-oriented culture** that supports experimentation, evaluation, adaptation and improvement of IT governance processes and practices. Seek external input, benchmarking and best practices to identify gaps, opportunities and areas for improvement.

ETHICAL & LEGAL COMPLIANCE

An IT governance framework is a set of policies, processes, roles and responsibilities that guide the creation, use and management of information technology (IT) assets and services in an organisation. It helps to ensure that IT supports the organisation's strategy, objectives and performance, while also managing the risks, costs and benefits of IT.

An IT governance framework should be aligned with the organisation's overall governance framework, which provides a holistic overview of how the organisation creates and manages its enterprise-wide information assets (records, information and data) .

Ethical and legal compliance is important for several reasons:

- It helps to build trust and reputation among stakeholders, which can enhance customer loyalty, employee engagement, partner collaboration and social responsibility.
- It helps to avoid or minimise legal liabilities, fines, sanctions or lawsuits that can result from violating laws, regulations or standards that apply to the organisation's IT activities.
- It helps to prevent or mitigate ethical issues or dilemmas that can arise from the use or misuse of IT, such as privacy breaches, data misuse, cyberattacks, bias or discrimination.
- It helps to foster a culture of ethics and integrity in the organisation, which can encourage innovation, creativity and excellence in IT.

ACHIEVING ETHICAL & LEGAL COMPLIANCE

Some general steps that can be followed are:

Identify and understand the legal, regulatory and ethical requirements that apply to the organisation's IT activities. These may include laws and regulations related to data protection, cybersecurity, intellectual property, consumer rights, human rights or environmental protection. They may also include ethical principles or codes of conduct that reflect the organisation's values or industry standards.

Assess and document the current state of compliance in the organisation's IT governance framework. This may involve conducting audits, reviews or surveys to evaluate how well the organisation's IT policies, processes and practices comply with the relevant requirements. It may also involve identifying any gaps, weaknesses or risks that need to be addressed.

Develop and implement a plan to improve compliance in the organisation's IT governance framework. This may involve updating or creating new IT policies, processes or practices that align with the relevant requirements. It may also involve providing training, guidance or support to staff or stakeholders on how to comply with the requirements. It may also involve monitoring, measuring or reporting on the progress or outcomes of compliance efforts.

Review and update the compliance plan regularly. This may involve revisiting the legal, regulatory or ethical requirements periodically to ensure they are up-to-date and relevant. It may also involve evaluating the effectiveness or impact of compliance efforts on the organisation's performance or stakeholder satisfaction. It may also involve seeking feedback or input from staff or stakeholders on how to improve compliance.

1.2. IT COMPLIANCE & REGULATORY STANDARDS

Today's business environment is becoming more complex, and organizations must negotiate the web of regulations and standards.

IT compliance and regulatory standards ensure that organizations adhere to a set of guidelines, laws, and best practices.

Organizations must define and implement policies that not only facilitate compliance but also engender ethical conduct, responsible innovation, and safeguards against risks.

THE REGULATORY FRAMEWORK

The regulatory framework for IT compliance and regulatory standards is the set of laws, rules, guidelines and best practices that govern how businesses use, store, process and transmit information technology (IT).

The framework varies depending on the type and nature of the data involved, such as personal data, health data, financial data or government data. The framework also depends on the geographic location of the business and its customers, as different regions and countries have different regulations.

IT compliance standards include:

GDPR: The General Data Protection Regulation (GDPR) is a set of IT regulations that the European Union (EU) enforces. It protects the security and privacy of data belonging to EU citizens and residents. It applies to any business that operates with such data, even if it is not located in the EU.

PCI DSS: The Payment Card Industry Data Security Standard (PCI DSS) governs the security of financial card data, such as credit card or debit card information. It applies to any business that stores, processes or transmits such data.

HIPAA: The Health Insurance Portability and Accountability Act (HIPAA) is an IT compliance standard for the health care industry. It regulates how medical organizations protect the sensitive information of their patients. It applies to any business that deals with health data.

NIST SP 800-171: The National Institute of Standards and Technology (NIST) Special Publication 800-171 is a set of IT security requirements for businesses that work with federal or state agencies. It ensures that government data is protected from unauthorized access or disclosure.

These are the most used IT compliance standards. There are many more that may apply to your business depending on your industry, location and data.

IMPLEMENTING STANDARDS

To follow the regulatory framework for IT compliance and regulatory standards, you need to:

Identify the IT compliance standards that apply to your business. You can do this by researching the laws and regulations of your industry and location, consulting with legal experts or using online resources.

Assess your current level of compliance. You can do this by conducting an IT security audit, using tools or services that measure your compliance status or hiring external auditors.

Implement security measures to meet the compliance requirements. You can do this by adopting security policies and procedures, using secure software and hardware, training your staff on security best practices or outsourcing security tasks to professionals.

Monitor and maintain your compliance status. You can do this by regularly reviewing your security policies and procedures, updating your software and hardware, testing your security systems or reporting your compliance activities.

Following standards can help protect business from security threats, legal penalties and reputational damage. It can also help you improve your customer trust and satisfaction.

IT COMPLIANCE POLICIES

IT compliance policies matter for several reasons:

They help the organization meet its legal and contractual obligations, such as the Sarbanes-Oxley Act (SOX) for financial reporting, the Gramm-Leach-Bliley Act (GLBA) for financial data protection, or the Payment Card Industry Data Security Standard (PCI DSS) for credit card transactions .

They enhance the organization's reputation and trustworthiness among its customers, partners, and regulators, by demonstrating its commitment to data security and privacy.

They reduce the likelihood and impact of cyberattacks, data breaches, and other incidents that could compromise the organization's data and systems, by implementing preventive and corrective measures.

They improve the efficiency and effectiveness of the organization's IT operations, by streamlining processes, reducing errors, and optimizing resources.

CREATING IT COMPLIANCE POLICIES

To create effective IT compliance policies, an organization should follow these steps:

1. **Identify the applicable laws, regulations, and standards** that affect its IT activities, such as SOX, GLBA, PCI DSS, HIPAA, GDPR, ISO 27001, NIST 800-53, etc.
2. **Assess the current state of its IT compliance posture**, by conducting audits, gap analyses, risk assessments, and maturity assessments.
3. **Define the desired state of its IT compliance posture**, by setting goals, objectives, and metrics for each compliance area.
4. **Develop the IT compliance policies** that outline the roles, responsibilities, procedures, controls, and tools for achieving compliance in each area.
5. **Implement the IT compliance policies** across the organization, by communicating them to all stakeholders, providing training and awareness programs, enforcing them through monitoring and reporting mechanisms, and reviewing them periodically for improvement.

BEST PRACTICES FOR IT COMPLIANCE POLICIES

Some of the best practices for IT compliance policies are:

- Align them with the organization's business strategy, objectives, and values.
- Base them on industry standards and frameworks, such as COBIT or ITIL.
- Tailor them to the organization's specific context, needs, and risks.
- Make them clear, concise, consistent, and comprehensive.

- Update them regularly to reflect changes in laws, regulations, standards, technologies, and threats.
- Involve all relevant stakeholders in their development and implementation.
- Document them properly and make them accessible to all authorized parties.
- Measure their performance and effectiveness using key indicators.

ETHICS & COMPLIANCE

As an IT professional, you face many challenges and opportunities in your work. You must deal with complex technical issues, rapidly changing technologies, diverse stakeholders, and increasing regulatory standards. You also must make ethical decisions that affect your organization, your customers, your colleagues, and yourself.

Ethics is not just about obeying the law or following rules. It is about doing what is right, even when no one is watching. Ethics is aligning your actions with your values and principles. It is creating a culture of trust, respect, and integrity in your workplace.

Compliance is not just about avoiding penalties or lawsuits. Compliance is about meeting the expectations and requirements of your customers, regulators, partners, and society. Compliance is about demonstrating your commitment to quality, security, privacy, and accountability in your IT services and products. Compliance is about enhancing your reputation as a responsible and reliable IT professional.

Ethics and compliance are not mutually exclusive. They are interrelated and interdependent. A values-based approach to ethics and compliance can help you achieve both objectives in a sustainable and effective way. A values-based approach means that you:

- Define and communicate your core values and ethical standards to guide your decision-making and behaviour.
- Implement policies, procedures, and training modules that support your values and ethical standards and comply with relevant laws and regulations.
- Monitor and measure your performance and progress in ethics and compliance using appropriate indicators and feedback mechanisms.

- Review and improve your ethics and compliance program regularly to ensure its relevance, adequacy, and effectiveness.
- Recognize and reward ethical conduct and compliance achievements and address any breaches or gaps promptly and fairly.

A values-based approach to ethics and compliance can benefit you in many ways. It can help you:

- Reduce the risk of breaching the Competition and Consumer Act 2010 (CCA) or other applicable laws and regulations.
- Improve your customer relations by acting in accordance with your obligations under the CCA or other applicable laws and regulations.
- Increase your staff awareness and engagement in ethics and compliance issues and responsibilities.
- Strengthen your corporate culture and identity as an ethical and compliant IT organization.
- Enhance your competitive advantage and market position as an IT organization that delivers quality, security, privacy, and accountability.

RISK MANAGEMENT & MITIGATION

IT compliance and regulatory standards govern how organizations use, protect, and share information and technology. These standards may come from different sources, such as laws, regulations, industry codes, contracts, or ethical principles.

IT compliance and regulatory standards include:

The General Data Protection Regulation (GDPR), which is a European Union law that protects the privacy and rights of individuals in relation to their personal data.

The Payment Card Industry Data Security Standard (PCI DSS), which is a set of security requirements for organizations that process, store, or transmit credit card information.

The ISO/IEC 27000 series, which is a family of international standards for information security management systems.

WHY ARE IT COMPLIANCE AND REGULATORY STANDARDS IMPORTANT?

IT compliance and regulatory standards help to ensure that organizations use information and technology in a responsible, ethical, and lawful manner. This can enhance the trust and reputation of the organization among its customers, partners, regulators, and other stakeholders.

Second, they help to prevent or reduce the impact of cyberattacks, data breaches, fraud, or other incidents that could compromise the confidentiality, integrity, or availability of information and technology.

This can protect the organization from financial losses, legal liabilities, or reputational damage. Third, they help to improve the performance and efficiency of the organization by providing guidance and best practices for managing information and technology.

MANAGING RISK IN IT COMPLIANCE AND REGULATORY STANDARDS?

Managing and mitigating risks in IT compliance and regulatory standards involves a systematic process of identifying, analysing, evaluating, treating, monitoring, and reviewing the risks. Some of the steps involved in this process are:

Establishing a governance framework for IT compliance and regulatory standards. This involves defining the roles, responsibilities, policies, procedures, and controls for ensuring that the organization meets its obligations and objectives in relation to information and technology.

Conducting a risk assessment for IT compliance and regulatory standards. This involves identifying the sources and causes of potential risks, estimating their likelihood and impact, and prioritizing them based on their severity.

Implementing risk treatment strategies for IT compliance and regulatory standards. This involves selecting and applying appropriate measures to avoid, reduce, transfer, or accept the risks. Some examples of risk treatment strategies are:

Implementing technical safeguards such as encryption, firewalls, antivirus software, or backup systems to protect information and technology from unauthorized access or damage.

Implementing administrative safeguards such as training, awareness, policies, procedures, or audits to ensure that staff follow the rules and requirements for information and technology.

Implementing legal safeguards such as contracts, agreements, or insurance to transfer or share the responsibility or liability for information and technology with other parties.

Monitoring and reviewing the effectiveness of risk management activities for IT compliance and regulatory standards. This involves measuring and reporting on the performance and outcomes of the risk management process, identifying any gaps or weaknesses, and adjusting or improvements as needed.

DATA PROTECTION & PRIVACY

We cover the following topics:

- Why data protection and privacy matter.
- How to embed a culture of privacy in your organization.
- How to implement privacy by design in your projects and decisions.
- How to establish good privacy practices, procedures and systems.
- How to communicate with your customers and stakeholders about privacy.
- How to deal with third parties that handle personal information on your behalf.
- Why data protection and privacy matter.

Data protection and privacy are not only legal obligations, but also ethical principles that respect the rights and dignity of individuals. By protecting personal information, you can:

- Comply with the laws and regulations that apply to your business, such as the Australian Privacy Principles (APPs), the General Data Protection Regulation (GDPR) or the California Consumer Privacy Act (CCPA).
- Avoid fines, penalties, lawsuits or reputational damage that can result from privacy breaches or violations.
- Enhance customer loyalty, satisfaction and retention by showing that you care about their privacy and security.
- Gain a competitive edge by offering personalized services or products that meet customer expectations and preferences.
- Foster innovation by creating new opportunities for data analysis, insights and solutions.
- How to embed a culture of privacy in your organization

Good privacy management stems from good privacy governance. You need to ensure that your leadership and governance arrangements create a culture of privacy that values personal information. To embed a culture of privacy, you should:

- Treat personal information as a valuable business asset to be respected, managed and protected. Outline how protecting personal information is important for your business.
- Appoint key roles and responsibilities for privacy management, including a senior member of staff with overall accountability for privacy. Also have staff responsible for managing privacy, including a key privacy officer, who are responsible for handling internal and external privacy enquiries, complaints, and access and correction requests.
- Adopt a 'privacy by design' approach. Ensure you consider the seven foundational principles of privacy by design in all your business projects and decisions that involve personal information.
- Allocate resources to support the development and implementation of a privacy management plan that aligns your business processes with your privacy obligations. Your plan should outline how you will implement and monitor the steps outlined in this Framework and meet your goals or objectives for managing privacy.

1.3. DATA RETENTION & DELETION

BALANCING LEGAL COMPLIANCE & PRIVACY

Data retention and deletion are important aspects of data management that affect both legal compliance and privacy protection.

Data retention refers to the practice of storing and managing data for a designated period, while data deletion refers to the practice of removing data from storage when it is no longer needed or required. Both practices have benefits and challenges for organizations that collect, process and store data.

IMPORTANCE OF DATA RETENTION

Data retention is essential for maintaining accurate records, complying with laws and regulations, and ensuring that information is available for eDiscovery and litigation purposes.

Different types of data may have different retention periods, depending on the business needs and the legal obligations of the organization. For example, financial records may need to be kept for several years, while customer data may need to be deleted after a certain period of inactivity.

Data retention policies are the established protocols for determining what data needs to be retained, how long it should be stored, how it should be formatted, who has the authority to dispose of it, and what procedure to follow in case of a policy violation. Data retention policies help organizations ensure legal and regulatory compliance, as well as enhance efficiency and security.

DATA DELETION

Data deletion is equally important for balancing legal compliance and privacy protection. Data deletion refers to the removal of data from storage when it is no longer needed or required by law. Data deletion helps organizations reduce storage costs, improve performance, minimize risks, and protect the privacy of individuals.

Data deletion policies are the established protocols for determining when data should be deleted, how it should be deleted, who has the authority to delete it, and what procedure to follow in case of a policy violation.

Data deletion policies help organizations comply with laws and regulations that mandate data minimization, such as the General Data Protection Regulation (GDPR) and the California Consumer Privacy Act (CCPA), as well as respect the rights and preferences of individuals.

BEST PRACTICE

To balance legal compliance and privacy protection in data retention and deletion, organizations should follow some best practices, such as:

Identify and classify the data your organization holds, and determine its value, sensitivity, and legal obligations.

Know which laws and regulations apply to your organization and your data and understand their requirements for data retention and deletion.

Delete data once it is no longer required or after the data retention period has been met, using secure methods that prevent unauthorized access or recovery.

Implement a permission-based framework for all retained data, ensuring that only authorized users can access, modify, or delete it.

Anonymize or encrypt data that contains personal or confidential information, to protect it from unauthorized disclosure or misuse.

Document your data retention and deletion policies and procedures, and communicate them clearly to your employees, customers, and stakeholders.

Monitor your data retention and deletion practices regularly and audit them periodically to ensure compliance and effectiveness.

THE DIGITAL FOOTPRINT

Data retention and deletion are the processes of storing and disposing of data that your organization collects, creates or receives. Data retention refers to how long you keep data for a specific purpose, such as legal compliance, business operations or customer service. Data deletion refers to how you remove data from your systems once it is no longer needed or required.

INFORMED CONSENT & PURPOSE LIMITATION

WHAT IS INFORMED CONSENT?

Informed consent means that you tell people who give you their personal information:

- who you are and how to contact you.
- what data you are collecting and why.
- how you will use, store, and protect their data.
- how long you will keep their data.
- how they can access, correct, or delete their data.
- how they can withdraw their consent at any time.

You should get their clear and voluntary agreement before you collect or use their data. You should also respect their choices and rights regarding their data.

PURPOSE LIMITATION

Purpose limitation means that you only use the data for the specific and legitimate purposes that you told people when you got their consent. You should not use the data for other purposes without getting their consent again or unless required by law.

INFORMED CONSENT

Best practices to apply informed consent and purpose limitation in data retention and deletion:

- Use a privacy-by-design approach to build these principles into your data processing activities from the start.
- Provide clear and easy-to-understand privacy notices and consent forms to inform people about your data practices.
- Limit the collection, use, retention, and disclosure of personal information to the minimum necessary to achieve your purposes.
- Implement reasonable security measures to protect personal information from misuse, loss, or unauthorised access.
- Establish a data retention policy that specifies how long you will keep different types of data and how you will dispose of them securely.
- Review your data regularly and delete or de-identify any data that is no longer needed or requested by people.

- Respect the rights of people to access, correct, or delete their data or withdraw their consent at any time.

DATA DELETION & THE RIGHT TO BE FORGOTTEN

WHAT IS THE RIGHT TO BE FORGOTTEN?

The right to be forgotten is the right of an individual to request the deletion of their personal data by an entity that might be storing it.

This right has been explicitly recognized, legislated, and exercised in several jurisdictions across the world, including the European Union, Argentina, and California.

The right to be forgotten is based on the principle that individuals have the right to control their own data and to protect their privacy. However, this right is not absolute and must be balanced with other rights and interests, such as freedom of expression, public interest, or legal obligations.

WHEN TO APPLY THE RIGHT TO BE FORGOTTEN

According to the General Data Protection Regulation (GDPR), which applies in the European Union, an individual has the right to have their personal data erased if:

- The personal data is no longer necessary for the purpose an organization originally collected or processed it.
- An organization is relying on an individual's consent as the lawful basis for processing the data and that individual withdraws their consent.
- An organization is relying on legitimate interests as its justification for processing an individual's data, the individual objects to this processing, and there is no overriding legitimate interest for the organization to continue with the processing.
- An organization is processing personal data for direct marketing purposes and the individual objects to that processing.
- An organization has processed personal data unlawfully (i.e., in breach of the lawfulness requirement of the first principle).
- An organization has a legal obligation to erase the data.
- An organization has processed personal data to offer information society services to a child.

There are some exceptions to this right, such as when the processing is necessary for:

- Exercising the right of freedom of expression and information.
- Complying with a legal obligation or performing a task carried out in the public interest or in the exercise of official authority.
- Reasons of public interest in the area of public health.
- Archiving purposes in the public interest, scientific or historical research purposes or statistical purposes.
- The establishment, exercise or defence of legal claims.

HOW CAN AN INDIVIDUAL EXERCISE THE RIGHT TO BE FORGOTTEN?

An individual can exercise their right by contacting the organization that holds their personal data and requesting its deletion. The organization must respond to this request without undue delay and within one month. The organization must also take reasonable steps to verify the identity of the person making the request.

If the organization decides not to delete the data, it must explain why and inform the individual of their right to complain to a supervisory authority or seek a judicial remedy.

WHAT ARE SOME BEST PRACTICES FOR ORGANIZATIONS REGARDING DATA DELETION?

Organizations that collect and process personal data should adopt some best practices regarding data deletion, such as:

- Having a clear and transparent policy on how long they retain personal data and when they delete it.
- Implementing appropriate technical and organizational measures to ensure secure and effective deletion of personal data when requested or required.
- Providing easy and accessible ways for individuals to request deletion of their personal data and informing them of their rights and options.
- Keeping records of deletion requests and actions taken in response to them.
- Training staff on how to handle deletion requests and comply with data protection laws.

ETHICAL CONSIDERATIONS IN EMERGING TECHNOLOGIES

Emerging technologies such as artificial intelligence, cloud computing, big data, and cybersecurity have enormous potential to transform various domains of human activity.

ETHICAL DILEMMAS AND PRINCIPLES IN DATA RETENTION AND DELETION

Data retention and deletion involve ethical dilemmas that require careful balancing of competing values and interests. Some of the common ethical dilemmas are:

How long should data be retained? Retaining data for too long can increase the risk of data breaches, misuse, or abuse, while deleting data too soon can limit the potential benefits of data analysis or reuse.

How should data be deleted? Deleting data securely and completely can prevent unauthorized access or recovery, while retaining some traces of data can facilitate auditing or verification.

Who should decide on data retention and deletion? Data controllers and processors may have different incentives or preferences for data retention and deletion than data subjects or stakeholders, who may have different levels of awareness or consent.

What are the trade-offs between data retention and deletion? Data retention and deletion may involve trade-offs between efficiency and effectiveness, innovation and protection, individual and collective interests, or short-term and long-term goals.

ADDRESSING ETHICAL DILEMMAS

To address these ethical dilemmas, some ethical principles can guide the decision-making process. Some of the widely accepted ethical principles are:

Respect for human dignity. Data retention and deletion should respect the inherent worth and dignity of every human being, regardless of their characteristics or circumstances.

Fairness and justice. Data retention and deletion should ensure equal treatment and opportunity for all data subjects and stakeholders, without discrimination or bias.

Beneficence and non-maleficence. Data retention and deletion should maximize the benefits and minimize the harms for data subjects, stakeholders, and society at large.

Autonomy and consent. Data retention and deletion should respect the choices and preferences of data subjects, who should be informed and empowered to exercise their rights over their data.

Transparency and accountability. Data retention and deletion should be clear, consistent, and explainable to data subjects, stakeholders, and regulators, who should be able to monitor and evaluate their compliance and outcomes.

CHAPTER 1 WORKSHOP: IT GOVERNANCE FRAMEWORKS

In this workshop, we will consider the importance of IT governance frameworks, the main compliance and regulatory standards that apply to IT, and the best practices for data retention and deletion.

It will apply your knowledge to a case study and discuss your findings with your peers.

The workshop is divided into three parts:

PART 1: IT GOVERNANCE FRAMEWORKS

IT governance frameworks are sets of principles, policies, processes, and practices that guide the management and oversight of IT in an organization. They help align IT with the organization's goals, strategies, and values, as well as ensure that IT delivers value, manages risks, and meets the expectations of stakeholders.

IT governance frameworks include:

- **COBIT**: A framework that covers all aspects of IT governance, from planning and implementation to monitoring and improvement. It provides a comprehensive set of controls, objectives, and performance indicators for IT processes.
- **ITIL**: A framework that focuses on the delivery and support of IT services, from service strategy and design to service operation and improvement. It defines a set of best practices, roles, and responsibilities for IT service management.
- **ISO/IEC 27000**: A series of standards that specify the requirements for establishing, implementing, maintaining, and improving an information security management system. It covers topics such as risk assessment, security policies, controls, audits, and incidents.

In this part of the workshop, you will learn about the benefits and challenges of implementing an IT governance framework, the key components and elements of each framework, and how to choose the most suitable framework for your organization.

PART 2: IT COMPLIANCE & REGULATORY STANDARDS

IT compliance and regulatory standards are rules and regulations that govern how IT should operate in certain domains or industries. They aim to protect the interests of customers, users, partners, regulators, and society at large. They also help ensure the quality, security, reliability, and availability of IT systems and data.

IT compliance and regulatory standards include:

- **GDPR: The General Data Protection Regulation** is a European Union law that regulates how personal data of individuals in the EU is collected, processed, stored, and transferred. It grants data subjects rights such as access, rectification, erasure, portability, and objection. It also imposes obligations on data controllers and processors such as consent, transparency, accountability, and security.

- **HIPAA: The Health Insurance Portability and Accountability Act** is a US law that regulates how health information of individuals is protected and shared. It establishes standards for the privacy and security of health data, as well as the rights of patients to access and control their own data. It also sets rules for health care providers, insurers, clearinghouses, and business associates who handle health data.

- **PCI DSS: The Payment Card Industry Data Security Standard** is a global standard that applies to any organization that processes, stores, or transmits cardholder data. It specifies a set of requirements for securing cardholder data against fraud and theft. It also defines a process for assessing compliance and reporting breaches.

In this part of the workshop, you will learn about the scope and objectives of each standard, the main requirements and obligations for IT compliance, and how to implement a compliance program in your organization.

PART 3: DATA RETENTION & DELETION

Data retention and deletion are two aspects of data lifecycle management that deal with how long data should be kept and when it should be disposed of. They are influenced by factors such as business needs, legal obligations, technical limitations, and ethical considerations.

Data retention is the process of keeping data for a specified period for a specific purpose. Data retention policies define the criteria for determining which data should be retained, how long it should be retained, where it should be stored, who can access it, and how it can be used.

Data deletion is the process of removing data from storage devices or media in a way that ensures it cannot be recovered or accessed by unauthorized parties. Data deletion policies define the criteria for determining which data should be deleted, when it should be deleted, how it should be deleted, who can delete it, and how it can be verified.

In this part of the workshop, you will learn about the benefits and risks of data retention and deletion, the factors that affect data retention and deletion decisions, and how to design and implement data retention and deletion policies in your organization. Case Study: To apply what you have learned in this workshop; you will work on a case study based on a fictional scenario.

You will assume the role of an IT governance consultant who has been hired by a company called ABC Inc. to help them improve their IT governance practices.

ABC Inc. is a multinational corporation that operates in various sectors, such as manufacturing, retail, and finance.

It has offices in several countries and employs thousands of people. It uses various IT systems to support its business processes and to communicate with its customers, partners, and regulators.

ABC Inc. is facing several challenges related to its IT governance, such as:

- Lack of a clear and consistent IT governance framework
- Inadequate compliance with various IT standards and regulations
- Poor data management and protection practices

Your task is to analyse the current situation of ABC Inc., identify the main issues and gaps in their IT governance, and propose a plan of action to address them.

You will work in groups of four or five, and use the following steps to guide your analysis and proposal:

1. Choose an IT governance framework that best suits the needs and goals of ABC Inc.
2. Identify the key compliance and regulatory standards that ABC Inc. should follow and explain why they are relevant and important.
3. Assess the current data retention and deletion policies of ABC Inc. and suggest how they can be improved or revised.
4. Present your findings and recommendations to the rest of the workshop participants, using a PowerPoint presentation or a similar tool.

You will have 15 minutes to work on each step, and 10 minutes to present your final proposal.

You will be evaluated based on the following criteria:

- The quality and accuracy of your analysis and proposal
- The clarity and coherence of your presentation
- The relevance and feasibility of your recommendations
- The creativity and originality of your approach

CHAPTER 2:
CYBERSECURITY & DATA PROTECTION

CHAPTER SUMMARY

Cybersecurity and data protection are essential for any organization that collects, processes, or stores personal or sensitive information. In this chapter, we will explore some of the key concepts and challenges related to these topics, such as:

International data transfers and privacy: How to comply with different laws and regulations when transferring data across borders, and how to protect the rights and interests of data subjects.

Privacy by design and default: How to embed privacy principles and practices into the design and operation of systems and services, and how to ensure that data minimization and consent are respected by default.

Surveillance and privacy: How to balance the legitimate needs of security and law enforcement with the fundamental rights of privacy and freedom of expression, and how to prevent or mitigate the risks of mass surveillance and data misuse.

AI accountability and transparency: How to ensure that artificial intelligence systems are fair, ethical, and explainable, and how to avoid or address the potential harms of bias, discrimination, and manipulation.

Data breach notification and communication: How to prepare for and respond to data breaches, and how to communicate effectively with stakeholders, regulators, and the public about the incident and its consequences.

Cybersecurity training and ethical hacking: How to educate and empower employees and users about cybersecurity best practices, and how to use ethical hacking techniques to test and improve the security of systems and networks.

This chapter provides a concise overview of these topics, as well as practical examples and recommendations on how to implement them in your organization. By reading this chapter, you will gain a better understanding of the current trends and challenges in cybersecurity and data protection, as well as the best practices and standards that can help you achieve a high level of compliance and performance.

2.1. CYBERSECURITY & DATA PROTECTION

Australian laws, such as the Privacy Act of 1988 and the Notifiable Data Breaches (NDB) scheme, mandate the protection of personal data. Organizations are obliged to establish robust cybersecurity policies and practices to safeguard sensitive information, thus ensuring compliance with legal requirements and ethical responsibilities alike.

Cybersecurity & Data Protection is therefore the practice of safeguarding your devices, accounts and data from cyber threats such as scams and malware.

To protect yourself from cyber threats, you should follow some basic cybersecurity best practices, such as:

- Turn on automatic updates for your software, apps and operating systems to fix any vulnerabilities that cybercriminals can exploit.
- Use strong passwords and authentication methods for your accounts, such as multi-factor authentication or biometrics, to prevent unauthorized access.
- Avoid clicking on pop-ups, unknown emails and links that may contain malware or phishing attempts to steal your information or money.
- Always connect to secure Wi-Fi networks that are encrypted and password-protected and avoid using public Wi-Fi for sensitive activities such as online banking or shopping.
- Encrypt your data, especially when it is stored or transmitted over the internet or other networks, to prevent cybercriminals from reading or modifying it.
- Collaborate and share information with other organisations, security agencies and law enforcement to improve your cyber resilience and awareness of potential threats.
- Manage your assets, such as software and data, by using centralised systems and configuration management to ensure visibility and control of your critical resources.
- Implement protective measures and controls for your cyber risks, such as firewalls, antivirus software and backup systems, based on the Australian Signals Directorate's (ASD) Strategies to mitigate targeted cyber intrusions or equivalent.

- Use detection systems and processes to monitor your devices and networks for any signs of cyberattacks, such as unusual activity or anomalies, and use data analytics to integrate sources of threats in real time.
- Plan for response and recovery in case of a cyber incident, by having a clear strategy, roles and responsibilities, communication channels and contingency plans.

This advice notwithstanding, you should always tailor your approach to your specific context, needs and risks. You should also keep yourself updated on the latest trends and developments in cyber security, as cyber threats are constantly evolving and becoming more sophisticated.

Australian laws, such as the Privacy Act of 1988 and the Notifiable Data Breaches (NDB) scheme, mandate the protection of personal data. Organizations are obliged to establish robust cybersecurity policies and practices to safeguard sensitive information, thus ensuring compliance with legal requirements and ethical responsibilities alike.

THE IMPERATIVE OF CYBERSECURITY POLICIES

Cybers- Cybersecurity policies are essential for protecting the digital assets and interests of individuals, organizations and nations from cyber threats and attacks.

Cybersecurity policies should:

- Be based on a comprehensive risk assessment and a clear understanding of the cyber threat landscape, as well as the legal, ethical and social implications of cyber activities.
- Aim to achieve a balance between security, privacy, accessibility and innovation, while respecting the rights and responsibilities of all stakeholders in the cyberspace.
- Promote the adoption of best practices and standards for cyber resilience, such as zero trust and attack surface management, which can help prevent, detect and mitigate cyber risks.
- Address the challenges and opportunities posed by emerging technologies, such as artificial intelligence, cloud computing and quantum computing, which can enhance or undermine cyber security.
- Be aligned with national and international laws and regulations, as well as with the norms and values of the global

community, to foster cooperation and trust among cyber actors.

- Be regularly reviewed and updated to reflect the dynamic nature of cyber threats and technologies, as well as the evolving needs and expectations of the cyber society.

These policies, often informed by industry best practices and regulatory mandates, guide organizations in implementing a multi-layered defence strategy to protect critical assets and sensitive data.

Such policies should *specifically* include:

- Acceptable Use Policy.
- Security Awareness and Training Policy.
- Change Management Policy.
- Incident Response Policy.
- Remote Access Policy.
- Vendor Management Policy.
- Password Creation and Management Policy.
- Network Security Policy.

THE PRIVACY ACT & DATA PROTECTION

The Privacy Act of 1988 is a cornerstone of data protection in Australia. It lays the foundation for safeguarding personal information, ensuring that organizations collect, use, and disclose data in a responsible and ethical manner. The Act sets out strict guidelines that organizations must follow, with serious consequences for violations. This legal framework serves as a reminder of the ethical duty organizations must respect the privacy of individuals and safeguard their personal information.

The Privacy Act covers the following:

- Know why your personal information is being collected, how it will be used and who it will be disclosed to.
- Have the option of not identifying yourself, or of using a pseudonym in certain circumstances.
- Ask for access to your personal information (including your health information)

THE NOTIFIABLE DATA BREACHES SCHEME

The Notifiable Data Breaches (NDB) scheme is a legal requirement for organisations and agencies that are covered by the Privacy Act 1988 to report data breaches that are likely to cause serious harm to the individuals whose personal information is involved.

A data breach occurs when personal information is lost, accessed or disclosed without authorisation. For example, when a device with customer information is stolen, a database with personal information is hacked, or personal information is mistakenly given to the wrong person.

The notification to individuals must include recommendations about the steps they should take in response to the data breach. The notification to the Office of the Australian Information Commissioner (OAIC) must be done using the online Notifiable Data Breach form.

The NDB scheme aims to protect the privacy and security of personal information and to enhance public confidence in how organisations handle personal information.

The NDB scheme also provides guidance and support for organisations and agencies on how to prevent, prepare for and respond to data breaches, drawing on research and best practice.

ETHICAL & LEGAL CONSIDERATIONS

Ethical and legal considerations in cybersecurity and data protection are essential to ensure the privacy, security and trust of individuals, organisations and society.

You should be aware of and comply with the relevant laws and regulations that apply to your jurisdiction, sector and activities, such as the Privacy Act 1988 (Cth) in Australia, which sets out 13 Australian Privacy Principles for handling personal information.

You should also follow the international standards and best practices for data privacy and security, such as ISO 27701, which relates to the way an organisation collects personal data and prevents unauthorised use or disclosure.

You should respect the confidentiality, integrity and availability of the data you collect, use, store and disclose, and only do so for legitimate purposes and with consent or authorisation from the data subjects or owners.

You should employ reasonable protection efforts in your use of technology to communicate with clients, colleagues and stakeholders, and prevent unauthorized disclosure of sensitive information.

You should act ethically and responsibly when dealing with data, especially when using artificial intelligence or machine learning, which present some extraordinary challenges in terms of law, ethics and technical advancement.

You should consider the potential impact of your actions on individuals, organisations and society, and balance the benefits and risks of data use and sharing.

You should be transparent and accountable for your data practices and report any breaches or incidents promptly and appropriately.

CONFIDENTIALITY, INTEGRITY, & AVAILABILITY

Confidentiality, integrity, and availability (CIA) are the three main objectives of cybersecurity that aim to protect data and information from unauthorized access, use, and disclosure.

Confidentiality ensures that only authorized users and processes can access or modify data. This can be achieved by using encryption, authentication, access control, and other security measures.

Integrity ensures that data is maintained in a correct state, and nobody can improperly modify it, either accidentally or maliciously. This can be achieved by using checksums, digital signatures, audit trails, and other security measures.

Availability ensures that authorized users can access data whenever they need to do so. This can be achieved by using backup systems, redundancy, load balancing, and other security measures.

Cybersecurity and data protection are broader topics that cover the legal, ethical, and technical aspects of ensuring the CIA of data in various contexts and domains.

The best advice on the topic of CIA in cybersecurity and data protection is to follow the relevant standards, guidelines, and best practices that apply to your specific industry, sector, or organization. Some examples are ISO/IEC 27001, NIST SP 800-53, GDPR, HIPAA, etc. .

THE EVOLVING THREAT LANDSCAPE

The evolving threat landscape is an perpetual top priority for security and risk management leaders, according to a Gartner survey.

The COVID-19 pandemic has created new challenges and opportunities for cyberattackers, who exploit vulnerabilities in remote work environments, digital meeting solutions, and unpatched systems.

Cyberresilience is the ability to anticipate, withstand, recover from, and adapt to adverse conditions, stresses, attacks, or compromises on systems that use or are enabled by cyberresources.

A defence in depth (DiD) architecture is an approach to cybersecurity that uses a series of layered defensive mechanisms to protect valuable data and information.

Artificial intelligence (AI) models can enhance the capabilities of both defenders and attackers in the cyber domain, requiring adaptive strategies to safeguard sensitive data and protect against potential breaches.

Security best practices include using strong passwords, enabling multi-factor authentication, updating software and firmware, encrypting data, backing up data, avoiding phishing emails, and educating users on cyber hygiene.

COLLABORATIVE APPROACH

Recognize that cybersecurity risks are global and require a coordinated, collaborative approach. Cyberattacks can affect any country, sector, or organization, and have severe economic and social consequences. Therefore, we need to ensure that risks to cybersecurity, data protection, privacy, and online safety are addressed at all levels and by all stakeholders.

Share knowledge, build capacity and expertise, and assess cybersecurity risks at the country level. To cope with the evolving nature and complexity of cyber threats, we need to foster a culture of learning and innovation among cybersecurity and data protection professionals. We also need to conduct regular risk assessments to identify the most critical assets and vulnerabilities and prioritize the appropriate measures to protect them.

Provide incentives for the private sector to invest in digital infrastructure and technology. The private sector plays a vital role in developing and deploying secure and resilient digital solutions for various domains, such as health, transport, energy, etc. Therefore, we need to create a favourable environment for private sector participation, such as by providing tax breaks, subsidies, grants, or public-private partnerships.

Unite data protection and cybersecurity skills. Data breaches can have multiple impacts on an organization's reputation, operations, finances, and legal compliance. Therefore, we need to ensure that both data protection and cybersecurity specialists work together to prevent and respond to data breaches, by combining their skills in areas such as encryption, authentication, access control, incident response, etc.

THE HUMAN ELEMENT

The human element is a crucial factor in cybersecurity and data protection, as humans are both the primary source of risks and the target of attacks.

According to ISACA, humans represent a mystery to be deciphered by security/cybersecurity experts because their behaviours, attitudes, beliefs, rituals and decisions constitute a little-understood universe for executives and their heads of security.

The human factor in information security can be seen as the weakest link in the chain or as the reliable and resilient factor of the system, depending on how organizations approach the challenge of educating and empowering their employees.

Harvard Business Review suggests that better cybersecurity starts with fixing employees' bad habits, such as using weak passwords, clicking on suspicious links, or sharing sensitive information online.

The human element of cybersecurity also involves ethical, legal, and social aspects, such as privacy, consent, accountability, and responsibility.

To address the human element of cybersecurity and data protection, organizations need to adopt a holistic approach that combines technical, organizational, and behavioural measures, such as encryption, policies, training, and awareness.

Some points include:

- Keep software up to date.
- Avoid opening suspicious emails.
- Keep hardware up to date.
- Use a secure file-sharing solution to encrypt data.
- Use anti-virus and anti-malware.
- Use a VPN to privatize your connections.
- Check links before you click.
- Don't be lazy with your passwords.

BALANCING INNOVATION & SECURITY

Balancing innovation and security is a key challenge for IT governance, policy, ethics and law in the field of cybersecurity and data protection.

Innovation can bring benefits such as improved efficiency, customer satisfaction, competitive advantage and new revenue streams, but it can also introduce risks such as data breaches, cyberattacks, regulatory violations and reputational damage.

Security can help protect data, systems, users and stakeholders from malicious threats, but it can also hinder innovation by imposing constraints, costs and delays on the development and deployment of new technologies, services and business models.

To balance innovation and security, organizations need to adopt a strategic approach that aligns their business objectives, risk appetite, governance framework and security posture. Some best practices for this approach are:

- Performing risk assessments to identify and prioritize cybersecurity concerns and opportunities for innovation.
- Establishing clear roles and responsibilities for innovation and security across the organization
- Implementing security by design principles to embed security into the innovation lifecycle from the start.
- Leveraging emerging technologies such as artificial intelligence (AI) to enhance both innovation and security capabilities.
- Fostering a culture of collaboration and trust between innovation and security teams

- Monitoring and evaluating the performance and impact of innovation and security initiatives.
- Adapting to changing customer needs, market conditions, regulatory requirements and threat landscapes

Balancing innovation and security require a holistic and dynamic approach that considers the trade-offs, synergies and interdependencies between them. By doing so, organizations can achieve both business growth and risk mitigation in the domain of cybersecurity and data protection.

2.2. INTERNATIONAL DATA TRANSFERS & PRIVACY

It is common knowledge that the boundaries of information transcend physical borders. The global nature of IT operations has led to an increasing flow of data across international borders. It has made necessary policies that govern international data transfers.

Different countries and regions have different laws and regulations that govern how personal data can be transferred and protected, such as the EU General Data Protection Regulation (GDPR), the Australian Privacy Act 1988 (Privacy Act), or the Singapore Personal Data Protection Act 2012 (PDPA).

Depending on the destination and origin of the data transfer, different mechanisms or safeguards may be required to ensure that the personal data is adequately protected and that the data subjects' rights are respected.

Some of the common mechanisms or safeguards for international data transfers include:

- **Adequacy decisions**. These are official recognitions by a data protection authority (such as the European Commission) that a third country or region offers a level of data protection that is equivalent or comparable to the one in the originating jurisdiction. For example, the EU has granted adequacy status to Japan, Canada, and New Zealand, among others.
- **Standard contractual clauses (SCCs)**. These are pre-approved sets of contractual terms that can be used by data exporters and importers to ensure that the personal data is subject to appropriate safeguards and remedies in case of breach. For example, the EU has issued new SCCs for different scenarios of data transfers under the GDPR, such as between controllers and processors, or between processors and sub-processors.
- **Binding corporate rules (BCRs).** These are internal codes of conduct adopted by multinational corporations or groups of companies that commit to apply consistent data protection standards and policies across their global operations. For example, BCRs can be approved by one or more data protection authorities in the EU under the GDPR, or by the Australian Information Commissioner under the Privacy Act.
- **Derogations or exceptions**. These are specific situations where personal data can be transferred without requiring any

additional safeguards, such as with the explicit consent of the data subject, for the performance of a contract, or for important public interest reasons. For example, under the GDPR, derogations can be used for occasional and non-repetitive transfers that are not large-scale or systematic.

International data transfers are subject to ongoing developments and challenges, such as the invalidation of the EU-US Privacy Shield framework by the Court of Justice of the European Union in 2020, or the adoption of new data localization laws by some countries that restrict cross-border data flows. Therefore, it is important to keep up to date with the latest guidance and best practices from relevant authorities and experts.

BORDERLESS DATA LANDSCAPE

The digital era has redefined how information is shared, stored, and processed. Organizations now operate within a borderless data landscape where data generated in one country might be stored in another, accessed by users from around the world, and transmitted across jurisdictions.

Be aware of the legal and regulatory frameworks that apply to your data transfers, such as the GDPR in the EU, the Privacy Shield in the US, or the OECD Declaration on Transborder Data Flows.

Use appropriate legal mechanisms and safeguards to ensure compliance with data protection principles and obligations, such as standard contractual clauses, binding corporate rules, codes of conduct, or certification schemes.

Consider the risks and benefits of transferring data across borders, considering the nature, purpose, and context of the data processing, as well as the expectations and rights of the data subjects.

Adopt privacy-enhancing technologies to minimize the amount and sensitivity of personal data that are transferred, such as encryption, pseudonymization, anonymization, or differential privacy.

Implement best practices for data governance, security, and accountability, such as data protection by design and by default, data protection impact assessments, data breach notification, or data protection officers.

INTERNATIONAL DATA FLOW

While international data transfers facilitate global collaboration and business operations, they also introduce complex legal and ethical challenges.

International data transfers are the exchange of personal and non-personal data between countries, which are essential for the development and deployment of AI systems.

However, international data transfers face many legal challenges due to the different data protection regimes and standards around the world.

For example, the EU's General Data Protection Regulation (GDPR) requires that data transfers to third countries or international organizations ensure an adequate level of data protection.

The adequacy of data protection can be assessed by the European Commission, or by using appropriate safeguards such as standard contractual clauses (SCCs), binding corporate rules (BCRs), or codes of conduct.

However, the validity of some of these safeguards has been challenged by recent court rulings, such as the Schrems II case, which invalidated the EU-US Privacy Shield framework and imposed stricter conditions on the use of SCCs.

Therefore, it is important for organizations that engage in international data transfers to conduct regular assessments of the risks and benefits of their data flows, and to implement suitable measures to ensure compliance with the applicable laws and regulations.

Some possible measures include encrypting or pseudonymizing the data, obtaining explicit consent from the data subjects, or using technical solutions such as federated learning or differential privacy to minimize the exposure of personal data.

International data transfers can also be facilitated by regional or bilateral agreements that harmonize data protection standards and provide mutual recognition of adequacy decisions, such as the EU-US Data Privacy Framework or the Atlantic Declaration

DATA PROTECTION LAWS & CROSS-BORDER TRANSFERS

Many countries have enacted data protection laws that place restrictions on the transfer of personal data across borders.

It is important to be aware of the different data protection regimes and standards that apply to the countries where you transfer personal data, and ensure that you comply with their requirements.

If you transfer personal data from the EU to a third country, you need to follow the rules of the EU Data Protection Directive, which prohibits such transfers unless the third country ensures an adequate level of protection or one of the exceptions applies.

The EU has recognised some countries as providing adequate protection, such as Canada, Switzerland, Argentina, Guernsey and the Isle of Man. You can transfer personal data to these countries without further restrictions.

For other countries, you need to rely on appropriate safeguards, such as standard contractual clauses, binding corporate rules, codes of conduct or certification mechanisms, to ensure that the personal data is protected consistently with the EU principles.

Alternatively, you can use one of the derogations, such as unambiguous consent, contractual necessity, public interest or vital interest of the data subject, to justify the transfer on a case-by-case basis.

If you transfer personal data from Australia to a third country, you need to follow the proposed *Cross-border Data Flows* principle, which requires you to take reasonable steps to ensure that the recipient will protect the personal data in accordance with the Australian Privacy Principles.

You can also remain accountable for any breaches of privacy by the recipient, unless you obtain consent from the data subject or inform them that they will not be able to seek redress under the Privacy Act.

You should also consider the *APEC Privacy Framework*, which provides a set of principles and guidelines for cross-border data transfers among APEC member economies.

You should conduct due diligence on the recipient's privacy practices and policies, and use contractual or other means to ensure that they will protect the personal data consistently with the APEC principles.

ETHICAL ISSUES IN INTERNATIONAL DATA TRANSFERS

Ethical considerations in international data transfers extend beyond mere legal compliance. Organizations have an ethical obligation to protect individuals' privacy and uphold the principles of transparency, accountability, and informed consent.

Ethical issues in international data transfers arise from the differences in data protection laws and standards among countries and regions.

Data exporters and importers need to ensure that they comply with the applicable regulations and respect the rights and interests of data subjects when transferring personal data across borders.

Some of the challenges and risks involved in international data transfers are:

- Lack of transparency and control over how data are processed, stored and shared by third parties in other jurisdictions.
- Inadequate safeguards or mechanisms to ensure data security, confidentiality and integrity.
- Legal uncertainties and conflicts arising from divergent or incompatible data protection regimes.
- Potential violations of data subjects' rights, such as access, rectification, erasure, objection, portability and consent.
- Ethical dilemmas related to the use of data for purposes that may not align with the values, expectations or interests of data subjects or society at large.

Some of the best practices and recommendations for addressing ethical issues in international data transfers are:

- Conducting a data protection impact assessment (DPIA) to identify and mitigate the risks and impacts of data transfers on data subjects and their rights.
- Choosing an appropriate legal basis for data transfers, such as adequacy decisions, standard contractual clauses (SCCs), binding corporate rules (BCRs), codes of conduct or certification mechanisms.
- Implementing technical and organizational measures to ensure data security, confidentiality and integrity, such as encryption, pseudonymization, access control, audit trails and breach notification.
- Providing clear and comprehensive information to data subjects about the purposes, scope, duration, recipients and rights related to data transfers.

- Obtaining valid and informed consent from data subjects when required or appropriate, and allowing them to withdraw or modify their consent at any time.
- Respecting the principles of data minimization, purpose limitation and accountability when transferring personal data across borders.
- Monitoring and reviewing the compliance and performance of data transfer arrangements on a regular basis and updating them as necessary to reflect changes in laws, technologies or circumstances.

BALANCING SECURITY & ACCESSIBILITY

Ethical international data transfer policies must strike a balance between data security and data accessibility.

While protecting data during cross-border transfers is paramount, policies should not unduly restrict the legitimate flow of information that supports business operations, research, and innovation.

Ensuring secure, encrypted channels for data transfer while maintaining accessibility is a key challenge.

In short, how to:

- Protect sensitive data from unauthorized access or misuse.
- Ensure data availability and reliability for authorized users.
- Balance the trade-offs between security measures and user convenience.
- Comply with relevant laws and regulations regarding data privacy and security.
- Educate and train users on data security best practices and policies.

ADEQUATE SAFEGUARDS & MECHANISMS

Organizations engaged in international data transfers must implement adequate safeguards and mechanisms to ensure data protection.

These safeguards could include using encryption during data transfer, obtaining explicit consent from data subjects, implementing strict access controls, and adhering to international standards for data security.

To summarise:

- The risk of data breaches or unauthorized access by third parties in the destination country.
- The lack of adequate legal protection or enforcement for data subjects' rights and remedies in the destination country.
- The possibility of conflicting or incompatible data protection laws or regulations between the source and destination countries.
- The challenges of ensuring accountability and compliance with data protection principles and standards across different jurisdictions.
- The potential impact of political, social, economic or environmental factors on the stability and security of data transfers.

TRANSPARENCY & USER EMPOWERMENT

Ethical policies call for transparency in international data transfers. Organizations should inform users about how their data will be transferred, where it will be stored, and how it will be protected.

Users should have the power to make informed decisions about their data and should be empowered to exercise their rights, such as withdrawing consent or requesting data deletion.

To summarise:

- How to ensure that users are aware of the risks and benefits of transferring their data across borders.
- How to provide users with meaningful choices and control over their data, especially when it involves sensitive or personal information.
- ow to protect users' rights and interests in case of data breaches, misuse, or legal conflicts involving their data.
- How to balance the need for transparency and accountability with the need for efficiency and innovation in data transfer.
- How to foster trust and cooperation among different stakeholders, such as governments, businesses, and civil society, in the global data ecosystem.

CROSS-BORDER COLLABORATION & COMPLIANCE

Ethical policies should facilitate compliance with international data protection laws while enabling organizations to collaborate across jurisdictions. This might involve setting up data sharing agreements, ensuring that data is shared only with trusted partners, and conducting due diligence on the privacy practices of collaborators.

The primary concerns about Cross-Border Collaboration & Compliance for international data transfer is:

- **Data privacy and security**. ensuring that the data is protected from unauthorized access, use, disclosure, or loss across different jurisdictions and regulations.
- **Data sovereignty and localization**. complying with the laws and regulations of the countries where the data is collected, stored, processed, or transferred, and respecting the rights and preferences of the data subjects.
- **Data quality and integrity**. maintaining the accuracy, completeness, consistency, and reliability of the data throughout its lifecycle and across different platforms and systems.
- **Data governance and accountability.** establishing clear roles and responsibilities for the data owners, custodians, processors, and users, and implementing policies and procedures to monitor and audit the data activities and outcomes.

DATA MINIMIZATION & PURPOSE LIMITATION

Ethical international data transfer policies should adhere to the principles of data minimization and purpose limitation.

Organizations should only transfer the data necessary for the intended purpose and ensure that the data is not used for any purpose beyond what was initially consented to.

Data minimization means collecting and processing only the data that is necessary for a specific purpose and deleting it when it is no longer needed.

Purpose limitation means using the data only for the purpose for which it was collected, and not for any other incompatible or unlawful purposes.

International data transfer involves moving personal data across borders, which may expose it to different legal regimes and risks.

The primary concerns about data minimization and purpose limitation for international data transfer are:

- How to ensure that the data is adequately protected in the destination country, especially if it has lower or different standards of data protection than the source country.
- How to obtain valid consent from the data subjects for the transfer, especially if they are not aware of or informed about the potential consequences of the transfer.
- How to comply with the applicable laws and regulations in both the source and destination countries, especially if they are conflicting or inconsistent.
- How to monitor and audit the data processing activities of the third parties involved in the transfer, especially if they are in remote or inaccessible locations.
- How to handle any data breaches, complaints, or requests from the data subjects or authorities related to the transfer, especially if they involve multiple jurisdictions and parties.

THE ROLE OF ETHICAL LEADERSHIP

Ethical leadership is pivotal in shaping international data transfer policies that prioritize privacy and responsible data handling.

Organizations should cultivate an ethical culture where leaders and employees alike understand the importance of data protection, compliance, and ethical data practices.

The Role of Ethical Leadership is a framework that guides organizations in managing data across borders with respect for human rights, privacy, and security.

The primary concerns about this framework are:

- How to ensure that the ethical principles are aligned with the legal and regulatory requirements of different jurisdictions.
- How to balance the interests and expectations of various stakeholders, such as customers, employees, partners, and regulators.
- How to monitor and evaluate the effectiveness and impact of the ethical practices on data transfer and use.
- How to foster a culture of ethical awareness and accountability among data handlers and users.

International data transfers require organizations to be both compliant and ethically responsible. Policies that guide these transfers must align with international data protection laws, respect users' privacy rights, and uphold principles of transparency, security, and consent.

As technology continues to connect the globe, the ethical handling of data across borders becomes an essential pillar of trust-building, encouraging collaboration, and ensuring that the benefits of digital innovation are realized without compromising the rights and dignity of individuals.

2.3. PRIVACY BY DESIGN & DEFAULT

Where personal data has become a valuable commodity and technology shapes every facet of our lives, there is a pressing need to safeguard individuals' privacy.

The concept of *"Privacy By Design & Default"* has emerged as a powerful framework that aims to integrate privacy considerations into the process of technological innovation.

Privacy by Design & Default is a concept that emphasizes the integration of privacy considerations into the design and development process of products, services, and systems.

The goal is to ensure privacy is considered at every stage of any development process, from initial design to final deployment and beyond.

Privacy by Design & Default is a proactive implementation approach aimed at preventing privacy breaches rather than reacting to them after the fact.

It is built around seven key principles:

1. Proactive not reactive, preventative not remedial.
2. Privacy as a default setting.
3. Privacy embedded into design.
4. Full functionality - positive-sum not zero-sum.
5. End-to-end security – full lifecycle protection.
6. Visibility and transparency – keep it open.
7. Respect for user privacy – keep it user centric.

Privacy by Design & Default has become an internationally accepted framework for protecting privacy. It has also been incorporated into Article 25 of the European Union General Data Protection Regulation (GDPR), which has made "data protection by design and default" a mandatory requirement in the European Union and the United Kingdom.

In NSW, the Privacy and Personal Information Protection Act 1998 (PPIP Act) and the Health Records and Information Privacy Act 2002 (HRIP Act) continue to provide the overarching privacy framework. Both the PPIP Act and HRIP Act are principles based and focus on the collecting, holding, using or disclosing of personal and health information.

ELEVATING PRIVACY TO THE FOREFRONT

Traditionally, privacy concerns were addressed reactively, after technologies were developed and deployed.

However, the rising tide of data breaches, unauthorized data usage, and invasive practices has underscored the urgency of prioritizing privacy from the outset.

Privacy by design and default takes a proactive approach where privacy considerations are an inherent part of the entire lifecycle of technology, from conception to implementation.

To summarise:

- How to ensure that privacy is embedded into the design and architecture of IT systems and business practices.
- How to minimize the amount and sensitivity of personal data collected, used and retained.
- How to provide clear and transparent notice and choice to individuals about how their data is handled.
- How to implement strong security measures to protect personal data from unauthorized access or disclosure.
- How to respect the rights and preferences of individuals regarding their data, such as access, correction and deletion.
- How to comply with the relevant laws and regulations on data protection and privacy.

THE FOUNDATION OF PRIVACY BY DESIGN

At its core, privacy by design seeks to promote the idea that privacy should be a central consideration throughout the entire process of technological development. It entails integrating privacy into the architecture, design, and functionality of products and services. Rather than being an add-on, privacy becomes a fundamental building block.

The primary concerns are:

- How to ensure that the privacy principles are embedded into the design and operation of information systems and technologies.
- How to balance the competing interests and expectations of various stakeholders, such as users, regulators, developers, and providers.

- How to measure and demonstrate the effectiveness and compliance of the privacy by design approach.
- How to address the challenges and opportunities posed by emerging technologies, such as artificial intelligence, biometrics, and blockchain.
- How to foster a culture of privacy awareness and responsibility among all actors involved in the information lifecycle.

PROACTIVE PRIVACY CONSIDERATIONS

Privacy by design principles encompass several proactive considerations. These include data minimization, ensuring that only the minimum necessary data is collected and retained; user consent, obtaining clear and informed consent for data collection and usage; access controls, allowing users to manage their data and control who has access to it; and transparency, ensuring that users are informed about how their data will be used.

The primary concerns are:

- How to identify and assess the potential privacy risks and impacts of a project or system at the early stages of design and development.
- How to implement appropriate technical and organizational measures to ensure that the privacy principles and rights of data subjects are respected by default.
- How to monitor and evaluate the effectiveness and compliance of the privacy-enhancing solutions throughout the lifecycle of the project or system.
- How to communicate and demonstrate the benefits and value of proactive privacy considerations to stakeholders, customers, regulators, and the public.

ENSURING SECURITY MEASURES

Privacy by design and default is intertwined with security. Robust security measures are essential to protect the confidentiality, integrity, and availability of data. Encryption, access controls, regular audits, and secure coding practices are vital components that reinforce the protection of user data and maintain trust.

The primary concerns are how to:

- Implement data minimization and pseudonymization techniques to reduce the risk of unauthorized access or disclosure of personal information.
- Ensure that privacy policies and notices are clear, concise and transparent, and that users have meaningful choices and control over their data.
- Conduct privacy impact assessments and audits to identify and mitigate potential privacy risks and comply with relevant laws and regulations.
- Design and maintain secure systems and networks that protect data from cyberattacks, breaches and leaks.
- Train and educate staff and stakeholders on privacy best practices and ethical principles.

RESPECTING USER AUTONOMY

User autonomy is a fundamental aspect of privacy by design. Individuals should have control over their personal information, and their choices should be respected.

This includes the ability to review, correct, or delete their data, as well as the freedom to opt in or out of data collection and sharing.

- Respecting user autonomy means giving users meaningful choices and control over their personal data and how it is used.
- Privacy by design and default means embedding privacy principles and safeguards into the design and operation of products, services and systems that process personal data.
- The primary concerns about respecting user autonomy for privacy by design and default are:
- How to ensure that users are informed and aware of the privacy implications and risks of using a product, service or system.
- How to provide users with clear, concise and easy-to-understand privacy notices, policies and settings.
- How to obtain valid and informed consent from users for the collection, use and sharing of their personal data, especially for sensitive or unexpected purposes.
- How to respect users' preferences and rights to access, correct, delete or restrict their personal data.

- How to avoid or minimize the collection, use and retention of personal data that is not necessary or relevant for the intended purpose.
- How to prevent or mitigate privacy harms such as identity theft, discrimination, surveillance or manipulation that may result from the processing of personal data.

CULTURAL & ETHICAL CONSIDERATIONS

Privacy by design also recognizes the significance of cultural and ethical nuances in data usage. What might be considered acceptable data practices in one culture could be deemed invasive in another.

Ethical considerations play a role in designing technologies that align with societal norms and values.

- How to balance the rights and interests of different stakeholders, such as data subjects, data controllers, data processors, and third parties.
- How to ensure that privacy is embedded in the design and implementation of systems, processes, and products, and not treated as an afterthought or a compliance issue.
- How to respect the diversity and context of different cultures, values, and norms, and avoid imposing a one-size-fits-all approach to privacy.
- How to foster a culture of privacy awareness and responsibility among all actors involved in the data lifecycle and promote ethical decision-making and accountability.
- How to address the challenges and opportunities posed by emerging technologies, such as artificial intelligence, biometrics, and blockchain, and ensure that they are used in a privacy-friendly and ethical manner.

THE ROLE OF DATA PROTECTION LAWS

Data protection laws, such as the European Union's General Data Protection Regulation (GDPR) and California Consumer Privacy Act (CCPA), have further underscored the importance of privacy by design principles.

These laws require organizations to demonstrate accountability, transparency, and user control over data. Privacy by design provides a framework for organizations to fulfill these legal obligations in an ethical and responsible manner.

A CULTURAL SHIFT & ETHICAL IMPERATIVE

Implementing privacy by design and default necessitates a cultural shift within organizations. It requires fostering a mindset where every stakeholder, from developers to designers to decision-makers, considers privacy implications in their roles.

This shift reflects an ethical imperative to uphold individuals' rights and dignity, even as technology continues to evolve.

To summarise:

- How to balance the benefits of data-driven innovation with the risks of data misuse and abuse.
- How to foster a culture of trust and accountability among data controllers and processors.
- How to ensure that privacy is embedded into the design and operation of products, services and systems.
- How to empower data subjects with meaningful choices and control over their personal data.
- How to comply with the evolving legal and regulatory frameworks for data protection and privacy.

COLLABORATION & EDUCATION

Privacy by design is not a solitary endeavour; it requires collaboration across departments and expertise. Legal teams, developers, designers, and privacy experts must collaborate to ensure that privacy principles are integrated seamlessly into the technological fabric. Furthermore, ongoing education is crucial to ensure that all stakeholders understand the importance of privacy and remain informed about best practices.

Therefore, in the pursuit of innovation and technological progress, organizations must not lose sight of their ethical responsibility to protect individuals' privacy. Privacy by design and default represents a paradigm shift that emphasizes proactive and ethical data handling.

By including privacy considerations into all aspects of technology development, organizations not only comply with legal obligations but also elevate privacy to a fundamental right.

As privacy by design becomes a cornerstone of digital ethics, it lays the foundation for a more respectful, secure, and trustworthy digital landscape where individuals can confidently engage with technology while preserving their privacy and autonomy.

2.4. SURVEILLANCE & PRIVACY

SECURITY & INDIVIDUAL RIGHTS

In the digitized environment, the deployment of surveillance technologies has become a cornerstone of modern security measures. From closed-circuit television (CCTV) cameras to advanced data analytics, surveillance plays a crucial role in maintaining public safety and preventing criminal activities.

Security and individual rights are closely linked in the digital age, as modern technologies can pose serious threats to privacy and human rights, as well as enable them.

Spyware and other hacking tools can turn personal devices into surveillance devices, allowing unauthorized access to data, communications, location and other sensitive information. Such tools can be used to target journalists, activists, opposition figures and human rights defenders, violating their right to privacy and freedom of expression, among others.

Encryption is a key enabler of privacy and human rights online, as it protects the confidentiality and integrity of data and communications from unauthorized interception or manipulation. Encryption can also facilitate the exercise of other rights, such as access to information, health, education and participation.

Surveillance of public spaces, both offline and online, can have chilling effects on the rights to freedom of expression, assembly and association, as well as the right to non-discrimination. Biometric data, digital identity systems and social media monitoring can enable the tracking and profiling of individuals or groups based on their opinions, activities or characteristics.

IT governance, policy, ethics and law should be guided by international human rights standards and principles when addressing the challenges and opportunities of security and individual rights in the digital age. This includes ensuring that any interference with privacy or other rights is lawful, necessary, proportionate and subject to independent oversight and remedy. It also includes promoting a human-centric approach to the design, development and deployment of digital technologies that respects human dignity, autonomy and agency.

SURVEILLANCE IN THE DIGITAL AGE

Surveillance in the digital age is a complex phenomenon that poses significant challenges to privacy and human rights.

State authorities can and do use intrusive hacking tools, such as spyware, to access and monitor people's devices and communications, often for illegitimate reasons, such as suppressing dissent and targeting journalists and activists.

Encryption is a vital tool for protecting human rights online, as it enables secure and confidential communication and data storage. However, encryption is under threat from attempts to weaken it or bypass it by mandating backdoors or client-side scanning.

Public spaces, both offline and online, are subject to widespread digital monitoring, enabled by large-scale data collection and analysis, biometric systems, digitized identity schemes and social media surveillance. These practices can have chilling effects on freedom of expression, association and assembly.

Journalists and the wider public need to be aware of the risks and implications of digital surveillance, as well as the legal and ethical frameworks that regulate it. They also need to adopt digital security practices, such as using encryption, VPNs, secure messaging apps and password managers, to protect themselves and their sources.

Digital surveillance requires effective oversight, accountability and transparency mechanisms, based on international human rights law and standards. It also requires public debate and participation, as well as resistance and contestation from civil society actors.

THE ROLE OF SURVEILLANCE POLICIES

The role of surveillance policies is to regulate the use of modern networked digital technologies that can pose threats to privacy and human rights, such as spyware, encryption, and biometric databases.

Surveillance policies should be based on international human rights law and standards and respect the principles of privacy and data protection.

Surveillance policies should also balance the legitimate interests of governments in protecting national security, public health, and law enforcement with the rights and freedoms of individuals and groups.

Surveillance policies should be transparent, accountable, and subject to democratic oversight and judicial review.

Surveillance policies should be proportionate, necessary, and effective in achieving their objectives, and avoid creating risks of abuse, misuse, or harm.

BALANCING PUBLIC SAFETY & PRIVACY

Balancing public safety and privacy in the context of surveillance and privacy is a complex and challenging issue that requires careful consideration of the ethical, legal, and social implications.

Surveillance technologies can offer significant benefits for public health, crime prevention, and national security, but they also pose potential risks for individual rights, data protection, and social trust.

Given the benefits. responsible surveillance practices should prioritize individual rights, transparency, and accountability. This means that surveillance should be lawful, necessary, proportionate, and subject to oversight and review.

Some examples of successful models that effectively mitigate privacy risks while maintaining public safety are:

- The European Union's General Data Protection Regulation (GDPR), which provides a comprehensive framework for data protection and privacy in the digital age.
- The Privacy by Design approach (discussed earlier), which embeds privacy principles into the design and operation of surveillance systems and technologies.
- The Citizen Lab's research and advocacy on digital surveillance and human rights, which exposes abuses and promotes accountability and reform.

WARRANTED VS. UNWARRANTED SURVEILLANCE

Warranted surveillance is the observation and/or monitoring of a person or group by the government or its agents with proper legal authorization, such as a warrant or a court order.

Whereas unwarranted surveillance is the observation and/or monitoring of a person or group by the government or its agents without proper legal authorization, such as a warrant or a court order.

Warranted surveillance can be justified on the grounds of national security, law enforcement, public safety, or other legitimate public interests, as long as it is conducted in accordance with the law and respects the privacy rights of the individuals or groups under surveillance.

Unwarranted surveillance can be considered unethical, illegal, or unconstitutional, as it violates the privacy rights of the individuals or groups under surveillance and undermines the principle of checks and balances that prevents the abuse of power by the government or its agents.

The ethics of surveillance depends on several factors, such as the type and amount of data collected, the purpose and duration of the surveillance, the methods and technologies used, the safeguards and oversight mechanisms in place, and the consent and awareness of the individuals or groups under surveillance.

Some examples of technologies that enable warranted or unwarranted surveillance are cell phones, GPS, automated license plate readers (ALPRs), wearable devices, wiretaps, keystroke logging, encryption backdoors, etc.

Some sources that discuss the topic of warranted vs. unwarranted surveillance in the broader context of "Surveillance & Privacy" are:

- The Ethics (or not) of Massive Government Surveillance
- The Fourth Amendment of the US Constitution in the Digital Age.
- NSA warrantless surveillance (2001–2007).

CONSENT & TRANSPARENCY

Consent and transparency are key ethical principles for conducting surveillance and privacy practices in a responsible manner. Consent means obtaining the agreement of the individuals whose personal information is collected, used or disclosed for a specific purpose, and respecting their choices and preferences.

Transparency means providing clear and comprehensive information about the purpose, methods, scope and outcomes of the surveillance and privacy activities, and being accountable for the data handling practices.

Consent and transparency can help to build trust, protect individual rights, prevent misuse or abuse of data, and comply with legal obligations.

However, consent and transparency may not always be possible or desirable in some situations, such as when covert surveillance is necessary for law enforcement, national security, public safety or research purposes.

In such cases, covert surveillance should be conducted with due regard to the proportionality, necessity and legality of the surveillance activities, and with appropriate safeguards to protect the data subjects' interests and rights.

Some examples of covert surveillance techniques are hidden cameras, audio recorders, GPS trackers, spyware, keystroke loggers, facial recognition software and social media analysis.

Some examples of legitimate covert surveillance uses are crime prevention and detection, counterterrorism, fraud investigation, employee monitoring, market research and journalism.

DATA MINIMIZATION & PURPOSE LIMITATION

Data minimization & purpose limitation are two core data protection principles that aim to ensure that personal data are only collected and processed for specific, explicit and legitimate purposes.

Data Minimization means that personal data should be adequate, relevant and limited to what is necessary for the purposes of processing. This helps to reduce the risks of data breaches, misuse, or unauthorized access.

Purpose Limitation means that personal data should not be further processed in a way that is incompatible with the original purposes for which they were collected. This helps to respect the rights and expectations of data subjects and to maintain transparency and accountability.

Data Minimization & Purpose Limitation are required by various data protection regulations, such as the EU General Data Protection Regulation (GDPR) and the California Privacy Rights Act (CPRA).

To implement Data Minimization & Purpose Limitation in data-driven systems, some best practices include:

- Define the purpose of data collection and processing as clearly and explicitly as possible and communicate it to data subjects and other stakeholders.
- Evaluate the necessity and proportionality of the data collected and processed and avoid collecting or retaining any data that are excessive or irrelevant for the purposes.
- Use technical and organizational measures, such as anonymization, pseudonymization, encryption, access control, or data retention policies, to minimize the amount and exposure of personal data.
- Review and update the purposes and methods of data processing regularly and delete or anonymize any data that are no longer needed or compatible with the purposes.

ACCOUNTABILITY & OVERSIGHT

Accountability and oversight are essential for ensuring that government surveillance regimes respect human rights and the rule of law.

According to a global report by experts from various fields, 84% of the 86 countries surveyed lacked even moderately effective oversight and accountability mechanisms to protect Internet users from indiscriminate surveillance.

Some of the actors and mechanisms that can play a role in police oversight include internal and executive control, parliamentary and judicial oversight, independent complaint bodies, NGOs, the media, and international monitors.

Police equipped with body-worn cameras (BWCs) are a controversial technology that can have both positive and negative impacts on police accountability, integrity, and oversight. They can increase transparency, deter misconduct, and provide evidence, but they can also raise privacy, security, and ethical concerns.

A human rights-based approach to policing requires that police serve the needs of the community, be accountable to the law, protect human rights, be transparent in activities, and shift from a 'warrior mindset' to a 'protector mindset'.

PREVENTING DISCRIMINATORY PRACTICES

Preventing discriminatory practices in surveillance and privacy is an ethical and legal imperative for IT professionals. Data privacy is about the rights and responsibilities of data subjects and data collectors regarding access, use and collection of data.

Data privacy breaches can cause harm to individuals and society, such as loss of trust, security, reputation and legitimacy.

IT professionals should follow ethical principles and best practices to protect data privacy, such as:

- Respect the law and the rights of data subjects, including their consent, access and correction rights.
- Minimize the collection and retention of personal data and use anonymization or pseudonymization techniques when possible.
- Implement appropriate technical and organizational measures to ensure the confidentiality, integrity and availability of data.
- Conduct regular privacy impact assessments and audits to identify and mitigate privacy risks.
- Educate and train staff and stakeholders on data privacy policies, standards and guidelines.
- Report and respond to data breaches promptly and transparently.

DATA SECURITY & PROTECTION

Data security and protection are essential aspects of surveillance and privacy, as they aim to safeguard personal data from unauthorized or malicious access, use or disclosure.

Data security and protection are not only technical issues, but also ethical and legal ones, as they involve respecting the rights and interests of individuals whose data are collected and analysed by surveillance technologies.

Data security and protection require organisations to comply with relevant laws and regulations, such as the Privacy and Data Protection Act 2014 (PDP Act) and the Information Privacy Principles (IPPs) in Victoria, or the Privacy Act 1988 (Privacy Act) and the Australian Privacy Principles (APPs) at the federal level.

Data security and protection also require organisations to adopt a privacy enhancing approach to surveillance, which involves conducting privacy impact assessments, implementing privacy by design principles, obtaining informed consent from data subjects, minimising data collection and retention, ensuring data quality and accuracy, providing transparency and accountability mechanisms, and enabling data access and correction rights.

Data security and protection can benefit organisations by enhancing public trust and confidence, reducing legal risks and liabilities, improving operational efficiency and effectiveness, and fostering innovation and competitiveness.

SAFEGUARDING WHISTLEBLOWERS & JOURNALISTS

Ensure whistleblower protection laws cover genuine public interest disclosures that do not pose real harm to national security, defence or law enforcement interests.

Use end-to-end encryption tools to communicate securely and confidentially with sources and colleagues, and to protect the integrity of information.

Use internet protocols like HTTPS to protect data as it passes between news websites and readers, and to prevent censorship and tampering.

Protect devices and online platforms from hacking and surveillance by government and private actors, using strong passwords, antivirus software and VPNs.

Seek legal advice and support from professional associations or NGOs if facing threats, harassment or prosecution for reporting on sensitive issues.

2.5. AI ACCOUNTABILITY & TRANSPARENCY

AI accountability and transparency are important aspects of responsible and ethical use of AI systems. It means that people responsible for the different phases of the AI system lifecycle should be identifiable and accountable for the outcomes of the AI systems, and human oversight of AI systems should be enabled.

AI transparency means that there should be transparency and responsible disclosure so people can understand when they are being significantly impacted by AI and can find out when an AI system is engaging with them. It also means that the algorithms used in AI solutions are not hidden or unable to be looked at more closely.

Some best practices for ensuring AI accountability and transparency are:

- Use a small set of inputs that is necessary for the desired performance of the model. This can make it easier to accurately pinpoint where the correlation or the causation between variables comes from.
- Give explainable AI methods priority over models that are hard to interpret (i.e., black box models).
- Build accountability into your AI by defining the basic conditions for accountability throughout the entire AI life cycle — from design and development to deployment and monitoring — and laying out specific questions for leaders and organizations to ask, and the audit procedures to use, when assessing AI systems.
- Follow AI model security standards to minimize the risks of data breaches, model tampering, or adversarial attacks, and to ensure that machine learning systems produce trustworthy and consistent results.
- Align your AI systems with human-centred values, fairness, privacy protection and security, reliability and safety, contestability, and human, societal and environmental wellbeing.

THE RISE OF AI REVOLUTIONIZING DECISION-MAKING

AI systems should be designed, developed and deployed with the aim of benefiting individuals, society and the environment, while respecting human rights, diversity and autonomy.

AI systems should be inclusive and accessible and should not involve or result in unfair discrimination against individuals, communities or groups.

AI systems should respect and uphold privacy rights and data protection and ensure the security of data.

AI systems should reliably operate in accordance with their intended purpose and be subject to regular testing and monitoring.

AI systems should be transparent and explainable, so people can understand when they are being significantly impacted by AI and can find out when an AI system is engaging with them.

AI systems should be contestable, meaning that there should be a timely process to allow people to challenge the use or outcomes of the AI system.

AI systems should be accountable, meaning that people responsible for the different phases of the AI system lifecycle should be identifiable and accountable for the outcomes of the AI systems, and human oversight of AI systems should be enabled.

To achieve these principles, some of the best practices are:

- Use a small set of inputs that is necessary for the desired performance of the model, to make it easier to pinpoint where the correlation or causation between variables comes from.
- Give explainable AI methods priority over models that are hard to interpret (i.e., black box models).
- Follow AI model security standards to minimize the risks of bias, inconsistency or tampering.
- Disclose the objectives, limitations and assumptions of the AI system to the users and stakeholders.

ACCOUNTABILITY & TRANSPARENCY

Accountability and transparency are essential for building trust in AI systems and ensuring that they are used for beneficial outcomes for individuals, society and the environment.

Accountability means that people responsible for the different phases of the AI system lifecycle should be identifiable and accountable for the outcomes of the AI systems, and human oversight of AI systems should be enabled.

Transparency means that there should be transparency and responsible disclosure so people can understand when they are being significantly impacted by AI and can find out when an AI system is engaging with them. It also means that the algorithms used in AI solutions are not hidden or unable to be looked at more closely.

To ensure accountability and transparency in AI systems, some best practices are:

- Use a small set of inputs that is necessary for the desired performance of the model. This can make it easier to accurately pinpoint where the correlation or the causation between variables comes from.
- Give explainable AI methods priority over models that are hard to interpret (i.e., black box models).
- Follow AI model security standards to minimize the risks of data breaches, model tampering, or adversarial attacks that can compromise the reliability and fairness of AI systems.
- Implement mechanisms for contestability, which means that when an AI system significantly impacts a person, community, group or environment, there should be a timely process to allow people to challenge the use or outcomes of the AI system.

AI ETHICS ACCOUNTABILITY

AI accountability policies are guidelines or standards that ensure AI systems are designed, developed and deployed in an ethical, responsible and trustworthy manner.

AI accountability policies should address the following aspects of AI systems: *human, societal and environmental wellbeing; human-centred values; fairness; privacy protection and security; reliability and safety; transparency and explainability; contestability; and accountability.*

These aspects are derived from Australia's AI Ethics Principles, which are designed to ensure AI is safe, secure and reliable for all Australians.

AI accountability policies should also be informed by relevant research and best practices from various sources, such as the OECD's Principles on AI, the EU's Ethics Guidelines for Trustworthy AI, and the Practical Guide to Building Ethical AI by Harvard Business Review.

AI accountability policies should be tailored to the specific context and objectives of each AI system and should be regularly reviewed and updated to reflect changing circumstances and expectations.

AI accountability policies should be communicated clearly and openly to all stakeholders, including users, customers, employees, regulators, and the public.

TRANSPARENCY

Transparency involves making the decision-making process of AI systems visible and understandable to users. Transparency ensures that users can understand how decisions are made and can hold the system accountable if something goes wrong.

Transparency decreases the risk of error and misuse, distributes responsibility, enables internal and external oversight, and expresses respect for people. It is not an all-or-nothing proposition, however. Companies need to find the right balance with regards to how transparent to be with which stakeholders.

To increase the accountability of high-risk AI systems, we need to develop technologies to increase their end-to-end transparency and fairness.

To build accountability into AI systems, we need to define the basic conditions for accountability throughout the entire AI life cycle — from design and development to deployment and monitoring — and ask specific questions when assessing AI systems.

TRACEABILITY OF DECISIONS

Traceability of Decisions is a key requirement for trustworthy AI, related to the need to maintain a complete account of the provenance of data, processes, and artifacts involved in the production of an AI model.

Traceability helps to ensure transparency, explainability and communication of the AI system, as well as technical robustness, safety, privacy, data governance, diversity, non-discrimination, fairness, environmental and societal well-being, and accountability.

Traceability of Decisions can be best achieved by using transparent and auditable algorithms, as well as providing clear explanations of how decisions are made and who is responsible for those decisions.

Traceability of Decisions can be supported by tools, practices, and data models that enable the documentation and verification of the AI model's lifecycle, from data collection and processing to model development and deployment.

Traceability of Decisions can be integrated into the design process of AI systems by following the Transparency by Design principles, which cover relevant contextual, technical, informational, and stakeholder-sensitive considerations.

ADDRESSING BIAS & DISCRIMINATION

Some action points on addressing bias and discrimination in AI accountability and transparency are:

- Use diverse and representative training data to avoid amplifying existing biases or creating new ones.
- Develop transparent and explainable models that can provide clear and understandable reasons for their decisions.
- Conduct regular evaluation and updating of AI systems to monitor their performance and identify any potential issues.
- Promote diversity in AI development teams to ensure that different perspectives and values are considered in the design and deployment of AI systems.
- Follow clear regulatory standards that define the ethical principles and legal obligations for AI systems.
- Implement third-party audits to verify the compliance and quality of AI systems.
- Respect user empowerment and consent by informing them of how their data is used and giving them control over their participation in AI systems.
- Ensure continuous monitoring and compliance by establishing mechanisms for feedback, redress, and accountability.

These are some of the best practices based on research and literature on the topic of AI ethics. However, addressing bias and discrimination in AI is not a one-time or one-size-fits-all solution. It requires ongoing collaboration, communication, and learning among all stakeholders involved in the development and use of AI systems.

EXPLAINABILITY A PILLAR OF ACCOUNTABILITY

Explainability is a key aspect of AI accountability and transparency, as it helps to ensure that decisions made by AI systems are understandable and justifiable by humans.

Explainability can also help to foster trust, fairness, reliability, safety, and ethical standards in AI applications.

Best practices for achieving explainability in AI are:

- Disclose the purpose, scope, and limitations of the AI system to the users and stakeholders.
- Provide clear and accessible explanations of how the AI system works, how it reaches its conclusions, and what factors influence its outcomes.
- Monitor and evaluate the performance and behaviour of the AI system over time, and update or retrain it as needed to ensure its accuracy and consistency.
- Implement mechanisms for feedback, review, and appeal for the users and stakeholders who are affected by the AI system's decisions.
- Ensure that the AI system complies with relevant laws, regulations, and ethical principles.

AVOIDING BLACK BOX PHENOMENON

The black box problem in AI refers to the lack of transparency and interpretability of complex AI systems, such as deep learning models, that make decisions without explanation or justification.

This problem poses risks for the trustworthiness, ethics, fairness, safety and accountability of AI applications, especially when they affect significant human goods, such as security, health care and justice.

To avoid the black box phenomenon and promote AI accountability and transparency, some possible strategies are:

- **Explainable AI (XAI).** a branch of AI that aims to provide human-understandable explanations of how and why AI systems make decisions.
- **Open-source models**. AI models that are publicly available and can be inspected, modified and verified by anyone.

- **Algorithm governance**. a set of policies and practices that ensure the quality, reliability, ethics and compliance of AI systems throughout their lifecycle.

These strategies can help increase the confidence, acceptance and adoption of AI systems by various stakeholders, such as users, regulators, customers and auditors.

HUMAN OVERSIGHT & CONTROL

Human oversight and control is a key requirement for ensuring AI accountability and transparency, which are essential for ethical, safe and reliable AI systems.

Human oversight and control can take various forms, such as human-in-the-loop, human-on-the-loop or human-in-command, depending on the level of autonomy and impact of the AI system. As such it should respect human rights, diversity and autonomy of individuals, and prevent unfair discrimination or harm caused by AI systems.

Human oversight and control should enable transparency and explainability of AI systems, so that people can understand how and why AI decisions are made and challenge them if necessary. It should involve human expertise, collaboration and participation from relevant stakeholders, such as developers, users, regulators and affected communities.

It is desirable that human oversight and control should be adaptive and responsive to the changing context and outcomes of AI systems and ensure that human values and interests are always prioritised.

ETHICAL CONSIDERATIONS IN AI TRAINING DATA

Ensuring that the data is representative and diverse and does not reflect existing biases or prejudices in society.

Obtaining the data with consent and respect for privacy and ensuring that the data is secure and protected from unauthorized access or misuse.

Being transparent and accountable about the sources, methods, and quality of the data, and providing mechanisms for feedback and correction

Aligning the data with the values and goals of the stakeholders and ensuring that the data is used for ethical and beneficial purposes.

INCENTIVES FOR RESPONSIBLE AI

Define clear lines of accountability for AI applications, ensuring that algorithms, attributes and correlations are open to inspection and that internal and external checks enable equitable outcomes for all participants.

Adopt voluntary ethics principles and frameworks that align with Australia's Artificial Intelligence Ethics Framework and reflect the latest research and best practice on responsible AI.

Invest in education and training for AI developers, users and regulators, fostering a culture of trust, transparency and ethical awareness in the AI ecosystem.

Engage with diverse stakeholders and communities to understand their needs, expectations and concerns regarding AI, and co-design solutions that are inclusive, accessible and beneficial.

Monitor and evaluate the impacts of AI on society, economy and environment, and adjust the governance measures accordingly to ensure the safety, security and reliability of AI systems.

EDUCATIONAL INITIATIVES EMPOWERING STAKEHOLDERS

The first thing to do is define the purpose and scope of your educational initiative, as well as the intended outcomes and impact for the stakeholders involved. Stakeholders may include learners, educators, parents, policymakers, researchers, and AI developers.

Then identify and address the ethical challenges and risks of using AI in education, such as fairness, bias, privacy, autonomy, agency, and inclusion. Consider using existing frameworks and guidelines for ethical AI in education, such as the ones proposed by Holmes et al. or Chaudhry et al..

Ensure that your educational initiative is transparent and accountable to the stakeholders. Transparency means providing clear explanations of how AI systems operate, why they make certain decisions, and what assumptions they rely on. Accountability means being responsible for the consequences of AI systems and being able to correct or mitigate any harms or errors. You may refer to the principles of AI accountability suggested by Dignum or the NTIA.

Engage with the stakeholders throughout the design, development, deployment, and evaluation of your educational initiative. Seek their feedback, input, and consent on how AI systems are used and how they affect their learning experiences and outcomes. Foster a culture of trust and collaboration among the stakeholders by being responsive, respectful, and inclusive.

Evaluate the effectiveness and impact of your educational initiative using appropriate methods and metrics. Monitor and measure how AI systems perform, how they influence learning processes and outcomes, and how they align with ethical standards and values. Report and communicate your findings and recommendations to the stakeholders and other relevant audiences.

2.6. DATA BREACH NOTIFICATION & COMMUNICATION

Data breaches have become an unfortunate reality, posing significant threats to individuals' privacy and organizations' sensitive information. In response, data breach notification and communication policies have emerged as vital tools to address these challenges.

These policies establish clear guidelines for organizations to follow when a breach occurs, ensuring affected individuals and relevant authorities are promptly informed. Ethical and legal considerations underscore the importance of transparent and timely communication during data breaches, fostering trust, accountability, and responsible data handling.

TRANSPARENCY, TRUST, & ACCOUNTABILITY

Transparency, trust and accountability are essential principles for managing data breaches involving personal information.

Data breach notifications are required by law under the Privacy Act 1988 (Cth) when a breach is likely to result in serious harm to affected individuals and remedial action cannot prevent or mitigate the harm.

Data breach notifications should inform the affected individuals and the Office of the Australian Information Commissioner (OAIC) of the following: *what happened, what information was involved, what are the risks and impacts, what are the steps taken or planned to address the breach, and what are the options for individuals to protect themselves.*

Data breach notifications must be timely, clear, concise and easy to understand. They should also be honest, respectful and empathetic. It is not uncommon for organisations to wait weeks or months before notifying those affected. Meanwhile their personal information is being sold on the dark web.

Data breach notifications can help reduce the potential harm to individuals, restore trust and confidence in the organisation, and demonstrate compliance with legal obligations and ethical standards.

Such notifications should be part of a broader data breach response plan that includes preparation, containment, assessment, notification, review and evaluation stages.

Data breach response plans must be aligned with best practices and guidance from relevant authorities, such as the OAIC, the Data Protection Commissioner and industry bodies.

THE MODERN DATA LANDSCAPE

The ubiquity of digital systems has led to an unprecedented accumulation of personal and sensitive data. From financial records and healthcare information to personal preferences and online behaviours, data has become a valuable asset, making it an attractive target for cybercriminals.

The modern data landscape is dynamic, with data being collected, stored, processed, and shared across multiple platforms, devices, and jurisdictions.

Data breaches are therefore a serious threat to the privacy and security of personal information, and can have significant legal, reputational, and financial consequences for organisations and individuals.

As mentioned, data breach notification and communication should follow the best practices outlined by the Office of the Australian Information Commissioner (OAIC) in its Data Breach Preparation and Response Guide, as well as any applicable laws or regulations in the relevant jurisdictions.

Some of the best practices for data breach notification and communication are:

- Notify the OAIC and affected individuals as soon as practicable after becoming aware of a data breach that is likely to result in serious harm, unless remedial action can prevent or mitigate the risk of harm.
- Use multiple communication channels to ensure that all affected individuals are notified, such as email, phone, SMS, website, social media, or postal mail.
- Use plain language that is clear, concise, and accurate, and avoid technical jargon or legal terms that may confuse or mislead the recipients.
- Provide a comprehensive explanation of what happened, what information was involved, what actions have been taken to contain and resolve the breach, what steps are being taken to prevent future breaches, and what assistance or support is available to the affected individuals.

- Use effective headlines that capture the attention and convey the urgency of the message, such as "Important: Data Breach Notification" or "Urgent: Action Required Following Data Breach".
- Inform the affected individuals about the next steps they should take to protect themselves from potential harm, such as changing passwords, monitoring accounts, contacting credit reporting agencies, or seeking legal advice.

Data breach notification and communication should be tailored to the specific circumstances and context of each breach, considering factors such as the nature and extent of the breach, the type and sensitivity of the information involved, the potential harm to the affected individuals, and the expectations and preferences of the recipients.

DATA BREACH NOTIFICATION POLICIES

Data breach notification policies are a structured framework that organizations must adhere to when a data breach occurs. These policies outline the necessary steps for identifying, mitigating, and communicating the breach to the affected individuals and relevant authorities.

Have a written data breach response plan that outlines the roles and responsibilities of the data breach response team, the steps to contain, assess, notify and review the breach, and the communication strategies for internal and external stakeholders.

Consider the safety and privacy of the individuals whose personal information has been compromised and avoid disclosing any confidential or sensitive information that could put them at further risk.

Comply with the requirements of the Privacy Act 1988 (Cth) and the Notifiable Data Breaches (NDB) scheme, which mandate notification to the affected individuals and the Office of the Australian Information Commissioner (OAIC) if a data breach is likely to result in serious harm.

Provide clear and timely information to the affected individuals about the nature and extent of the breach, the steps taken to mitigate the harm, the actions they can take to protect themselves, and the contact details for further assistance.

Review the incident and identify the causes and contributing factors of the breach and implement measures to prevent or reduce the likelihood of future breaches.

PROMOTING TRANSPARENCY

At the core of data breach notification policies lies the principle of transparency. Organizations are ethically obligated to communicate openly about breaches, ensuring individuals are aware of potential risks to their personal data.

Promoting transparency in data breach notification and communication is essential for building trust with customers and complying with legal obligations.

Transparency involves being honest and clear about what personal information has been compromised, how the breach occurred, what actions have been taken to contain and remediate the breach, and what steps are being taken to prevent future breaches.

Transparency also involves notifying the affected individuals and the relevant authorities as soon as possible and providing them with guidance on how to reduce or avoid the potential harm from the breach.

Transparency can help reduce the reputational impact of a data breach, as well as mitigate the risk of legal action or regulatory enforcement.

Therefore, to promote transparency, organisations should have a data breach response plan that outlines the roles and responsibilities of staff, the procedures for identifying and assessing breaches, the criteria for determining whether a breach is notifiable, and the communication strategies for informing stakeholders.

Organisations should also follow the best practices of data privacy, such as explaining how they use personal information, extracting insights rather than identifiable information, and facilitating the flow of consented data for customer benefit.

TIMELINESS THE ETHICAL IMPERATIVE

Ethical data breach notification policies stress the urgency of timely communication. Delayed notification can exacerbate the impact of a breach, allowing cybercriminals more time to exploit compromised data.

Timeliness is an ethical imperative in data breach notification because it can reduce or prevent the harm to the affected individuals and restore the trust in the organisation that handles their personal information.

The Privacy Act 1988 (Cth) requires organisations to notify individuals and the Commissioner of eligible data breaches as soon as practicable after becoming aware of them, unless an exception applies.

An eligible data breach occurs when there is any unauthorised access, disclosure or loss of personal information that is likely to result in serious harm to any of the individuals to whom the information relates.

To determine whether a data breach is likely to result in serious harm, organisations should consider the nature and sensitivity of the personal information involved, the circumstances of the breach, and the potential consequences for the individuals.

Timely notification and communication can help individuals to take steps to protect themselves from the harm, such as changing passwords, monitoring accounts, or contacting their financial institutions.

Timely notification and communication can also demonstrate that the organisation is taking the data breach seriously, is committed to protecting the privacy of its customers or clients and is transparent and accountable for its actions.

To achieve timeliness in data breach notification and communication, organisations should have a data breach response plan that outlines the roles and responsibilities of staff, the steps to contain, assess, notify and review a data breach, and the communication strategies and channels to use.

Organisations should also train their staff on how to identify and report a data breach, and regularly review and update their data breach response plan to ensure its effectiveness.

BALANCING LEGAL COMPLIANCE & ETHICAL VALUES

Data breach notification policies often align with legal requirements imposed by data protection regulations. However, ethical considerations go beyond legal mandates, emphasizing the moral responsibility of organizations to safeguard individuals' data and rights.

Balancing legal compliance and ethical values in data breach notification and communication is a complex and challenging task that requires careful consideration of various factors, such as:

- The applicable laws and regulations in different jurisdictions that may impose different obligations and standards for data breach notification and communication, such as the type, timing, content, and format of the notification.
- The ethical values and expectations of the stakeholders that may go beyond the legal requirements and demand more transparency, accountability, and responsiveness from the organization.
- The potential risks and benefits of disclosing or withholding certain information about the data breach, such as the cause, scope, severity, and consequences of the breach, as well as the remedial measures taken or planned by the organization.

Based on research and best practice, some of the general principles and guidelines for balancing legal compliance and ethical values in data breach notification and communication are:

- Be proactive and prepared - develop a data breach response plan that outlines the roles, responsibilities, procedures, and resources for data breach notification and communication. Conduct regular training and testing to ensure that the plan is effective and up-to-date.
- Be timely and accurate - notify the affected stakeholders as soon as possible after discovering a data breach, without unreasonable delay. Provide accurate and factual information about the data breach, without speculation or exaggeration. Update the information as new facts emerge or circumstances change.
- Be clear and concise - use plain and simple language that is easy to understand by the intended audience. Avoid technical jargon or legal terms that may confuse or mislead the stakeholders. Use appropriate channels and formats to communicate the information, such as email, phone call, letter, website, social media, etc.
- Be respectful and empathetic - acknowledge the impact and harm caused by the data breach to the stakeholders. Express sincere apology and regret for the incident. Demonstrate genuine concern and care for the stakeholders' well-being

and security. Offer assistance and support to help them cope with the aftermath of the data breach.

- Be honest and accountable - admit responsibility and liability for the data breach, if applicable. Explain the root cause and contributing factors of the data breach. Disclose the actions taken or planned to investigate, contain, recover, and prevent future breaches. Cooperate with relevant authorities and regulators in their inquiries or investigations. Accept feedback and criticism from the stakeholders and address their questions or concerns.

INDIVIDUAL EMPOWERMENT

Notification policies empower affected individuals by providing them with information about the breach. This empowers them to take proactive measures to protect themselves from potential identity theft or fraud.

Individual empowerment is therefore the ability of individuals to exercise control over their personal information and protect their privacy rights.

Data breach notification and communication is the process of informing individuals and relevant authorities when their personal information has been compromised by a data breach.

As a professional with expertise in IT governance, policy, ethics and law, you should advise on the following aspects of individual empowerment in data breach notification and communication:

- The legal and ethical obligations to notify individuals and authorities of a data breach, such as the Privacy Act 1988 (Cth) and the Notifiable Data Breaches (NDB) scheme in Australia or the General Data Protection Regulation (GDPR) in the European Union.
- The best practices to prepare for and respond to a data breach, such as developing a data breach response plan, identifying the lead supervisory authority, assessing the risk and impact of the breach, containing and mitigating the breach, and evaluating and improving the response.
- The effective ways to communicate with individuals and authorities about a data breach, such as providing clear and timely information, describing the nature and extent of the

breach, explaining the actions taken and the remedies available, and recommending steps to protect personal information.

- The benefits of reporting a data breach voluntarily or proactively, such as demonstrating accountability and transparency, strengthening data protection processes, preventing future breaches, minimising reputational and financial harm, and maintaining public trust.

MINIMIZING PANIC & MISINFORMATION

Data breaches involving personal information can put affected individuals at risk of serious harm and damage an organisation's reputation as a data custodian.

When a data breach occurs, a quick and effective response can have a positive impact on people's perceptions of an organisation's trustworthiness.

An effective response to a data breach is one that successfully reduces or removes the risk of harm to individuals, and that aligns with legislative requirements and community expectations.

To minimise panic and misinformation, organisations should communicate security breach notifications to customers in a clear, timely and comprehensive manner.

Some best practices for communicating security breach notifications are:

- Scan local data breach laws and comply with any notification obligations.
- Incorporate the right sentiment, such as empathy, honesty and accountability.
- Use plain language and avoid technical jargon or legal terms.
- Give a comprehensive explanation of what happened, what information was affected, what actions were taken, and what risks are involved.
- Use effective headlines and subject lines that capture attention and convey urgency.
- Inform about the next steps, such as how customers can protect themselves, how to contact the organisation for more information or assistance, and what measures the organisation is taking to prevent future breaches.

STRENGTHENING TRUST & REPUTATION

Be prepared for a data breach by developing and implementing an effective data breach response strategy that aligns with legislative requirements and community expectations.

Notify the relevant authorities and regulators of any data breach that is likely to cause serious harm to affected individuals, unless you can demonstrate otherwise.

Notify the affected individuals and the Office of the Information Commissioner (OIC) of any data breach that is likely to cause serious harm to them, as this is good privacy practice and promotes openness and transparency.

Contain the breach as quickly as possible and take steps to prevent a repeat by reviewing your information security policies and procedures.

Reduce the reputational impact of a data breach by effectively minimising the risk of harm to affected individuals, and by demonstrating accountability in your data breach response.

COLLABORATION WITH AUTHORITIES

Collaboration with authorities is an essential aspect of data breach notification and communication, as it can help mitigate the risks and impacts of a breach, as well as demonstrate compliance with legal and ethical obligations.

Depending on the jurisdiction and the nature of the breach, there may be different authorities that need to be notified, such as data protection regulators, law enforcement agencies, sector-specific regulators, or contractual partners.

The notification should be made as soon as possible after becoming aware of the breach and should include relevant information such as the nature and extent of the breach, the personal data affected, the potential consequences for the data subjects, the measures taken or proposed to address the breach, and the contact details of the data protection officer or other point of contact.

The notification should also be clear, concise, transparent, and written in plain English, avoiding technical jargon or legal terms that may confuse or mislead the data subjects or the authorities.

The notification should be made through appropriate channels, such as online portals, email, phone, or post, depending on the preferences and requirements of the authorities. The notification should also be documented and recorded for future reference and evidence.

Collaboration with authorities should not end with the notification, but should continue throughout the breach response process, by providing updates, seeking guidance, cooperating with investigations, and implementing recommendations.

CONTINUOUS IMPROVEMENT & LEARNING

Continuous Improvement & Learning (CIL) is a key aspect of data breach notification and communication, as it helps organisations to prevent, prepare for and respond to data breaches effectively.

CIL involves reviewing and learning from data breach incidents, identifying the root causes, implementing prevention plans, and updating policies and procedures accordingly.

CIL also involves communicating the lessons learned and the actions taken to relevant stakeholders, such as affected individuals, regulators, partners, and employees.

CIL can help organisations to reduce the risk of harm to individuals, comply with the Privacy Act 1988 (Cth) and the Notifiable Data Breaches (NDB) scheme, and maintain trust and reputation as data custodians.

Some sources of information and guidance on CIL for data breach notification and communication are:

- Data breach preparation and response - Office of the Australian Information Commissioner
- Part 3: Responding to data breaches – four key steps | OAIC
- Data Breach Response: The Continuous Improvement Cycle - Tanner De Witt Solicitors

EDUCATIONAL INITIATIVES EMPOWERING USERS

Educate users on how to protect their personal information and prevent data breaches, such as using strong passwords, avoiding phishing emails, and reporting suspicious activities.

Inform users about their rights and obligations under the Privacy Act 1988 (Cth) and the Notifiable Data Breaches (NDB) scheme, which require organisations to notify individuals and the Commissioner of eligible data breaches that are likely to result in serious harm.

Provide clear and timely communication to users in the event of a data breach, following the four key steps: *contain, assess, notify, and review*. Use appropriate channels and methods to reach the affected users, such as letters, emails, websites, or media releases.

Offer support and assistance to users who may be affected by a data breach, such as providing identity theft prevention tips, identity monitoring services, or counselling services.

Engage with users and seek feedback on how to improve data security practices and policies and demonstrate a commitment to privacy and trust.

2.7. CYBERSECURITY TRAINING & ETHICAL HACKING

RESILIENT DEFENSES & RESPONSIBLE PRACTICES

Offensive cyber security training involves teaching students how to perform penetration testing, ethical hacking and other techniques to identify and exploit vulnerabilities in systems and networks.

This type of training can have many benefits, such as improving the security posture of organizations, enhancing the skills and knowledge of cyber security professionals, and contributing to the advancement of cyber security research and innovation.

However, such training also poses significant ethical risks, such as misuse or abuse of the acquired skills, violation of privacy or confidentiality, damage to systems or data, or harm to individuals or society at large.

Therefore, you should follow some ethical principles for designing responsible offensive cyber security training, such as:

- **Principle 1: Respect for autonomy**. You should respect the autonomy of your students and other stakeholders by informing them about the objectives, methods, risks and benefits of the training, and obtaining their consent before engaging in any offensive cyber security activities.
- **Principle 2: Beneficence and non-maleficence**. You should aim to maximize the benefits and minimize the harms of the training for your students and other stakeholders by ensuring that the training is relevant, proportionate, necessary and effective.
- **Principle 3: Justice**. You should ensure that the training is fair and equitable for your students and other stakeholders by avoiding discrimination, bias, favouritism or exploitation, and providing equal opportunities for participation and learning.
- **Principle 4: Accountability**. You should be accountable for your actions and decisions in the training by adhering to relevant laws, regulations, standards and codes of conduct, and being transparent, honest and responsible for the outcomes and impacts of the training.
- **Principle 5: Education**. You should educate your students and other stakeholders about the ethical implications of offensive cyber security by raising their awareness, fostering their

critical thinking, and encouraging their ethical reasoning and decision-making.

In addition to these principles, you should also follow some good practices for cyber resilience that can help you protect your assets, detect threats, respond to incidents and recover from disruptions. Some of these practices are:

- Developing a cybersecurity strategy and governance framework that aligns with your organizational goals and objectives, and involves board engagement and oversight.
- Implementing a cyber risk management process that identifies, assesses, treats and monitors cyber risks, including those related to third parties such as vendors or partners.
- Collaborating and sharing information with other organizations, security agencies and law enforcement entities to enhance your situational awareness, threat intelligence and incident response capabilities.
- Managing your assets effectively by maintaining an inventory of your critical internal and external assets (e.g. software and data), and ensuring their visibility, availability and integrity.
- Implementing protective measures and controls based on the Australian Signals Directorate's (ASD) Strategies to mitigate targeted cyber intrusions (or equivalent), as well as additional controls such as encryption for data in transit.
- Using detection systems and processes that enable continuous monitoring of your systems and networks, and leverage data analytics to integrate sources of threats in real time.

THE DIGITAL LANDSCAPE A BREEDING GROUND FOR THREATS

The rapid digitization of business processes, coupled with the proliferation of internet-connected devices, has created an expansive attack surface for cybercriminals.

Data breaches, ransomware attacks, and other cyber threats have become pervasive, requiring organizations to adopt proactive measures to defend their assets.

Identify the unique risks introduced by emerging technologies such as artificial intelligence and machine learning and evaluate your current framework to address them effectively and efficiently.

Ensure that your organization follows ethical principles and values when adopting and implementing new technologies and avoid any violations or compromises that could harm your reputation, customers, or stakeholders.

Implement data security measures to protect the integrity and accuracy of the data used and generated by new technologies, especially when they are involved in crucial predictions or decisions.

Monitor and review the performance and outcomes of new technologies regularly and seek feedback from relevant parties to ensure alignment with your business objectives and stakeholder expectations.

THE ROLE OF CYBERSECURITY TRAINING POLICIES

Cybersecurity training policies are essential for raising employee awareness of potential threats and their responsibility in protecting the company's data.

Cybersecurity training policies should be aligned with the organization's cyber security guidelines and information security manual, and cover topics such as authorized use of systems, protection of systems, reporting of incidents, and personnel security.

Said policies should provide tailored content for different groups of personnel, such as privileged users, who may require additional training on how to prevent and respond to cyberattacks.

These policies should be updated regularly to reflect the changing threat landscape and the latest best practices in cyber security.

They should be supported by effective assessment and feedback mechanisms to measure the impact of the training and identify areas for improvement.

THE HUMAN ELEMENT IN CYBERSECURITY

Elevating the human element in cybersecurity means strengthening the awareness, skills and behaviours of the people who interact with digital systems and data.

According to a report by Verizon, human errors and actions accounted for 82% of all cyberattacks in 2022 . Therefore, it is crucial to train and educate employees on how to prevent and respond to cyber threats.

Some best practices for elevating the human element in cybersecurity are:

- Offering continuous training opportunities for all staff members, from the CEO to the receptionist, on their role in protecting the organization from cyber risks.
- Deploying advanced email protections, such as spam filters, phishing simulations and email encryption, to reduce the chances of falling victim to malicious messages.
- Revisiting the approach to password security, such as enforcing strong and unique passwords, using password managers and changing passwords regularly.
- Updating multifactor authentication controls, such as using biometric or token-based verification methods, to add an extra layer of security for accessing sensitive data or systems.
- Using insider threat protection technology, such as user behaviour analytics or data loss prevention tools, to monitor and detect abnormal or suspicious activities by authorized users.

ETHICAL HACKING A PROACTIVE APPROACH TO SECURITY

Ethical hacking is the use of hacking skills and techniques with good intentions and with the full consent and approval of the target.

Ethical hackers help organizations identify and fix vulnerabilities in their IT systems, networks, and applications before malicious hackers can exploit them.

Ethical hacking is a valued component of cybersecurity, but it is not the same as cybersecurity. Cybersecurity is a broader term that encompasses all the policies, practices, and tools that protect IT environments from cyber threats. Ethical hacking is a proactive approach that involves system testing to find and address weaknesses.

Ethical hacking requires a high level of technical skills, ethical standards, and legal compliance. Ethical hackers must follow certain principles, such as obtaining the target's consent, defining the scope of their activities, reporting their findings, and respecting the target's privacy and security.

It can benefit organizations in various ways, such as improving their security posture, enhancing their reputation, complying with regulations, and saving costs.

Ethical hacking can also benefit society by raising awareness of cyber risks, promoting ethical values, and contributing to cyber resilience.

THE RESPONSIBILITY OF RESPONSIBLE HACKING

Responsible hacking is the practice of using hacking skills for ethical, legal or beneficial purposes, such as testing the security of systems, finding vulnerabilities, or exposing wrongdoing.

Responsible hacking requires adhering to certain principles and standards, such as obtaining consent, respecting privacy, avoiding harm, reporting findings, and complying with laws and regulations.

Responsible hacking also entails being aware of the risks and consequences of hacking activities, such as legal liability, reputational damage, or retaliation from malicious actors.

As an IT professional, you should advise your clients or employers on how to implement responsible hacking practices in their cybersecurity training and ethical hacking programs.

Some of the best practices for responsible hacking include:

- Establishing clear policies and procedures for ethical hacking activities, such as defining the scope, objectives, methods, and reporting mechanisms.
- Obtaining written authorization from the owners or operators of the systems to be hacked and ensuring that the hacking activities do not violate any contractual or legal obligations.
- Conducting regular security assessments and audits to identify and remediate vulnerabilities, and using only approved tools and techniques that minimize the impact on the systems.
- Educating and training staff on ethical hacking skills and principles and ensuring that they follow the code of conduct and professional standards of the industry.
- Collaborating with other stakeholders, such as law enforcement agencies, regulators, or industry associations, to share information, best practices, and lessons learned.

Some of the sources that you can refer to for more information on responsible hacking are:

- Cybersecurity Laws and Regulations Report 2023 Australia, which covers common issues in cybersecurity laws and regulations in Australia.
- Cybersecurity. Who is responsible? which discusses the roles and responsibilities of different actors in cybersecurity.
- Who is Liable when Business Emails are Hacked? which explains the legal implications of hacking business emails in Australia.

MITIGATING LEGAL & REPUTATIONAL RISKS

Ethical hacking is a valuable practice that can help organizations improve their cybersecurity posture and prevent malicious attacks.

However, ethical hackers also face legal and reputational risks if they do not follow certain principles and guidelines.

Some of the best practices for mitigating legal and reputational risks in ethical hacking are:

- Obtain written consent from the client or the target organization before conducting any penetration testing or vulnerability assessment. This consent should specify the scope, duration, and objectives of the ethical hacking activity, as well as the roles and responsibilities of both parties.
- Follow the principle of least privilege and only access the minimum amount of data and systems necessary to perform the ethical hacking task. Avoid accessing, modifying, or deleting any sensitive or personal information that is not relevant to the security assessment.
- Report any findings or incidents to the client or the target organization in a timely and transparent manner. Provide clear and actionable recommendations on how to address the identified vulnerabilities or threats. Do not disclose any information to third parties without prior authorization.
- Adhere to the relevant laws, regulations, standards, and codes of ethics that apply to the ethical hacking domain. Respect the privacy, confidentiality, and intellectual property rights of the client or the target organization and their stakeholders.
- Maintain a high level of professionalism and integrity throughout the ethical hacking process. Do not engage in any

malicious, fraudulent, or illegal activities that could harm the client or the target organization or their reputation.

BUILDING A CULTURE OF CYBERSECURITY

Building a culture of cybersecurity involves transforming the way everyone works, the way leaders lead, the way processes execute, and the way issues are managed.

A strong cybersecurity culture helps protect the enterprise's most important asset: its data. Human error or behaviour causes 90% of all cyberattacks. Therefore, employees need to be aware of the security risks and the processes for avoiding them.

Creating a robust cybersecurity culture means being transparent, clear and consistent in messaging. Be constructive in your approach to training. Don't reprimand employees for getting things wrong, treat it as a learning curve and use it to build a culture where no question is too basic.

Some practical ways to build a cybersecurity culture are: *setting clear security rules, investing in ongoing employee cybersecurity training, strengthening security with regular penetration tests, backing up words with actions, and leading by example in cybersecurity*.

A cybersecurity culture is not a one-time effort, but a continuous process that requires constant monitoring, evaluation and improvement. It should be aligned with the organization's goals, values and mission.

STAYING AHEAD OF EVOLVING THREATS

Staying ahead of evolving threats in cybersecurity training and ethical hacking requires a holistic approach that aligns IT governance, policy, ethics and law with the organisation's strategy and objectives.

Data ethics is a key aspect of IT governance that seeks to preserve the trust of users, clients, employees and partners by ensuring appropriate data management practices across the value chain, from collection to analytics to insights.

IT governance frameworks, such as ISO 38500, COBIT and ITIL, can help organisations implement effective IT governance programmes that address IT risks, legal and regulatory obligations, stakeholder expectations and return on IT investment.

Ethical hacking is a form of IT security testing that simulates malicious attacks on systems or networks to identify vulnerabilities and weaknesses that could be exploited by real hackers.

Ethical hacking should follow certain principles and guidelines, such as obtaining prior consent from the system owner, respecting the privacy and confidentiality of data, reporting the findings and recommendations to the system owner, and avoiding any harm to the system or network.

BALANCING PREVENTION & INNOVATION

To balance prevention and innovation in cybersecurity training and ethical hacking, some of the best practices are:

- Conducting internal trainings for staff members and technical developers on fundamental ethics and ethical codes of conduct.
- Conducting follow-up audits to assess the level of compliance with the core ethical principles.
- Adopting a risk-based approach to ethical hacking, prioritizing the most critical assets and threats.
- Employing a diverse team of ethical hackers with different backgrounds, perspectives, and skills.
- Collaborating with other stakeholders, such as regulators, researchers, customers, etc., to share knowledge and insights.
- Seeking external guidance or consultation from experts or authorities when facing ethical dilemmas or uncertainties.

CONTINUOUS LEARNING & SKILL DEVELOPMENT

Enrol in a reputable and accredited ethical hacking certification program that covers the latest tools, techniques, and methodologies used by ethical hackers. For example, the Certified Ethical Hacker (CEH) credential from EC-Council is the most trusted ethical hacking certification that employers worldwide value.

Practice your ethical hacking skills in a safe and legal environment using hands-on labs, practice ranges, mock engagements, and cyber competitions. These will help you gain experience, confidence, and recognition in the field. The CEH v12 program offers a comprehensive learning framework that includes all these elements.

Stay updated on the latest trends, threats, and technologies in cybersecurity and ethical hacking by reading blogs, newsletters, journals, podcasts, and webinars. You can also join online communities and forums where you can network with other ethical hackers and learn from their experiences.

Engage in continuous learning and skill development by taking advantage of online courses, workshops, webinars, podcasts, and other resources that cover topics such as malware analysis, cloud and IoT hacking, social engineering, ransomware, supply chain attacks, etc. You can also participate in skill challenges and hackathons to test your knowledge and abilities.

CHAPTER 2 WORKSHOP:
CYBERSECURITY & DATA PROTECTION

This is a 20-minute workshop exercise for IT professionals who want to learn more about cybersecurity and data protection. The exercise is based on the topics covered in Chapter 2 of the IT Governance, Policy, Ethics and Law textbook.

The exercise consists of three parts: reading, discussion and reflection.

PART 1: READING

Read the following article that summarizes the main concepts and challenges of cybersecurity and data protection. The article is written in plain English and uses subheads to make it more readable.

Cybersecurity and data protection are two interrelated aspects of IT governance that aim to ensure the confidentiality, integrity and availability of data and systems. Cybersecurity refers to the measures taken to prevent, detect and respond to cyberattacks that can compromise data and systems. Data protection refers to the legal and ethical obligations to respect the rights and interests of data subjects, such as customers, employees and citizens, when collecting, processing and sharing their personal data.

Cybersecurity and data protection face several challenges in the current digital environment, such as:

- **International data transfers and privacy**: Data flows across borders are essential for global business and innovation, but they also pose risks for data protection, as different countries have different laws and standards for privacy. How can IT professionals ensure that data transfers comply with the applicable regulations and respect the preferences of data subjects?
- **Privacy by design and default**: Privacy by design is an approach that embeds privacy principles into the design and development of systems, products and services. Privacy by default is a setting that ensures that the most privacy-friendly options are selected by default. How can IT professionals implement privacy by design and default in their projects and processes?
- **Surveillance and privacy**: Surveillance is the monitoring of activities, behaviors and communications of individuals or groups, often for security or intelligence purposes. Surveillance

can be conducted by governments, corporations or other actors, using various technologies, such as cameras, drones, biometrics or online tracking. How can IT professionals balance the benefits and risks of surveillance for privacy and human rights?

- **AI accountability and transparency**: AI is the use of machines or software that can perform tasks that normally require human intelligence, such as reasoning, learning or decision making. AI can enhance efficiency, innovation and personalization, but it can also pose challenges for accountability and transparency, as AI systems may be complex, opaque or biased. How can IT professionals ensure that AI systems are accountable and transparent to their users, stakeholders and regulators?

- **Data breach notification and communication**: A data breach is an unauthorized or accidental disclosure, alteration or loss of data that may harm the rights or interests of data subjects or other parties. Data breaches can be caused by cyberattacks, human errors or technical failures. How can IT professionals notify and communicate with the affected parties in a timely, clear and responsible manner?

- **Cybersecurity training and ethical hacking**: Cybersecurity training is the education and awareness of IT professionals and other staff on the best practices and standards for cybersecurity. Ethical hacking is the authorized use of hacking techniques to test the security of systems or networks. How can IT professionals improve their cybersecurity skills and knowledge through training and ethical hacking?

PART 2: DISCUSSION

Form groups of three or four participants and discuss the following questions based on the article:

- Which of the topics do you find most relevant or interesting for your work or industry? Why?
- Which of the topics do you find most challenging or difficult to deal with? Why?
- What are some examples of good or bad practices that you have encountered or heard of in relation to any of the topics?
- What are some recommendations or tips that you would give to other IT professionals or organizations regarding any of the topics?

PART 3: REFLECTION

Write a short paragraph reflecting on what you have learned from the article and the discussion. Consider the following points:

- What are some key takeaways or insights that you have gained from the exercise?
- How will you apply what you have learned to your work or projects?
- What are some questions or issues that you would like to explore further or learn more about?

CHAPTER 3:
CLOUD COMPUTING & OUTSOURCING

CHAPTER SUMMARY

Cloud computing and outsourcing are two ways of delivering IT services to organizations. Cloud computing is the use of remote servers and networks to store, process and access data, software and applications over the internet. Outsourcing is the contracting of a third-party provider to perform IT functions that would otherwise be done in-house.

The main benefits of cloud computing and outsourcing are:

Cost savings. Organizations can reduce their capital and operational expenses by paying only for the resources they use and avoiding the maintenance and upgrade costs of owning IT infrastructure.

Scalability. Organizations can easily adjust their IT capacity and performance according to their changing needs and demands, without having to invest in new hardware or software.

Flexibility. Organizations can access their IT services from anywhere, anytime and on any device, if they have an internet connection.

Innovation. Organizations can leverage the expertise and innovation of the cloud and outsourcing providers, who offer the latest technologies and solutions in the market.

However, cloud computing and outsourcing also include these challenges:

Security. Organizations must entrust their sensitive data and information to the cloud and outsourcing providers, who may not have adequate security measures or policies to protect them from unauthorized access, theft or loss.

Privacy. Organizations must comply with the privacy laws and regulations of the countries where their data is stored or processed, which may differ from their own or conflict with each other.

Reliability. Organizations must depend on the availability and performance of the internet and the cloud and outsourcing providers, who may experience downtime, outages or service degradation due to technical issues or natural disasters.

Control. Organizations must relinquish some control over their IT functions and resources to the cloud and outsourcing providers, who may not meet their expectations or requirements in terms of quality, service level or customization.

Therefore, organizations must carefully weigh the pros and cons of cloud computing and outsourcing, and adopt appropriate governance, policy, ethics and law frameworks to ensure that they achieve their strategic objectives and manage their risks effectively.

3.1 CLOUD COMPUTING & OUTSOURCING

CLOUD COMPUTING & OUTSOURCING

Cloud computing and outsourcing are two concepts that have become increasingly popular in the business world. Cloud computing refers to the delivery of computing services, such as servers, storage, databases, networking, software, analytics, and intelligence, over the internet. Outsourcing refers to the practice of contracting out a business process or function to a third-party provider.

Both cloud computing and outsourcing can offer many benefits to businesses, such as cost savings, scalability, flexibility, innovation, and access to specialised skills and expertise. However, they also come with certain risks and challenges, such as security, compliance, governance, performance, quality, and vendor management.

STRATEGY

Before adopting cloud computing and outsourcing, you should have a clear strategy that aligns with your business goals and objectives.

You should identify the business problems you want to solve, the opportunities you want to seize, and the value you want to create with cloud computing and outsourcing. You should also assess your current capabilities and gaps, and determine which processes or functions are suitable for cloud computing and outsourcing.

SOLUTION SELECTION PROCESS

Once you have a strategy in place, you should conduct a thorough market research and evaluation of potential cloud computing and outsourcing providers. You should compare different options based on criteria such as cost, quality, reliability, security, compliance, scalability, flexibility, innovation, and customer service. You should also check the reputation and track record of the providers and ask for references and testimonials from their previous or existing clients.

CONTRACT NEGOTIATION

After selecting your preferred cloud computing and outsourcing providers, you should negotiate a contract that clearly defines the scope, terms, conditions, roles, responsibilities, expectations, deliverables, service levels, metrics, incentives, penalties, dispute resolution mechanisms, termination clauses, and exit strategies. You should also ensure that the contract protects your intellectual property rights, data ownership rights, privacy rights, and confidentiality obligations.

TRANSITION APPROACH

Once you have a contract in place, you should plan and execute a smooth transition from your current state to your desired state with cloud computing and outsourcing. You should communicate the change to your internal stakeholders and external partners and provide them with adequate training and support. You should also establish a project management team that oversees the transition process and coordinates with the cloud computing and outsourcing providers.

RISK ASSESSMENTS AND SECURITY

One of the biggest challenges of cloud computing and outsourcing is managing the risks associated with data security and privacy. You should conduct regular risk assessments to identify and mitigate any potential threats or vulnerabilities that may compromise your data or systems. You should also implement appropriate security controls and measures to protect your data from unauthorized access or use. You should also comply with relevant laws and regulations regarding data protection and privacy.

IMPLEMENTATION OF CONTROLS

Another challenge of cloud computing and outsourcing is ensuring that the services provided meet your quality standards and expectations. You should implement appropriate controls and measures to monitor and evaluate the performance and outcomes of the cloud computing and outsourcing providers. You should also establish feedback mechanisms and improvement processes to address any issues or gaps that may arise.

ONGOING OVERSIGHT

Finally, you should maintain an ongoing oversight of the cloud computing and outsourcing arrangements to ensure that they continue to deliver value to your business. You should review the contract periodically to ensure that it remains relevant and aligned with your changing needs and goals. You should also maintain a good relationship with the cloud computing and outsourcing providers based on trust, transparency, and collaboration.

POLICIES TO ADDRESS DATA SECURITY & PRIVACY

Cloud computing and outsourcing offer many benefits for organisations, such as cost savings, scalability, flexibility and innovation. However, they also pose significant challenges for data security and privacy, as organisations lose direct control over their data and rely on third-party providers to protect it. Therefore, organisations need to adopt appropriate policies and practices to ensure that their data is secure and compliant with relevant laws and regulations.

Some of the policies that organisations should consider are:

- **Conduct a risk assessment** before choosing a cloud or outsourcing provider. This involves identifying the sensitivity of the data to be stored or processed, the potential threats and vulnerabilities, the legal and regulatory obligations, and the security measures offered by the provider. Organisations should also evaluate the provider's track record, transparency, governance and cyber supply chain risk management.
- **Choose a provider that is located in Australia or has data centres in Australia** (or wherever you are located). This reduces the jurisdictional risks associated with foreign laws and authorities that may access or interfere with the data without the organisation's knowledge or consent. If this is not possible, organisations should ensure that they understand the legal implications of using an offshore provider and obtain appropriate contractual guarantees and safeguards.
- **Establish clear roles and responsibilities for data security and privacy**. This involves defining who is accountable for what aspects of data protection, such as encryption, backup, access control, incident response, auditing and reporting. Organisations should also implement a shared responsibility

model that specifies what the provider and the organisation are expected to do to ensure data security and privacy.

- **Implement data protection measures throughout the data lifecycle**. This includes applying encryption, anonymisation, pseudonymisation or other techniques to protect data at rest, in transit and in use. Organisations should also monitor and audit data access and usage, enforce strong authentication and authorisation policies, and educate their staff and customers about data security and privacy best practices.
- **Review and update policies regularly**. This involves keeping abreast of changes in technology, threats, laws and regulations that may affect data security and privacy. Organisations should also conduct periodic audits and assessments of their providers' performance and compliance and update their policies accordingly.

DATA PRIVACY & COMPLIANCE

Cloud computing and outsourcing are increasingly popular ways for organisations to reduce costs, improve efficiency and access innovative services. However, they also pose significant challenges for data privacy and compliance. When organisations entrust their sensitive data to external vendors, they need to ensure that they meet their legal and ethical obligations to protect the data from unauthorised access, use, disclosure, modification or loss.

RISKS OF CLOUD COMPUTING AND OUTSOURCING

Cloud computing and outsourcing involve transferring data to third-party service providers who may store, process or manage the data in different locations, jurisdictions or countries. This exposes the data to various risks, such as:

- Loss of control over the data and its security
- Lack of transparency and accountability of the service providers
- Incompatibility or conflict between different privacy laws and regulations
- Breach of contractual or fiduciary obligations to data subjects or stakeholders
- Exposure to cyberattacks, natural disasters or human errors
- Difficulty in accessing, retrieving or deleting the data

- Legal liability or reputational damage in case of a privacy incident

These risks may vary depending on the nature, sensitivity and volume of the data, as well as the type, level and location of the cloud service or outsourcing arrangement. Therefore, organisations need to assess the materiality of these risks before engaging in cloud computing or outsourcing.

ASSESSMENT OF MATERIALITY

Materiality is a concept that helps organisations determine whether a risk is significant enough to warrant attention or action. According to APRA's information paper on outsourcing involving cloud computing services, materiality depends on the potential impact of a risk on the organisation's business objectives, financial position, reputation, regulatory compliance or prudential supervision.

To assess the materiality of cloud computing or outsourcing risks, organisations should consider the following factors:

- The nature and purpose of the data: Is it personal, confidential, sensitive or critical?
- The classification and protection of the data: How is it labelled, encrypted, backed up or destroyed?
- The ownership and responsibility of the data: Who owns, controls, accesses or audits the data?
- The location and jurisdiction of the data: Where is it stored, processed or transferred? What laws or regulations apply?
- The service level and quality of the service provider: How reliable, secure, compliant or accountable are they?
- The contractual and legal terms of the service agreement: What are the rights, obligations, liabilities and remedies of both parties?

Based on these factors, organisations should classify their cloud computing or outsourcing arrangements into low, heightened or extreme inherent risk categories. For low-risk arrangements not involving off-shoring, APRA does not expect organisations to consult with them prior to entering into the arrangement. For heightened risk arrangements, APRA expects to be consulted after the organisation's internal governance process is completed. For extreme risk arrangements, APRA expects organisations to avoid them unless they can demonstrate that they have adequate controls and mitigation strategies in place.

RISK MANAGEMENT CONSIDERATIONS

Risk management is a process that helps organisations identify, analyse, evaluate, treat, monitor and review their risks. For cloud computing and outsourcing risks, organisations should adopt a comprehensive and systematic approach that covers the following aspects:

- **Strategy**. Organisations should align their cloud computing or outsourcing decisions with their business strategy, objectives and values. They should also consider their risk appetite, tolerance and capacity.
- **Governance**. Organisations should establish clear roles and responsibilities for managing cloud computing or outsourcing risks. They should also ensure effective oversight, communication and escalation mechanisms.
- **Solution selection process**. Organisations should conduct due diligence on potential service providers before selecting them. They should also compare different options and alternatives based on their costs, benefits and risks.
- **APRA access and ability to act**. Organisations should ensure that APRA has timely access to their data and information held by service providers. They should also ensure that APRA can act in case of a prudential issue or concern.
- **Transition approach**. Organisations should plan and execute a smooth transition from their existing systems or processes to the new cloud service or outsourcing arrangement. They should also test and verify the functionality and performance of the new solution.
- **Risk assessments and security**. Organisations should conduct regular risk assessments on their cloud computing or outsourcing arrangements. They should also implement appropriate security measures to protect their data from unauthorised access, use, disclosure, modification or loss.
- **Implementation of controls**. Organisations should implement effective controls to manage their cloud computing or outsourcing risks. These may include contractual, technical, operational, organisational or legal controls.
- **Ongoing oversight**. Organisations should monitor and review their cloud computing or outsourcing arrangements on an

ongoing basis. They should also measure and report on their performance, compliance and incidents.

- **Business disruption**. Organisations should prepare and test contingency plans for business continuity and disaster recovery in case of a disruption to their cloud service or outsourcing arrangement. They should also ensure that they have adequate backup and recovery options.
- **Audit and assurance**. Organisations should conduct independent audits and obtain assurance on their cloud computing or outsourcing arrangements. They should also verify the adequacy and effectiveness of their controls and mitigation strategies.

APRA NOTIFICATION AND CONSULTATION

As mentioned earlier, APRA expects organisations to notify and consult with them on their cloud computing or outsourcing arrangements depending on their materiality. APRA's information paper on outsourcing involving cloud computing services provides detailed guidance on when and how to do so.

In summary, organisations should notify APRA of any material outsourcing arrangement within 20 business days of entering into the contract. They should also consult APRA before entering into any heightened risk arrangement or making any significant changes to an existing arrangement.

APRA's notification and consultation process aims to ensure that organisations manage their cloud computing or outsourcing risks in a prudent manner and in accordance with the relevant prudential standards and guidance.

DATA SOVEREIGNTY CONCERNS

Data sovereignty is the concept that data is subject to the laws and regulations of the country where it is stored or processed.

This can pose challenges for cloud computing and outsourcing, as data may cross borders and jurisdictions when it is transferred or accessed by different parties.

DATA SOVEREIGNTY

Different countries have different rules and laws regarding data protection, privacy, security, access, retention and deletion. Some examples are:

- **The European Union's General Data Protection Regulation (GDPR),** which applies to any organization that processes personal data of EU residents, regardless of where the data is stored or processed.
- **The United States' Cloud Act**, which allows US law enforcement to access data stored by US-based cloud providers, even if the data is located outside the US.
- **China's Cybersecurity Law**, which requires data related to critical information infrastructure to be stored within China and subject to security review before being transferred abroad.

These rules and laws may conflict or contradict each other, creating legal uncertainty and compliance risks for cloud users and providers.

To avoid potential violations or penalties, it is important to understand the data sovereignty landscape of the countries where your data is stored or processed, as well as the countries where your cloud providers or outsourcing partners are based or operate.

CLOUD PROVIDERS & OUTSOURCING PARTNERS

Not all cloud providers and outsourcing partners are equal when it comes to data sovereignty. Some factors to consider are:

- The location of their data centres and servers, and whether they offer options to choose or restrict where your data is stored or processed.
- The jurisdiction they are subject to, and whether they comply with the relevant data protection laws and regulations of your country and the countries where your data is stored or processed.
- The transparency and accountability they provide regarding their data practices, policies and procedures, such as how they handle data requests from authorities, how they notify you of data breaches or incidents, and how they audit and certify their data security and privacy standards.

- The contractual terms and conditions they offer, such as whether they guarantee data sovereignty rights, responsibilities and remedies, whether they allow you to audit or monitor their data activities, and whether they indemnify you for any data sovereignty issues or disputes.

To choose cloud providers and outsourcing partners that meet your data sovereignty needs and expectations, it is advisable to conduct due diligence, compare different options, negotiate favourable terms and conditions, and seek legal advice if necessary.

DATA SOVEREIGNTY BEST PRACTICE

Even if you choose cloud providers and outsourcing partners that respect data sovereignty, you still need to implement some best practices to ensure your data is protected and compliant. Some examples are:

- Classify your data according to its sensitivity, value and regulatory requirements, and apply different levels of protection and control accordingly.
- Encrypt your data at rest and in transit, using strong encryption algorithms and keys that you manage and control.
- Backup your data regularly and store copies in different locations or jurisdictions, preferably under your own custody or with trusted third parties.
- Monitor your data activities and access logs, using tools such as cloud observability platforms or security information and event management systems.
- Educate your employees and stakeholders about data sovereignty issues and policies and train them on how to handle data securely and responsibly.

Data sovereignty is a complex and evolving issue that affects cloud computing and outsourcing. By following this advice, you can mitigate data sovereignty risks and leverage the benefits of cloud computing and outsourcing.

CONTRACTUAL AGREEMENTS AND RISK MITIGATION

Cloud computing and outsourcing involve significant risks that need to be carefully managed through contractual agreements and risk mitigation strategies. In this article, I will discuss some of the key aspects of these topics and provide some practical tips for organisations that are considering or already using cloud computing and outsourcing services.

CLOUD COMPUTING RISKS AND CONTRACTS

Cloud computing is the delivery of computing services such as servers, storage, databases, networking, software, analytics, and intelligence over the Internet. Cloud computing can offer many benefits such as scalability, flexibility, reliability, security, and innovation. However, it also poses some challenges and risks such as:

Data privacy and security. Cloud computing involves transferring data to third-party providers who may have different policies, standards, and practices regarding data protection. Data may also be subject to different laws and regulations depending on where it is stored and processed. Data breaches, unauthorised access, or loss of data can have serious consequences for organisations and their customers.

Service availability and performance. Cloud computing relies on the Internet and the service provider's infrastructure to deliver the expected level of service. However, network failures, outages, disruptions, or degradation can affect the availability and performance of cloud services. This can result in reduced productivity, customer dissatisfaction, or loss of revenue.

Vendor lock-in and dependency. Cloud computing can create a high degree of dependency on the service provider's platform, tools, and features. This can make it difficult or costly to switch to another provider or to migrate data back to the organisation's own systems. Vendor lock-in can also limit the organisation's ability to negotiate better terms or prices or to take advantage of new technologies or opportunities.

Compliance and governance. Cloud computing can introduce new complexities and challenges for complying with laws, regulations, standards, and policies that apply to the organisation's data and activities. For example, cloud computing may involve cross-border data transfers that require specific agreements or authorisations. Cloud computing may also affect the organisation's governance processes such as auditing, monitoring, reporting, or decision-making.

To address these risks, organisations need to establish clear and comprehensive contractual agreements with their cloud service providers that define the roles, responsibilities, expectations, and obligations of both parties.

Service level agreements (SLAs): SLAs specify the minimum level of service that the provider must deliver in terms of availability, performance, reliability, security, support, etc. SLAs also define how the service level will be measured, monitored, and if necessary corrective action taken.

THE CHALLENGE OF VENDOR MANAGEMENT

Cloud computing and outsourcing are two trends that have transformed the IT landscape in recent years. They offer many benefits, such as cost savings, scalability, flexibility, and innovation.

However, they also pose significant challenges for IT governance, policy, ethics and law experts who need to manage multiple vendors and ensure compliance, security, quality, and value.

Here are some best practices for vendor management in cloud computing and outsourcing:

Establish a clear strategy and governance framework for sourcing decisions. Define the objectives, scope, criteria, and processes for selecting, contracting, and monitoring vendors. Align the sourcing strategy with the business goals and priorities and communicate it to all stakeholders.

Evaluate the risks and benefits of different sourcing models and options. Consider the trade-offs between single-sourcing, multi-sourcing, co-sourcing, and insourcing. Assess the impact of cloud computing and outsourcing on the IT organization's role, capabilities, and culture. Identify the legal, regulatory, ethical, and social implications of outsourcing and cloud computing.

Choose vendors that match your needs and expectations. Conduct due diligence on potential vendors' qualifications, reputation, performance, and capabilities. Use a balanced scorecard approach to compare vendors based on multiple criteria, such as cost, quality, innovation, reliability, security, compliance, and customer satisfaction.

Negotiate contracts that protect your interests and foster collaboration. Define the scope of work, service levels, deliverables, milestones, penalties, incentives, and dispute resolution mechanisms. Include clauses that address data ownership, privacy, security, confidentiality, intellectual property rights, liability, indemnification, termination, and exit strategies. Establish clear roles and responsibilities for both parties and assign dedicated contact persons.

Monitor vendor performance and relationship regularly. Use key performance indicators (KPIs) and service level agreements (SLAs) to measure vendor performance against agreed standards and expectations. Conduct periodic reviews and audits to evaluate vendor compliance with contractual obligations and best practices. Provide feedback and recognition to vendors and address issues promptly. Seek opportunities to improve vendor performance and relationship through continuous improvement initiatives.

Leverage vendor capabilities to drive innovation and value creation. Encourage vendors to share their expertise, insights, and best practices with you. Involve vendors in strategic planning and problem-solving activities. Explore new ways to collaborate with vendors to create synergies and co-create solutions that benefit both parties.

By following these best practices, you can manage vendors effectively in cloud computing and outsourcing environments. You can also enhance your IT governance, policy, ethics and law expertise by staying updated on the latest trends, developments, and standards in the field.

ETHICAL AND LEGAL IMPLICATIONS OF DATA BREACHES

As discussed in earlier chapters, data breaches are incidents where unauthorized parties access, copy, modify or destroy data that belongs to someone else.

Data breaches can have serious consequences for the victims, such as identity theft, financial loss, reputational damage, legal liability and emotional distress.

Data breaches can also affect the trust and confidence of customers, partners, regulators and the public in the organizations that handle data.

Cloud computing and outsourcing are two common ways that organizations use to store, process and manage their data. Cloud computing is the delivery of computing services over the internet, such as servers, storage, databases, software and analytics. Outsourcing is the practice of contracting out a business function or process to a third-party provider. Both cloud computing and outsourcing can offer benefits such as cost savings, scalability, flexibility and innovation. However, both also pose challenges and risks for data security and privacy.

ACCOUNTABILITY

Who is responsible for the data breach? Is it the organization that owns the data, the cloud service provider or the outsourcing vendor? How can they be held accountable for their actions or inactions? What are their obligations to notify the affected parties and to mitigate the harm? How can they prevent or reduce the likelihood of future data breaches?

COMPLIANCE

What are the laws and regulations that apply to the data breach? How do they differ across jurisdictions and sectors? How can the organization ensure compliance with the relevant standards and frameworks? What are the penalties and sanctions for non-compliance?

TRANSPARENCY

How transparent is the organization about its data practices? Does it inform its stakeholders about how it collects, uses, shares and protects their data? Does it disclose its cloud computing and outsourcing arrangements and the associated risks? Does it communicate clearly and promptly about any data breaches that occur?

TRUST

How does the organization maintain or restore trust with its stakeholders after a data breach? How does it demonstrate its commitment to data security and privacy? How does it address the concerns and expectations of its stakeholders?

ETHICS

How does the organization balance its business interests with its ethical values and social responsibilities? How does it respect the rights and interests of its data subjects? How does it ensure fairness, justice and accountability in its data decisions? How does it contribute to the common good and public interest?

These are some of the key questions that organizations need to consider when dealing with data breaches in cloud computing and outsourcing. By following ethical principles and legal requirements, organizations can not only protect their data assets but also enhance their reputation and competitiveness in the digital economy.

CHAPTER 3 WORKSHOP: CLOUD COMPUTING & OUTSOURCING

INTRODUCTION

Cloud computing and outsourcing are two popular strategies for IT organizations to reduce costs, increase flexibility, and access specialized skills and services. However, they also pose significant challenges and risks for IT governance, policy, ethics, and law. In this workshop exercise, you will learn about the benefits and drawbacks of cloud computing and outsourcing, and how to apply best practices and frameworks to manage them effectively.

LEARNING OBJECTIVES

By the end of this workshop exercise, you will be able to:

- Define cloud computing and outsourcing and explain their main types and models.
- Identify the advantages and disadvantages of cloud computing and outsourcing for IT organizations.
- Analyse the impact of cloud computing and outsourcing on IT governance, policy, ethics, and law.
- Apply relevant standards, guidelines, and frameworks to ensure compliance, security, privacy, quality, and performance of cloud computing and outsourcing services.
- Evaluate the risks and opportunities of cloud computing and outsourcing for your own IT organization.

ACTIVITIES

The workshop exercise consists of three main activities:

Activity 1: Cloud Computing and Outsourcing Quiz

Activity 2: Cloud Computing and Outsourcing Case Study

Activity 3: Cloud Computing and Outsourcing Action Plan

Each activity will take about 20 minutes to complete. You will work in small groups of 3-4 participants and share your results with the whole group at the end of each activity.

ACTIVITY 1: CLOUD COMPUTING AND OUTSOURCING QUIZ

In this activity, you will test your knowledge of cloud computing and outsourcing concepts and terminology. You will answer 10 multiple-choice questions on a paper or online quiz. The questions are based on the following topics:

- Definition and types of cloud computing
- Definition and types of outsourcing
- Benefits and challenges of cloud computing
- Benefits and challenges of outsourcing
- Cloud computing service models (IaaS, PaaS, SaaS)
- Cloud computing deployment models (public, private, hybrid, community)
- Outsourcing models (offshore, nearshore, onshore)
- Outsourcing contracts (fixed-price, time-and-materials, outcome-based)

You will have 10 minutes to complete the quiz individually. Then, you will compare your answers with your group members, and discuss any disagreements or doubts. Finally, you will review the correct answers with the facilitator.

ACTIVITY 2: CLOUD COMPUTING AND OUTSOURCING CASE STUDY

In this activity, you will analyse a real-world scenario of an IT organization that uses cloud computing and outsourcing services. You will read a short case study that describes the organization's background, goals, challenges, and current situation. The case study is based on the following topics:

- The organization's industry, size, structure, culture, and strategy
- The organization's IT vision, mission, objectives, functions, and processes
- The organization's cloud computing and outsourcing providers, services, agreements, and performance
- The organization's IT governance, policy, ethics, and law issues related to cloud computing and outsourcing.

You have 10 minutes to read the case study individually. Then, you will work with your group members to answer the following questions:

- What are the main benefits and drawbacks of cloud computing and outsourcing for the organization?

- What are the main IT governance, policy, ethics, and law challenges that the organization faces due to cloud computing and outsourcing?
- How would you rate the organization's compliance, security, privacy, quality, and performance of its cloud computing and outsourcing services?
- What are some best practices or frameworks that the organization could use to improve its cloud computing and outsourcing management?

Finally, present your answers to the whole group, and receive feedback from the facilitator.

ACTIVITY 3: CLOUD COMPUTING AND OUTSOURCING ACTION PLAN

In this activity, apply what you learned from the previous activities to your own IT organization.

Create a simple action plan to address one or more issues related to cloud computing or outsourcing that affect your IT organization.

The action plan should include the following elements:

- A clear statement of the problem or opportunity that you want to address
- A SMART goal that describes what you want to achieve
- A list of actions that you need to take to reach your goal
- A timeline that specifies when you will complete each action
- A list of resources that you need or have available to support your actions
- A list of indicators that you will use to measure your progress and success

You have 10 minutes to create your action plan individually.

Then, you will share your action plan with your group members, and receive feedback from them.

Finally, you will present your action plan to the whole group, and receive feedback from the facilitator.

CONCLUSION

Cloud computing and outsourcing are powerful tools for IT organizations to achieve their goals, but they also require careful planning, management, and oversight.

In this workshop exercise, you learned about the benefits and drawbacks of cloud computing and outsourcing, and how to apply best practices and frameworks to ensure compliance, security, privacy, quality, and performance of cloud computing and outsourcing services.

You also created an action plan to address a specific issue related to cloud computing or outsourcing that affects your own IT organization.

Thank you for your participation and attention.

CHAPTER 4:
DIGITAL ETHICS & RESPONSIBLE AI

CHAPTER SUMMARY

Digital ethics and responsible AI are two important topics in the field of IT governance, policy, ethics and law. They deal with the moral principles and values that guide the design, development, use and impact of digital technologies and artificial intelligence (AI) systems.

In this chapter, we explore the key issues and challenges related to these topics:

Ethical AI and algorithm bias. How can we ensure that AI systems are fair, transparent, accountable and trustworthy? How can we prevent or mitigate the harmful effects of algorithmic discrimination, manipulation and exploitation on individuals and society?

Emerging technologies and ethical regulation. How can we balance the benefits and risks of new and disruptive technologies, such as biotechnology, nanotechnology, blockchain and quantum computing? How can we foster innovation and collaboration while protecting human rights, privacy and security?

Whistleblower protection and digital ethics. How can we support and protect those who expose unethical or illegal practices in the digital domain, such as data breaches, cyberattacks, surveillance and censorship? How can we create a culture of ethical awareness and responsibility among digital professionals and users?

Ethical considerations in AI art. How can we appreciate and evaluate the artistic expressions and creations of AI systems, such as music, poetry, painting and sculpture? How can we respect the intellectual property rights and moral rights of human and non-human artists?

4.1. DIGITAL ETHICS & RESPONSIBLE AI

Artificial intelligence (AI) is transforming the world in many ways, from improving health care and education to enhancing productivity and innovation. However, AI also poses significant challenges and risks, such as potential bias, discrimination, privacy breaches, security threats, and ethical dilemmas.

How can we ensure that AI is used for good and not evil? How can we design and implement AI systems that are fair, transparent, accountable, reliable, and respectful of human values?

FOLLOW THE AI ETHICS PRINCIPLES

Many countries and organizations have developed ethical principles or guidelines for AI, such as Australia's 8 AI Ethics Principles, the IEEE's Ethically Aligned Design, or the Berkman Klein Centre's report on ethical principles in eight categories. These principles provide a common framework and a shared language for understanding and addressing the ethical issues of AI. They also help to build public trust and consumer loyalty in AI-enabled services.

The principles cover various aspects of AI, such as human wellbeing, human-centred values, fairness, privacy protection and security, reliability and safety, transparency and explainability, contestability, and accountability. By following these principles and committing to ethical AI practices, you can achieve safer, more reliable and fairer outcomes for all stakeholders.

ENSURE HUMAN CONTROL AND OVERSIGHT

AI systems should not operate autonomously without human control and oversight. Human beings should always have the final say in the design, development, implementation and evaluation of AI systems. Human control ensures that AI systems are aligned with human values and goals, and that they can be corrected or stopped if they cause harm or deviate from their intended purpose.

Human control can be exercised through various means, such as control panels, status displays, feedback mechanisms, audits, reviews, or appeals. Human control also implies human responsibility: people who are involved in different phases of the AI system lifecycle should be identifiable and accountable for the outcomes of the AI systems.

EXPLAINABLE & COMPREHENSIBLE AI

AI systems should be transparent and explainable so that people can understand when they are being significantly impacted by AI and can find out how an AI system is engaging with them or making decisions that affect them. Transparency and explainability are essential for ensuring fairness, accountability, contestability, and trust in AI systems.

Explainable AI (XAI) refers to the ability of an AI system to provide explanations of its decisions or actions in a human-understandable way.

Comprehensible AI (CAI) refers to the ability of a human being to comprehend the explanations provided by an AI system. XAI and CAI are closely related and mutually dependent: an explanation is only useful if it can be comprehended by the intended audience.

To implement XAI and CAI, you should use clear and simple language, visual aids, examples, analogies, or other methods that can help convey the logic, data, assumptions, limitations, uncertainties, or trade-offs of an AI system. You should also provide different levels of detail or granularity for different users or purposes: for example, a high-level summary for a general audience or a low-level technical description for an expert audience.

CONDUCT BIAS AND FAIRNESS ASSESSMENTS

AI systems should not involve or result in unfair discrimination against individuals, communities or groups. Bias is a deviation from accuracy or fairness that can negatively affect the performance or outcomes of an AI system. Bias can arise from various sources, such as data quality or quantity, algorithm design or implementation, human judgement or intervention.

To prevent or mitigate bias in AI systems, you should conduct bias and fairness assessments at different stages of the AI system lifecycle. These assessments involve identifying potential sources of bias, measuring the extent or impact of bias, and applying appropriate techniques to reduce or eliminate bias.

Some examples of bias detection and mitigation techniques are:

- **Data collection**: ensure diversity and representativeness of data samples; use multiple sources of data; avoid data leakage or contamination; anonymize or pseudonymize sensitive data; obtain informed consent from data subjects.
- **Data processing**: clean and normalize data; handle missing values or outliers; balance data classes; apply feature selection or extraction; use data augmentation or synthesis.
- **Algorithm development**: choose appropriate models or methods; avoid overfitting or underfitting; use regularization or cross-validation; tune hyperparameters; compare performance metrics; test on unseen data.
- **Algorithm deployment**: monitor and evaluate results; collect and analyse feedback; update or retrain models; document and report findings; disclose limitations or uncertainties.

ESTABLISH AN AI ETHICS COMMITTEE

AI ethics is a complex and dynamic field that requires multidisciplinary and multi-stakeholder collaboration and consultation. An AI ethics committee is a group of people who have relevant expertise, experience, or interest in AI ethics, and who can provide guidance, advice, or oversight on AI ethics issues or cases.

An AI ethics committee can help you to:

- Identify and prioritize the ethical issues or risks of AI systems.
- Develop and implement ethical policies, standards, or codes of conduct for AI systems.
- Review and approve AI projects, proposals, or applications.
- Resolve ethical dilemmas or conflicts involving AI systems.
- Educate and raise awareness on AI ethics among employees, customers, partners, or the public.
- Engage and consult with external stakeholders, such as regulators, experts, civil society, or users.

An AI ethics committee should be diverse and inclusive, representing different perspectives, backgrounds, roles, or interests. It should also be independent and impartial, avoiding conflicts of interest or undue influence. It should follow clear and transparent procedures and criteria for decision making, communication, and reporting.

PROVIDE TRAINING ON AI ETHICS

AI ethics is not only a matter of technical skills or knowledge, but also of attitudes, values, and behaviours. To foster a culture of ethical AI in your organization, you should provide training on AI ethics to all employees who are involved in or affected by AI systems. Training on AI ethics can help you to:

- Increase the awareness and understanding of the ethical principles, issues, and challenges of AI systems.
- Enhance the skills and competencies for applying ethical principles, practices, or tools to AI systems.
- Promote the adoption and implementation of ethical standards, policies, or codes of conduct for AI systems.
- Encourage the reflection and discussion on the ethical implications or consequences of AI systems.
- Inspire the innovation and creativity for developing ethical solutions or alternatives for AI systems.

Training on AI ethics should be tailored to the specific needs, roles, or levels of your employees. It should also be interactive, engaging, and relevant, using real-world examples, scenarios, or cases that illustrate the ethical aspects of AI systems. It should also be updated regularly to reflect the latest developments or trends in AI ethics.

ALGORITHMIC BIAS & ITS IMPLICATIONS

Algorithmic bias is the application of an algorithm that produces unfair or discriminatory outcomes for individuals or groups, often due to problems with the data, the AI system, or the societal context.

Algorithmic bias can have negative impacts on human rights, such as the right to equality and non-discrimination, the right to privacy, and the right to an effective remedy.

SOURCES OF ALGORITHMIC BIAS

Algorithmic bias can arise from sources such as:

Data quality. The data used to train or test an AI system may be incomplete, inaccurate, outdated, unrepresentative, or skewed by human biases.

Data processing. The methods used to preprocess, clean, label, or augment the data may introduce or amplify biases in the data.

Model design. The choice of algorithm, parameters, features, or performance metrics may affect how the AI system learns from the data and makes decisions.

Model interpretation. The way the AI system's outputs are presented, explained, or used may influence how they are understood and acted upon by humans.

Societal context. The historical, cultural, or institutional factors that shape the problem domain, the stakeholders, and the expectations of fairness and accountability.

EXAMPLES OF ALGORITHMIC BIAS

Such bias has been observed in various domains and applications of AI-informed decision making, such as:

Criminal justice. Risk assessment tools that predict the likelihood of recidivism or bail violation may be biased against certain racial or ethnic groups.

Advertising. Online platforms that display targeted ads based on user profiles may be biased against women or minorities in showing job opportunities or financial products.

Recruitment. Resume screening tools that filter candidates based on their qualifications or suitability may be biased against applicants with certain names, genders, or backgrounds.

Healthcare. Diagnostic tools that detect diseases or recommend treatments may be biased against patients with certain characteristics or conditions.

Policing. Facial recognition tools that identify suspects or persons of interest may be biased against people with darker skin tones or non-binary genders.

HOW TO ADDRESS ALGORITHMIC BIAS

Algorithmic bias is a complex and multifaceted problem that requires a multidisciplinary and multi-stakeholder approach to address. Some possible strategies to mitigate algorithmic bias are.

Data auditing. Reviewing the data sources, collection methods, and quality measures to ensure that the data is relevant, reliable, and representative of the target population.

Data augmentation. Adding more data from underrepresented groups or generating synthetic data to balance the data distribution and reduce sampling bias.

Model validation. Testing the model on different subsets of the data or using different performance metrics to evaluate its accuracy, robustness, and fairness across different groups.

Model explanation. Providing transparent and interpretable explanations of how the model works, what factors influence its decisions, and what uncertainties or limitations it has.

Human oversight. Involving human experts, stakeholders, or users in reviewing, monitoring, or challenging the model's decisions and providing feedback or corrections.

Ethical guidelines. Following best practices and principles for responsible and ethical use of AI, such as those developed by the Australian Human Rights Commission, Gradient Institute, Consumer Policy Research Centre, CHOICE, and CSIRO's Data61.

In short, algorithmic bias is a serious challenge for AI-informed decision making that can affect human rights and social justice. It is important to understand the sources, examples, and implications of algorithmic bias and to adopt appropriate measures to prevent or reduce it. By doing so, we can ensure that AI is used in a way that is fair, accountable, and transparent for all.

RESPONSIBLE AI FRAMEWORKS

Artificial Intelligence (AI) is a powerful technology that can bring many benefits to society, but which also pose many risks and challenges.

WHAT IS RESPONSIBLE AI?

Responsible AI is a term that refers to the design, development, deployment and use of AI systems that uphold human values and align with ethical principles.

Responsible AI aims to ensure that AI systems are trustworthy, fair, reliable, safe, private, secure, inclusive, transparent and accountable.

WHY DO WE NEED RESPONSIBLE AI FRAMEWORKS?

AI systems are increasingly influencing and impacting people's lives at scale, from healthcare to education, from finance to entertainment. However, AI systems can also cause unintended or harmful consequences, such as bias, discrimination, privacy breaches, security threats, misinformation or manipulation.

To prevent or mitigate these risks, and to ensure that AI systems serve the public good, we need to establish clear and consistent standards and guidelines for building and using AI responsibly. Responsible AI Frameworks provide such standards and guidelines, as well as tools and practices to implement them.

BUILDING RESPONSIBLE AI FRAMEWORKS?

There is no one-size-fits-all solution for building Responsible AI Frameworks. Different organizations may have different goals, values, stakeholders and contexts that require different approaches. However, based on my experience and research, I suggest the following steps for building Responsible AI Frameworks:

- Define the purpose and scope of the AI system. What problem are you trying to solve? Who are the intended users and beneficiaries? What are the potential harms or risks?

- Identify the relevant ethical principles and values that should guide the AI system. For example, you can refer to existing frameworks such as Microsoft's Responsible AI Standard, Accenture's Principles of a Responsible AI Framework, or Cisco's Responsible AI Framework.
- Translate the ethical principles and values into practical and measurable goals and requirements for the AI system. For example, you can use methods such as impact assessments, data governance, human oversight or explainability techniques.
- Implement the goals and requirements throughout the AI system lifecycle, from design to deployment to evaluation. For example, you can use tools such as data quality checks, fairness metrics, privacy-preserving methods or reliability tests.
- Monitor and review the performance and impact of the AI system regularly. For example, you can use feedback mechanisms, audits or accountability processes.

In short, responsible AI is not only a moral duty but also a competitive advantage. By building and using AI systems that respect human values and ethical principles, we can create trust in AI and realize its full potential for society. I hope my advice on Responsible AI Frameworks will help you achieve this goal.

FAIRNESS & ACCOUNTABILITY

Promote a culture of fairness and accountability in IT governance. IT governance is not only about processes and activities, but also about people and culture.

Foster a culture of fairness and accountability in your organization, where everyone involved in IT governance respects the rights, interests and expectations of others. You should also encourage ethical behaviour in all its forms, such as honesty, integrity, professionalism and social responsibility.

By doing this, you can ensure that your IT governance is fair, respectful and trustworthy.

TRANSPARENCY & EXPLAINABILITY

Transparency means that the processes, methods, data and outcomes of IT systems are clear and accessible to the relevant stakeholders.

Transparency helps to avoid hidden biases, errors or malicious actions that could compromise the quality, reliability or fairness of IT systems. Transparency also fosters trust and confidence among the users, customers, regulators and society at large.

Explainability means that the logic, reasoning and assumptions behind the decisions or actions of IT systems are understandable and interpretable by humans. Explainability helps to ensure that the IT systems are aligned with the values, goals and expectations of the stakeholders. Explainability also enables feedback, learning and improvement of the IT systems over time.

There are several ways to achieve Transparency and Explainability in IT systems, depending on the context, purpose and design of the system. Some of the best practices include:

Adopting a human-centric approach that involves the stakeholders in the development, deployment and evaluation of the IT system.

Applying ethical principles and standards that guide the design, implementation and operation of the IT system.

Implementing governance frameworks and processes that monitor, audit and review the IT system regularly.

Providing documentation, communication and education that explain the IT system clearly and accurately to the stakeholders.

Using methods and tools that enable the extraction, visualization and interpretation of the IT system's logic, reasoning and assumptions.

ETHICAL DECISION-MAKING & CONSENT

Data is a valuable asset for any organisation, but it also comes with certain ethical responsibilities. Data ethics is the practice of using data in ways that preserve the trust of users, customers, employees and partners. Data ethics goes beyond legal compliance and considers the broader impact of data activities on people and society.

WHAT IS ETHICAL DECISION-MAKING?

It is the process of choosing the best course of action among different alternatives, based on ethical principles and values. Ethical decision-making involves:

- Recognising the nature of the issue and its ethical components.
- Getting the facts and identifying the stakeholders.
- Evaluating alternative actions and their consequences.
- Making a decision that is consistent with your ethical values and obligations.
- Testing your decision against ethical standards and expectations.
- Acting on your decision and communicating it to others.
- Reflecting on the outcome and learning from it.

Ethical decision-making is not always easy or straightforward. It may involve dilemmas, trade-offs, uncertainties and conflicts. It may also require courage, integrity, accountability and empathy.

WHAT IS CONSENT?

Consent is the voluntary agreement of a person to a proposed action or use of their personal information. Consent can be express or implied, depending on the context and the nature of the information. Consent can also be withdrawn at any time, unless there is a legal or contractual obligation to continue.

Consent is an important aspect of data ethics, as it respects the autonomy, dignity and privacy of individuals. Consent also helps to build trust and confidence between organisations and their data subjects.

HOW TO OBTAIN CONSENT?

To obtain valid consent, you need to:

- Inform the person about the purpose, scope, duration, benefits and risks of the proposed action or use of their information.
- Provide clear, accurate, relevant and timely information that is easy to understand.
- Avoid coercion, deception, manipulation or undue influence.
- Respect the person's right to refuse or withdraw consent without negative consequences.
- Document the consent process and keep records.

How to apply ethical decision-making and consent in IT governance, policy, ethics and law?

Here are some practical tips on how to apply ethical decision-making and consent in IT governance, policy, ethics and law:

- Use de-identified data where possible. De-identified data is not personal information and does not require consent. However, you need to ensure that de-identification is done properly and that re-identification risks are minimised.
- Adopt a privacy-by-design approach. Privacy-by-design means integrating privacy into your organisation's culture, processes and systems from the beginning to the end of a project. Privacy-by-design helps to prevent privacy breaches, reduce compliance costs and enhance customer loyalty.
- Follow the Australian Privacy Principles (APPs). The APPs are a set of legal obligations that apply to organisations that collect, use, disclose or store personal information. The APPs cover areas such as collection, notification, access, correction, security, quality, use limitation and cross-border disclosure.
- Consult with stakeholders. Stakeholders are people who have an interest or stake in your data activities. They may include users, customers, employees, partners, regulators or community groups. Consulting with stakeholders helps to identify their needs, expectations and concerns. It also helps to gain their input, feedback and support.
- Collaborate across disciplines and organisations. Data ethics is a multidisciplinary field that requires collaboration across different functions, sectors and industries. Collaboration helps to share knowledge, expertise and best practices. It also helps to address common challenges and opportunities.

ADDRESSING SOCIAL IMPACT

The ethical considerations surrounding AI extend beyond individual decisions to broader societal impact. Responsible AI frameworks encourage organizations to assess the potential social, economic, and cultural consequences of their AI systems. This assessment enables organizations to anticipate and mitigate potential negative outcomes, ensuring that AI serves the greater good.

4.2. ETHICAL AI & ALGORITHM BIAS

ETHICAL AI & ALGORITHM BIAS

Artificial intelligence (AI) is a powerful technology that can enhance decision-making, optimize processes, and create new value in various domains.

However, AI also poses ethical challenges that need to be addressed by IT professionals who design, develop, deploy, or use AI systems. One of the most pressing ethical issues in AI is algorithm bias, which is a kind of error or unfairness that can arise from the use of AI.

WHAT IS ALGORITHM BIAS AND WHY DOES IT MATTER?

Algorithm bias is a situation where an AI system produces outcomes that are systematically skewed or inaccurate, often resulting in unfair or discriminatory treatment of individuals or groups based on their characteristics, such as race, gender, age, or disability. Algorithm bias can have negative impacts on human rights, such as the right to equality, privacy, dignity, and justice.

Algorithm bias can occur for several reasons, such as:

- The data used to train or test the AI system is not representative of the target population or context, leading to overfitting or underfitting.
- The algorithm design or implementation is flawed or contains hidden assumptions or preferences that favour certain outcomes or groups over others.
- The interpretation or application of the AI results is influenced by human biases or prejudices, either intentionally or unintentionally.

Some examples of algorithm bias in real-world scenarios are:

- A facial recognition system that performs poorly on people of colour, resulting in false positives or negatives that can affect security, access, or identification.
- A hiring system that screens candidates based on their resumes but excludes qualified applicants who have non-traditional backgrounds or names that indicate their ethnicity or gender.

- A credit scoring system that assigns lower scores to people who live in certain neighbourhoods or have certain occupations, affecting their access to loans or insurance.

HOW CAN IT PROFESSIONALS ADDRESS ALGORITHM BIAS?

As IT professionals who are involved in the development or use of AI systems, we have a responsibility to ensure that our AI systems are ethical and aligned with human rights principles. We can do this by following some best practices, such as:

- Conducting a thorough analysis of the data sources, algorithms, and outcomes of the AI system, and identifying potential sources and impacts of bias.
- Applying appropriate methods and tools to mitigate or reduce bias in the data collection, processing, analysis, and validation stages of the AI system.
- Implementing transparency and accountability mechanisms to explain how the AI system works, what data it uses, what assumptions it makes, and what results it produces.
- Engaging with relevant stakeholders, such as users, customers, regulators, and experts, to solicit feedback, address concerns, and ensure compliance with ethical standards and legal requirements.
- Monitoring and evaluating the performance and impact of the AI system on an ongoing basis and updating or correcting it as needed.

Algorithm bias is a serious ethical challenge that can undermine the trustworthiness and value of AI systems. IT professionals have a key role to play in ensuring that our AI systems are ethical and respect human rights. By following some best practices, we can create AI systems that are fair, accurate, and beneficial for all.

THE IMPORTANCE OF ETHICAL AI POLICIES

AI poses significant challenges and risks, such as potential bias, discrimination, privacy breaches, and accountability gaps. Therefore, it is essential to develop and implement ethical AI policies that can ensure the safe, secure, and responsible use of AI for the benefit of individuals, society, and the environment.

WHAT ARE ETHICAL AI POLICIES?

Ethical AI policies are guidelines or principles that aim to align the design, development, and deployment of AI systems with human values and rights. Ethical AI policies can help to:

- Achieve safer, more reliable, and fairer outcomes for all stakeholders affected by AI applications.
- Reduce the risk of negative impacts or harms caused by AI systems.
- Build public trust and confidence in AI systems and their providers.
- Encourage innovation and competitiveness in the AI sector.
- Comply with existing laws and regulations related to AI.

Ethical AI policies can be developed and implemented by various actors, such as governments, businesses, researchers, civil society, and international organizations. Ethical AI policies can also vary in their scope, level of detail, and enforceability.

EXAMPLES OF ETHICAL AI POLICIES

Several countries and regions have developed or are developing ethical AI policies to guide their AI strategies and initiatives. For example:

Australia has published its AI Ethics Framework, which includes eight voluntary AI Ethics Principles that cover human, social, and environmental wellbeing; human-centred values; fairness; privacy protection and security; reliability and safety; transparency and explainability; contestability; and accountability.

The **European Union** has proposed its Artificial Intelligence Act, which is a comprehensive legal framework that aims to regulate high-risk AI systems and promote trustworthy AI based on four ethical principles: respect for human dignity and autonomy; prevention of harm; fairness; and democratic values.

The **United States** has issued its Executive Order on Maintaining American Leadership in Artificial Intelligence, which directs federal agencies to foster public trust and confidence in AI technologies by promoting reliable, robust, trustworthy, secure, portable, and interoperable AI systems.

In addition to governments, many private sector companies have also adopted their own ethical AI policies or principles to demonstrate their commitment to responsible AI practices. For example:

Microsoft has established its *Responsible AI Standard*, which is a set of requirements and processes that help its teams design, develop, deploy, and operate AI systems in a manner consistent with its six ethical principles: fairness; reliability and safety; privacy and security; inclusiveness; transparency; and accountability.

Google has published its *Responsible AI Practices*, which is a collection of best practices and tools that help its engineers build AI systems that are aligned with its seven principles: socially beneficial; avoid creating or reinforcing unfair bias; be built and tested for safety; be accountable to people; incorporate privacy design principles; uphold high standards of scientific excellence; and be made available for uses that accord with these principles.

ADVICE ON ETHICAL AI POLICIES

Ethical AI policies should be informed by evidence-based research and best practices from various disciplines and sectors. Such policies should be co-designed and co-implemented with the participation of diverse stakeholders, including those who are directly or indirectly affected by AI systems.

Ethical AI policies should be regularly reviewed and updated to reflect the evolving nature and impact of AI technologies. They should be complemented by mechanisms for oversight, enforcement, evaluation, and feedback.

Ethical AI policies should be communicated clearly and transparently to all relevant parties, including the public.

By following these advice points, you can ensure that your ethical AI policies are not only sound and robust but also responsive and adaptable to the changing needs and expectations of your customers, partners, employees, regulators, and society at large.

TRANSPARENCY & EXPLAINABILITY

Today, artificial intelligence (AI) systems are increasingly used to make decisions that affect our lives, such as health care, education, employment, and justice.

However, many of these systems are not transparent or explainable, meaning that we do not know how they work or why they produce certain outcomes. This poses ethical and legal challenges for the users, developers, and regulators of AI systems.

Transparency and explainability are two related but distinct concepts that can help us understand and trust AI systems. Transparency refers to the ability to access and inspect the data, algorithms, and processes that underlie an AI system. Explainability refers to the ability to provide understandable and meaningful reasons for the decisions or actions of an AI system.

WHY ARE TRANSPARENCY AND EXPLAINABILITY IMPORTANT?

They are important for several reasons:

- They can enhance the accountability and responsibility of the actors involved in the development and deployment of AI systems, such as developers, providers, users, and regulators.
- They can foster the trust and confidence of the public and the stakeholders in the benefits and risks of AI systems.
- They can enable the verification and validation of the quality, reliability, and safety of AI systems.
- They can facilitate the identification and correction of errors, biases, or harms caused by AI systems.
- They can empower the users and affected parties to exercise their rights and interests, such as informed consent, access, rectification, objection, or redress.

HOW CAN WE ACHIEVE TRANSPARENCY AND EXPLAINABILITY?

There is no one-size-fits-all solution for achieving transparency and explainability of AI systems. Different types of AI systems may require different levels and methods of transparency and explainability, depending on their purpose, context, and impact. Moreover, there may be trade-offs or tensions between transparency and explainability and other values or objectives, such as privacy, security, efficiency, or innovation.

Therefore, we need to adopt a context-sensitive and risk-based approach to determine the appropriate degree and mode of transparency and explainability for each AI system. We also need to balance the interests and expectations of different stakeholders, such as developers, providers, users, regulators, and affected parties.

Some possible strategies to enhance the transparency and explainability of AI systems are:

- Adopting ethical principles and standards for the design and development of AI systems that incorporate transparency and explainability as key requirements.
- Developing technical methods and tools that can generate explanations for the inputs, outputs, or processes of AI systems in a human-readable and understandable way.
- Providing clear and accessible information and documentation about the data sources, algorithms, assumptions, limitations, uncertainties, and potential impacts of AI systems.
- Implementing mechanisms for auditing, monitoring, testing, reviewing, or certifying the compliance and performance of AI systems with respect to transparency and explainability criteria.
- Establishing channels for communication, consultation, feedback, or complaint between the developers, providers, users, regulators, and affected parties of AI systems.
- Creating legal frameworks and institutions that can ensure the respect and protection of the rights and interests of the users and affected parties of AI systems.

Transparency and explainability are essential for ensuring the ethical and legal use of AI systems. They can help us understand how AI systems work and why they make certain decisions or actions.

They can also help us ensure that AI systems are accountable, trustworthy, reliable, safe, fair, and beneficial for society.

MITIGATING BIAS

IDENTIFY AND ASSESS POTENTIAL SOURCES OF BIAS

The first step to mitigate bias is to identify and assess the potential sources of bias in the IT system or decision. This can be done by conducting a thorough analysis of the data, algorithms, processes and outcomes involved in the system or decision. Some questions to ask are:

- What are the objectives and criteria of the system or decision?
- What are the data sources, methods and quality of the data collection and processing?

- What are the assumptions, limitations and trade-offs of the algorithms and models used?
- How are the results interpreted, communicated and acted upon?
- Who are the stakeholders, beneficiaries and potential victims of the system or decision?
- What are the ethical, legal and social implications of the system or decision?

Some tools that can help with this step are:

- IBM's AI Fairness 360 toolkit, which provides a set of metrics, algorithms and visualizations to detect and mitigate bias in datasets and machine learning models.
- IBM's AI Factsheets, which provide a standardized way to document the characteristics, capabilities and limitations of AI systems.
- IBM Watson OpenScale, which provides a platform to monitor, explain and improve AI performance, fairness and compliance.

IMPLEMENT BIAS MITIGATION STRATEGIES

The second step is to implement bias mitigation strategies that address the identified sources of bias. This can be done by applying various techniques, such as:

- Data augmentation, transformation or sampling to improve the representativeness, diversity and balance of the data.
- Algorithm selection, modification or regularization to reduce the complexity, opacity or sensitivity of the models.
- Human review, feedback or intervention to provide oversight, validation or correction of the results.
- Stakeholder engagement, consultation or participation to ensure transparency, accountability and inclusiveness of the system or decision.

Some examples of bias mitigation strategies are:

Conflicts and Biases in the Boardroom, which provides guidance on how to address conflicts of interest and common biases that impact board decisions.

Algorithmic bias detection and mitigation: Best practices ... - Brookings, which provides policy recommendations on how to detect and mitigate algorithmic bias in consumer harms.

AI Ethics Part 2: Mitigating bias in our algorithms - CMO, which provides best practices on how to build fairness and bias metrics and run a model governance process.

EVALUATE AND MONITOR BIAS MITIGATION OUTCOMES

The third step is to evaluate and monitor the outcomes of the bias mitigation strategies. This can be done by measuring, testing and reporting on the performance, fairness and trustworthiness of the system or decision. Some questions to ask are:

- How effective are the bias mitigation strategies in achieving the objectives and criteria of the system or decision?
- How fair are the system or decision outcomes for different groups of stakeholders?
- How trustworthy are the system or decision processes and results for different audiences?
- How robust are the system or decision against changes in data, algorithms or contexts?
- How adaptable are the system or decision to new requirements, feedback or challenges?

Some tools that can help with this step are:

- IBM Watson OpenScale, which provides a platform to monitor, explain and improve AI performance, fairness and compliance.
- IBM Watson Discovery, which provides a service to analyse text data for sentiment, emotion, tone and personality insights.
- IBM Watson Assistant, which provides a service to build conversational agents that can interact with users and provide feedback.

Mitigating bias in IT governance is a complex and ongoing challenge that requires a holistic and proactive approach. By following these three steps - identify and assess potential sources of bias, implement bias mitigation strategies, and evaluate and monitor bias mitigation outcomes - IT leaders can ensure that their systems and decisions are more ethical, fair and trustworthy.

ETHICAL AI IN CRITICAL DOMAINS

Certain domains, such as criminal justice and healthcare, hold significant ethical ramifications for AI usage. Biased algorithms in predictive policing can lead to unjust targeting, while healthcare AI biased against certain demographics might exacerbate health disparities. Ethical AI policies should emphasize thorough evaluation and validation of algorithms in these critical contexts.

IDENTIFY THE ETHICAL PRINCIPLES FOR AI

The first step to build ethical AI is to identify the ethical principles that should guide its development and use. There are many sources of ethical principles for AI, such as the OECD Principles on AI, the World Economic Forum's 9 Ethical AI Principles for Organizations, or the Ethics of Artificial Intelligence course by Coursera. These principles usually include values such as fairness, transparency, accountability, privacy, security, human oversight, and social good.

However, these principles are not enough by themselves. They need to be translated into concrete norms and practices that can be implemented and governed in specific contexts and domains. For example, what does fairness mean for an AI system that diagnoses diseases or recommends treatments? How can transparency be achieved for an AI system that predicts criminal behaviour or assesses legal risks? How can accountability be ensured for an AI system that controls autonomous vehicles or drones?

To answer these questions, we need to conduct a thorough ethical analysis of the AI system and its impacts and implications for the stakeholders involved.

CONDUCT AN ETHICAL ANALYSIS OF THE AI SYSTEM

The second step to build ethical AI is to conduct an ethical analysis of the AI system and its impacts and implications for the stakeholders involved. This analysis should consider the following aspects:

- **The purpose and goals of the AI system**. What problem does it aim to solve? What benefits does it provide? What risks does it entail?
- **The data and algorithms of the AI system**. What data is used to train and test the AI system? How is it collected, processed, stored, and shared? What algorithms are used to

analyse the data and generate outputs? How are they designed, validated, and updated?

- **The outputs and outcomes of the AI system**. What outputs does the AI system produce? How are they interpreted and used? What outcomes do they lead to? How are they measured and evaluated?
- **The stakeholders of the AI system**. Who are the stakeholders of the AI system? How are they affected by its outputs and outcomes? What are their needs, preferences, values, and expectations?
- **The ethical issues of the AI system**. What ethical issues arise from the AI system's purpose, data, algorithms, outputs, outcomes, and stakeholders? How can they be identified, prioritized, and addressed?

To conduct this analysis, we need to use critical skills and methods that can help us clarify and ethically evaluate the AI system in different domains of life. We also need to consult with relevant experts and stakeholders to ensure that we capture their perspectives and concerns.

IMPLEMENT ETHICAL SOLUTIONS FOR THE AI SYSTEM

The third step is to implement ethical solutions for the AI system that can address the ethical issues identified in the previous step. These solutions may include:

- **Ethical design**. Applying ethical principles and values in the design process of the AI system, such as user-centered design or value-sensitive design.
- **Ethical development**. Applying ethical standards and guidelines in the development process of the AI system, such as code of ethics or best practices.
- **Ethical testing**. Applying ethical criteria and methods in the testing process of the AI system, such as audits or impact assessments.
- **Ethical deployment**. Applying ethical rules and regulations in the deployment process of the AI system, such as policies or laws.
- **Ethical governance**. Applying ethical mechanisms and structures in the governance process of the AI system, such as oversight boards or ethics committees.

To implement these solutions, we need to use appropriate tools and techniques that can help us operationalize ethics in practice. We also need to monitor and evaluate the impacts and outcomes of the AI system on a regular basis.

Ethical AI is not only a moral duty but also a strategic advantage for organizations that want to create value and trust with their customers, employees, partners, regulators, and

4.3. EMERGING TECHNOLOGIES & ETHICAL REGULATION

THE DAWN OF EMERGING TECHNOLOGIES

Emerging technologies such as artificial intelligence (AI), internet of things (IoT), and cloud computing are transforming the world in many ways. They offer new opportunities for innovation, efficiency, and convenience, but they also pose new challenges for cybersecurity and ethical regulation.

CYBERSECURITY: PROTECTING DATA AND SYSTEMS

One of the main challenges of emerging technologies is to protect the data and systems that they rely on from the possibility of cyberattack. Cyberattacks can cause harm to organizations, users, and society by compromising the confidentiality, integrity, and availability of information and services.

For example, cyberattacks can steal personal data, manipulate AI decisions, disrupt IoT devices, or sabotage cloud infrastructures.

To prevent and mitigate cyberattacks, organizations need to adopt a holistic approach to cybersecurity that covers all aspects of their emerging technologies. This includes:

- Designing secure systems from the start, following best practices and standards for security engineering.
- Implementing robust security controls, such as encryption, authentication, authorization, firewalls, antivirus, and backups.
- Monitoring and testing the security of systems regularly, using tools such as vulnerability scanners, penetration testers, and audits.
- Educating and training staff and users on security awareness, policies, and procedures.
- Responding quickly and effectively to security incidents, using incident response plans and teams.

ETHICAL REGULATION TO ENSURE HUMAN-CENTRIC VALUES

Another challenge of emerging technologies is to ensure that they respect human-centric values, such as *privacy, fairness, transparency, accountability, dignity*, and *autonomy*.

Emerging technologies can have positive or negative impacts on these values depending on how they are designed, deployed, and used.

For example, emerging technologies can enhance privacy by enabling data protection or erode privacy by enabling data collection. They can promote fairness by reducing biases or create unfairness by amplifying biases. They can increase transparency by providing explanations or decrease transparency by hiding decisions. They can support accountability by assigning responsibilities or hinder accountability by creating ambiguities. They can uphold dignity by respecting human rights or violate dignity by harming human rights. They can empower autonomy by giving choices or undermine autonomy by taking choices away.

To ensure that emerging technologies respect human-centric values, organizations need to adopt an ethical approach to emerging technologies that considers the potential impacts and consequences of their actions. This includes:

- Conducting ethical assessments of emerging technologies before, during, and after their development and use, using frameworks and tools such as ethical principles, guidelines, checklists, impact assessments, and audits.
- Engaging with stakeholders and experts from different disciplines and backgrounds to gain diverse perspectives and insights on the ethical issues and implications of emerging technologies.
- Implementing ethical governance mechanisms, such as codes of conduct, ethics committees, ethics officers, ethics reviews, and ethics audits.
- Educating and training staff and users on ethical awareness, values, and standards.
- Responding quickly and effectively to ethical dilemmas or complaints involving emerging technologies.

Emerging technologies are morally neutral; neither inherently good nor bad. It is how they are used by people that defines the ethics.

ETHICS AT THE TECHNOLOGICAL FRONTIER

Technology is advancing at an unprecedented pace, creating new opportunities and challenges for society.

WHY ETHICS MATTER IN TECHNOLOGY

Technology is not neutral. It can have positive or negative impacts on human rights, privacy, security, democracy, equality, and well-being. Technology can also be used for good or evil purposes, depending on who controls it and how it is deployed. Therefore, it is essential to consider the ethical implications of new technology before there is a problem, as well as to monitor and address any issues that may arise along the way.

Ethics is not only a matter of morality, but also of *responsibility* and *accountability*. Technology developers, producers, users, and regulators have a duty to ensure that technology is designed, implemented, and governed in a way that respects human dignity, values, and interests. Ethics can also help to foster trust, innovation, and social good in the technological frontier.

THINKING ETHICALLY ABOUT TECHNOLOGY

There is no standard solution for ethical dilemmas in technology. However, there are some general principles and frameworks that can guide ethical decision-making and action. Here are some of them:

- The Ethical Principles for Artificial Intelligence (AI) proposed by the European Commission, which include respect for human autonomy, prevention of harm, fairness, transparency, diversity, non-discrimination, environmental and societal well-being, and accountability.
- The Embedded EthiCS program at Harvard University, which integrates ethics into computer science education and research by embedding philosophy faculty into computer science courses and projects.
- The Trustworthy AI framework by Deloitte, which outlines six dimensions of trust for AI systems: ethical, robust, reliable, explainable, secure, and transparent.
- The Ethics of Technology Wikipedia page, which provides an overview of the sub-field of ethics addressing the ethical questions specific to the Technology Age.
- The 14 Tech-Related Ethical Concerns And How They Can Be Addressed article by Forbes, which identifies some of the most pressing ethical issues in technology today and offers some possible solutions.

PRACTICAL ADVICE FOR ETHICAL TECHNOLOGY

In addition to following the above principles and frameworks, here are some practical tips for ethical technology that I have learned from my own experience:

- Involve diverse stakeholders in the design, development, deployment, and evaluation of technology. Seek input from experts, users, customers, regulators, civil society groups, and affected communities. Incorporate feedback loops and mechanisms for redress.
- Conduct regular risk assessments and impact assessments for technology. Identify potential harms and benefits for individuals, groups, and society. Mitigate risks and maximize benefits. Monitor outcomes and adjust accordingly.
- Explain how technology works and why it makes certain decisions or recommendations. Provide clear and accessible information about the data sources, algorithms, assumptions, limitations, uncertainties, and trade-offs of technology. Enable users to understand, question, challenge, or opt out of technology.
- Protect the privacy and security of data and systems. Use encryption, anonymization, pseudonymization, or other techniques to safeguard data from unauthorized access or misuse. Implement robust security measures to prevent cyberattacks or breaches. Respect data rights and preferences of users.
- Promote ethical culture and leadership in technology organizations. Establish codes of conduct, policies, guidelines, standards, or best practices for ethical technology. Provide training, education, awareness-raising, or mentoring programs for staff. Encourage ethical reflection and dialogue among teams. Reward ethical behaviour and sanction unethical behaviour.

RESPECTING PRIVACY & DATA SECURITY

Privacy and data security are essential aspects of cyber security. They involve protecting the personal, financial, or otherwise sensitive information of individuals and organizations from unauthorized access, theft, damage or misuse.

Privacy and data security also ensure that the systems and networks that store and process this information are fully operational and resilient to cyber threats. This advice is based on research and best practice from various sources, such as the Australian Cyber Security Centre (ACSC), Coursera, Harvard Business Review and others.

WHY PRIVACY AND DATA SECURITY MATTER

Privacy and data security matter for several reasons:

- They protect the rights and interests of individuals and organizations. Privacy is a fundamental human right that allows people to control their own information and how it is used. Data security ensures that the information is accurate, reliable, and accessible only to those who are authorized to use it.
- They enable trust and confidence in digital services and transactions. Privacy and data security enhance the reputation and credibility of organizations that provide or use digital services, such as online banking, shopping, social media, gaming and more. They also foster customer loyalty and satisfaction by ensuring that their data is handled with care and respect.
- They reduce the risks and costs of cyber incidents. Privacy and data security help prevent or mitigate the impact of cyber threats, such as scams, malware, ransomware, phishing, denial-of-service attacks and more. These threats can cause significant harm to individuals and organizations, such as identity theft, fraud, financial loss, reputational damage, legal liability, operational disruption and more.

HOW TO RESPECT PRIVACY AND DATA SECURITY

There are many ways to respect privacy and data security in the digital world. Here are some of the most important ones.

Turn on automatic updates for your devices and software. Updates are improved versions of software that fix bugs or vulnerabilities that cybercriminals can exploit to access or damage your data. Updates also provide new features and functionalities that can enhance your privacy and security settings. You should enable automatic updates for your computers, mobile phones, tablets and other internet-connected devices, as well as for your applications, programs and operating systems.

Use strong passwords and multi-factor authentication for your accounts. Passwords are the first line of defense for your online accounts, such as email, banking, shopping, social media, gaming and more. You should use strong passwords that are long, complex, unique and hard to guess. You should also use multi-factor authentication (MFA) whenever possible. MFA is an extra layer of security that requires you to provide something you know (such as a password), something you have (such as a code sent to your phone) or something you are (such as a fingerprint) to access your account.

Be **aware of scams and malware** and how to avoid them. Scams are messages sent by cybercriminals designed to trick you into giving up your sensitive information or activating malware on your device. Malware is malicious software that can steal or damage your data or control your device or account. You should be careful when opening emails, texts or messages from unknown or suspicious sources. You should also avoid clicking on links or attachments that look suspicious or too good to be true. You should also install reputable antivirus software on your devices and scan them regularly for malware.

Encrypt your data and use secure connections when transmitting or storing it. Encryption is a process that scrambles your data into an unreadable format that can only be decoded by authorized parties. Encryption protects your data from being intercepted or accessed by unauthorized parties when you send or receive it over the internet or store it on your device or cloud service. You should use encryption tools or software to encrypt your data before transmitting or storing it. You should also use secure connections when accessing online services or websites. Secure connections have a padlock icon or start with https:// in the address bar.

Follow the principles of ethical regulation when developing or using emerging technologies. Emerging technologies are new or innovative technologies that have the potential to transform society in positive or negative ways. Examples of emerging technologies include artificial intelligence (AI), biotechnology, blockchain, quantum computing and more. Ethical regulation is a set of principles or guidelines that aim to ensure that emerging technologies are developed and used in a way that respects human dignity, rights, values, and interests. Ethical regulation also considers the social, environmental, economic, and legal implications of emerging technologies.

Privacy and data security are vital for cyber security in the digital age. They protect the information of individuals and organizations from cyber threats and enable trust and confidence in digital services and transactions. To respect privacy and data security, you should follow some of the best practices and advice that I have shared in this article, such as turning on automatic updates, using strong passwords and MFA, avoiding scams and malware, encrypting your data, and using secure connections, and following ethical regulation principles when developing or using emerging technologies. By doing so, you will not only protect yourself and your data, but also contribute to a safer and more secure digital world for everyone.

QUANTUM COMPUTING & CRYPTOGRAPHY

Quantum computing is a revolutionary technology that harnesses the principles of quantum mechanics to perform calculations that are beyond the reach of classical computers. Quantum computers have the potential to transform many fields, such as cryptography, drug discovery, artificial intelligence, and more.

Quantum computing nonetheless poses a serious threat to the security of our digital systems, especially those that rely on encryption to protect privacy and confidentiality. Encryption is the process of transforming information into a secret code that can only be decrypted by authorized parties. Encryption is widely used in online banking, email, e-commerce, and other applications that involve sensitive data.

The problem is that most of the encryption methods we use today are based on mathematical problems that are hard to solve for classical computers, but easy for quantum computers. For example, RSA encryption, which is one of the most popular encryption systems in the world, relies on the difficulty of factoring large numbers into their prime factors. However, a quantum algorithm called Shor's algorithm can factor large numbers efficiently using a quantum computer. This means that RSA encryption could be broken by a quantum computer in the near future.

Therefore, we need to prepare for the advent of quantum computing by developing and adopting new encryption methods that are resistant to quantum attacks. These methods are called post-quantum cryptography or quantum-proof cryptography. Post-quantum cryptography aims to create encryption methods that are based on mathematical problems that are hard to solve for both classical and quantum computers.

POST-QUANTUM CRYPTOGRAPHY RESEARCH

Post-quantum cryptography is an active area of research in mathematics and computer science. There are several families of post-quantum cryptographic algorithms that have been proposed and studied in the literature, such as lattice-based cryptography, code-based cryptography, multivariate cryptography, hash-based cryptography, and more.

Each family has its own advantages and disadvantages in terms of security, efficiency, compatibility, and practicality. For example, lattice-based cryptography offers high security and versatility, but requires large key sizes and complex operations. Code-based cryptography offers fast encryption and decryption but requires large public keys and suffers from structural weaknesses. Hash-based cryptography offers simple and provable security but has limited functionality and requires stateful signatures.

In 2016, NIST launched a public competition to standardize post-quantum cryptographic algorithms for public-key encryption, digital signatures, and key exchange. The competition received 69 submissions from researchers around the world. After several rounds of evaluation and feedback, NIST announced the first group of winners in July 2022. These are:

- **CRYSTALS-KYBER**. A lattice-based encryption scheme that uses the learning with errors (LWE) problem as its security assumption. It offers high security, efficiency, and versatility.
- **FrodoKEM**. Another lattice-based encryption scheme that uses the learning with errors (LWE) problem as its security assumption. It offers high security and simplicity.
- **SPHINCS+**. A hash-based signature scheme that uses the Merkle tree construction as its security assumption. It offers provable security and stateless signatures.
- **FALCON**. A lattice-based signature scheme that uses the short integer solution (SIS) problem as its security assumption. It offers high security and performance.

NIST also announced four additional algorithms that are under consideration for inclusion in the standard. These are:

- **BIKE**. A code-based encryption scheme that uses the McEliece cryptosystem as its basis. It offers fast encryption and decryption.

- **Classic McEliece**. Another code-based encryption scheme that uses the McEliece cryptosystem as its basis. It offers high security and simplicity.
- **Rainbow**. A multivariate signature scheme that uses systems of quadratic equations as its basis. It offers small signatures and fast verification.
- **Dilithium**: Another lattice-based signature scheme that uses the module learning with rounding (MLWR) problem as its security assumption. It offers high security and efficiency.

NIST expects to finalize its post-quantum cryptographic standard in about two years. The standard will provide guidance for developers, vendors, and users on how to implement and use post-quantum cryptography in their systems.

POST-QUANTUM CRYPTOGRAPHY CHALLENGES AND OPPORTUNITIES

Post-quantum cryptography is not only a technical challenge but also a social and economic one. There are many factors that affect the adoption and deployment of post-quantum cryptography in the real world, such as:

- **Compatibility**. Post-quantum cryptographic algorithms need to be compatible with existing protocols, standards, platforms, devices, and applications that use encryption. For example, post-quantum encryption schemes need to be integrated with the Transport Layer Security (TLS) protocol, which secures the communication between web browsers and servers. Post-quantum signature schemes need to be compatible with the X.509 certificate format, which authenticates the identity of websites and other entities. Post-quantum key exchange schemes need to be compatible with the Diffie-Hellman protocol, which establishes a shared secret key between two parties.
- **Performance**. Post-quantum cryptographic algorithms need to be efficient and scalable in terms of computation, communication, and storage. For example, post-quantum encryption schemes need to have fast encryption and decryption times, low latency, and low bandwidth consumption. Post-quantum signature schemes need to have fast signing and verification times, small signature sizes, and low storage requirements. Post-quantum key exchange schemes need to have fast key generation and agreement

times, low communication overhead, and low memory consumption.

- **Security**. Post-quantum cryptographic algorithms need to be secure against both classical and quantum attacks. For example, post-quantum encryption schemes need to provide confidentiality, integrity, and authenticity of the encrypted data. Post-quantum signature schemes need to provide unforgeability, non-repudiation, and verifiability of the signed data. Post-quantum key exchange schemes need to provide secrecy, freshness, and forward secrecy of the shared key.
- **Usability**. Post-quantum cryptographic algorithms need to be user-friendly and transparent in terms of functionality, reliability, and trustworthiness. For example, post-quantum encryption schemes need to have clear and intuitive interfaces, robust error handling, and graceful degradation. Post-quantum signature schemes need to have clear and intuitive verification methods, robust revocation mechanisms, and trustworthy certification authorities. Post-quantum key exchange schemes need to have clear and intuitive key agreement methods, robust authentication mechanisms, and trustworthy key distribution centres.

These factors pose significant challenges for the development and deployment of post-quantum cryptography in the real world. However, they also offer opportunities for innovation and collaboration among researchers, developers, vendors, users, regulators, and policymakers. By working together, we can ensure that our digital systems are secure against the quantum threat and ready for the quantum future.

Quantum computing is a powerful technology that can bring many benefits to humanity, but also poses a serious threat to the security of our digital systems. To protect our privacy and confidentiality in the quantum era, we need to develop and adopt post-quantum cryptography as soon as possible.

Post-quantum cryptography is a new field of cryptography that aims to create encryption methods that are resistant to quantum attacks. NIST is leading a global effort to standardize post-quantum cryptographic algorithms for public-key encryption, digital signatures, and key exchange.

Post-quantum cryptography faces many technical, social, and economic challenges in its adoption and deployment in the real world. However, it also offers many opportunities for innovation and collaboration among various stakeholders.

ETHICAL FRAMEWORKS FOR AUTONOMOUS SYSTEMS

Autonomous systems are technologies that can perform tasks without human intervention or supervision, such as self-driving cars, drones, robots, or artificial intelligence (AI) systems. These technologies have the potential to bring many benefits to society, such as improving safety, efficiency, productivity, and innovation. However, they also pose ethical challenges that need to be addressed, such as ensuring respect for human dignity, rights, and values; preventing harm and discrimination; ensuring accountability and transparency; and fostering trust and social acceptance.

This section considers how to design and regulate autonomous systems in an ethical way, drawing on research and best practice from various sources. It uses the term "autonomous intelligent systems" (A/IS) to refer to systems that combine autonomy and intelligence, such as AI or robotics.

GENERAL PRINCIPLES FOR ETHICAL A/IS

One of the most comprehensive and influential sources of ethical guidance for A/IS is the *IEEE Global Initiative on Ethics of Autonomous and Intelligent Systems,* which has developed a document called *Ethically Aligned Design* .

The general principles are:

- **Human Rights**. A/IS shall be created and operated to respect, promote, and protect internationally recognized human rights.
- **Well-being**. A/IS creators shall adopt increased human well-being as a primary success criterion for development.
- **Data Agency**. A/IS creators shall empower individuals with the ability to access and securely share their data, to maintain people's capacity to have control over their identity.
- **Effectiveness**. A/IS creators and operators shall provide evidence of the effectiveness and fitness for purpose of A/IS.
- **Transparency**. The basis of a particular A/IS decision should always be discoverable.
- **Accountability**. A/IS shall be created and operated to provide an unambiguous rationale for all decisions made.

- **Awareness of Misuse**. A/IS creators shall guard against all potential misuses and risks of A/IS in operation.
- **Competence**. A/IS creators shall specify, and operators shall adhere to the knowledge and skill required for safe and effective operation.

These general principles are further elaborated in subsequent sections of Ethically Aligned Design, with specific contextual, cultural, and pragmatic explorations which impact their implementation.

ETHICS-EMBEDDING A/IS

Another approach to ensure ethical behaviour of A/IS is to embed ethics into their design and operation. This means that A/IS should be able to reason about ethical values and principles, and act accordingly in different situations.

This requires a combination of different theories and methods from ethics, such as deontology (duty-based ethics), consequentialism (outcome-based ethics), virtue ethics (character-based ethics), or value-sensitive design.

An example of an ethics-embedding A/IS is an ethical controller, which is a module that integrates machine ethics into the decision-making process of an autonomous system. An ethical controller can evaluate the ethical implications of different actions, based on predefined ethical rules or values, and select the most ethically acceptable one. For instance, an ethical controller can help a self-driving car decide how to avoid a collision while minimizing harm to passengers, pedestrians, or other vehicles.

ETHICAL REGULATION OF A/IS

Besides designing ethical A/IS, it is also important to regulate them in an ethical way. This means that there should be clear and consistent laws, policies, standards, and codes of conduct that govern the development, deployment, use, and oversight of A/IS. These regulations should aim to protect the public interest, ensure social justice, promote innovation, and foster collaboration among different stakeholders.

An example of an ethical regulation of A/IS is the European Commission's Ethics Guidelines for Trustworthy AI, which provide a framework for achieving trustworthy AI that is lawful, ethical, and robust.

The guidelines identify seven key requirements for trustworthy AI:

- **Human agency and oversight**. AI should empower human beings and respect their autonomy.
- **Technical robustness and safety**. AI should be reliable, secure, resilient, and accurate.
- **Privacy and data governance**. AI should respect privacy rights and ensure data quality and integrity.
- **Transparency.** AI should be understandable, explainable, and traceable.
- **Diversity, non-discrimination, and fairness**. AI should avoid bias and ensure fairness and inclusion.
- **Societal and environmental well-being**. AI should benefit society and the environment.
- **Accountability**. AI should be auditable, responsible, and liable.

The guidelines also provide a set of assessment tools to help implement these requirements in practice.

Ethical frameworks for A/IS are essential to ensure that these technologies are aligned with human values and interests, and that they contribute to the common good. Ethical frameworks for A/IS should include general principles, ethics-embedding methods, and ethical regulations, as well as mechanisms for monitoring, evaluation, and feedback. By following these frameworks, we can create and use A/IS that are trustworthy, beneficial, and sustainable.

CULTURAL AND SOCIAL IMPLICATIONS

Emerging technologies, such as artificial intelligence, biotechnology, nanotechnology, and quantum computing, have the potential to transform our society. They can bring benefits such as improved health, productivity, security, and communication.

They also pose ethical challenges and risks, such as privacy, security, accountability, human dignity, and social justice.

1. Understand the context and stakeholders of the technology. Before developing or deploying any emerging technology, it is important to understand the context and the stakeholders involved. Who are the users, beneficiaries, and potential victims of the technology? What are their needs, values, expectations, and concerns? How will the technology affect their lives, rights, and relationships? What are the legal, regulatory, and cultural norms that govern the technology? These questions can help identify the ethical issues and dilemmas that may arise from the technology.

2. Engage in ethical deliberation and dialogue. Ethical deliberation and dialogue are essential for addressing the cultural and social implications of emerging technologies. Ethical deliberation is the process of reflecting on the moral values and principles that guide our actions and decisions. Ethical dialogue is the process of communicating and exchanging views with others who may have different perspectives and interests. Ethical deliberation and dialogue can help foster mutual understanding, respect, trust, and collaboration among the stakeholders of the technology.

3. Apply ethical frameworks and principles. Ethical frameworks and principles are tools that can help guide our ethical deliberation and dialogue. Ethical frameworks are systematic approaches that provide criteria for evaluating the ethical aspects of a technology. Ethical principles are general rules that express the moral values and obligations that we should follow. Some examples of ethical frameworks are utilitarianism, deontology, virtue ethics, and care ethics. Some examples of ethical principles are autonomy, beneficence, non-maleficence, justice, and fairness.

4. Implement ethical design and governance. Ethical design and governance are practices that can help ensure that emerging technologies are developed and deployed in a responsible and accountable manner. Ethical design is the process of incorporating ethical considerations into the design process of a technology. Ethical governance is the process of establishing and enforcing rules and standards for the use and oversight of a technology. Ethical design and governance can help prevent or mitigate the negative impacts of emerging technologies on society.

5. Monitor and evaluate the outcomes and impacts of the technology. Monitoring and evaluation are processes that can help assess the outcomes and impacts of emerging technologies on society. Monitoring is the process of collecting data and information about the performance and behaviour of a technology. Evaluation is the process of analysing and interpreting the data and information to determine the effects and consequences of a technology. Monitoring and evaluation can help identify the benefits and harms of emerging technologies, as well as the gaps and challenges that need to be addressed.

4.4. WHISTLEBLOWER PROTECTION & DIGITAL ETHICS

DIGITAL ETHICS

WHAT ARE DIGITAL ETHICS?

Digital ethics are the principles and values that guide our behaviour and decisions in the digital world.

They are based on universal human rights, such as privacy, freedom of expression, and dignity. They also reflect the specific norms and expectations of different communities, cultures, and professions.

WHY ARE DIGITAL ETHICS IMPORTANT?

Digital ethics help us to use digital technologies in a responsible and beneficial way, without harming ourselves or others. They also protect the public interest and the common good, especially when we face ethical dilemmas or conflicts of interest.

HOW DO WE UPHOLD DIGITAL ETHICS?

Upholding digital ethics requires us to be aware, informed, and accountable. Here are some practical tips to help you do that:

- Be aware of the ethical implications of your actions and choices in the digital domain. Think about how they affect yourself, your colleagues, your clients, your stakeholders, and the society at large.
- Be informed about the relevant laws, regulations, policies, standards, and codes of conduct that apply to your profession and your context. Follow them and respect them, but also question them and challenge them if they are outdated, unfair, or inconsistent with digital ethics.
- Be accountable for your actions and choices in the digital domain. Document them, justify them, and communicate them clearly and transparently. Accept feedback, criticism, and consequences. Learn from your mistakes and improve your practices.

WHISTLEBLOWER PROTECTION

This is a crucial aspect of digital ethics, especially for cybersecurity professionals. Whistleblowers are people who expose wrongdoing or misconduct in their organizations or sectors, often at great personal risk. They can play a vital role in safeguarding the public interest and promoting accountability.

However, whistleblowers often face retaliation, harassment, intimidation, or legal action from their employers or other parties. For example, they may have signed a non-disclosure agreement (NDA) as a condition of employment.

Whistleblowers may also face ethical dilemmas or conflicts of interest when deciding whether, how, when, and to whom to disclose information.

To protect whistleblowers and support their ethical disclosure:

Create a culture of trust and openness in our organizations and sectors. Encourage reporting of wrongdoing or misconduct internally or externally. Provide clear channels and procedures for doing so. Protect the identity and confidentiality of whistleblowers.

Advocate for legal frameworks and policies that protect whistleblowers from retaliation or prosecution. Recognize their contribution to the public interest and reward them accordingly.

Educate ourselves and others about the rights and responsibilities of whistleblowers. Seek guidance from experts or authorities when in doubt. Support whistleblowers who need help or advice.

Upholding digital ethics is not easy, but it is essential for cybersecurity professionals. It helps us to use our skills and knowledge in a positive and constructive way, without compromising our integrity or values. It also helps us to protect whistleblowers who expose wrongdoing or misconduct in our organizations or sectors. By following these tips, we can uphold digital ethics and contribute to a safer and fairer digital world.

EXTENDING PROTECTION TO THE DIGITAL REALM

Whistleblowing is the act of reporting misconduct, fraud, corruption, or other wrongdoing within an organization or to the public. Whistleblowing can have positive impacts on democracy and business, as it can expose and prevent harm, improve accountability, and foster a culture of integrity. However, whistleblowing can also entail significant risks for the whistleblower, such as retaliation, harassment, discrimination, legal action, or physical harm.

USE ANONYMOUS COMMUNICATION TOOLS

One of the main challenges for whistleblowers is to protect their identity and avoid being traced or identified by their adversaries. This is especially difficult in the digital realm, where every online activity can leave a trail of data that can be used to track or deanonymize the whistleblower. Therefore, whistleblowers should use anonymous communication tools that can hide their IP address, encrypt their traffic, and prevent network surveillance. Some examples of such tools are:

Tor. Tor is a free software that allows users to browse the web anonymously by routing their traffic through a network of volunteer servers around the world. Tor can also access hidden services that are not indexed by regular search engines, such as whistleblower platforms or secure dropboxes.

Signal. Signal is a free app that allows users to send end-to-end encrypted messages and calls to other Signal users. Signal does not store any metadata or logs of its users' communications, and it supports disappearing messages and screen lock features.

ProtonMail. A free email service that offers end-to-end encryption and zero-access encryption, meaning that even ProtonMail cannot read or access its users' emails. ProtonMail also supports self-destructing emails and anonymous accounts.

These tools can help whistleblowers communicate securely and anonymously with their recipients, such as journalists, regulators or watchdogs. However, they are not foolproof, and they require careful usage and configuration. Whistleblowers should always verify the authenticity and trustworthiness of their recipients, avoid using personal or identifiable information, and follow the best practices and guidelines provided by the tools.

SEEK LEGAL ADVICE AND PROTECTION

Another challenge for whistleblowers is to navigate the complex and often unclear legal landscape of whistleblowing. Different countries and jurisdictions have different laws and regulations regarding whistleblowing, which may offer different levels of protection and incentives for whistleblowers. For example, some countries have dedicated whistleblower laws that protect whistleblowers from retaliation and provide them with rewards or compensation for their disclosures. Other countries may have sector-specific laws that cover only certain types of whistleblowing, such as in financial services or health care. Some countries may have no laws at all or even criminalize whistleblowing.

Therefore, whistleblowers should seek legal advice and protection before, during and after their disclosures. They should consult with qualified lawyers who specialize in whistleblowing cases and who can advise them on their rights and obligations, the potential risks and benefits, and the best strategies to protect themselves legally. They should also be aware of the existing channels and mechanisms for reporting misconduct, such as internal reporting systems, external regulators or ombudsmen, or public interest disclosures. They should choose the most appropriate channel based on their situation and goals and follow the relevant procedures and protocols.

Whistleblowers should also be aware of the international initiatives and frameworks that aim to protect and support whistleblowers globally. For example:

The EU Whistleblower Directive. The EU Whistleblower Directive is a law that requires all EU member states to implement national legislation that protects whistleblowers who report breaches of EU law in various domains, such as environmental protection, consumer protection, public health or data protection. The directive also provides for safe reporting channels, confidentiality measures, anti-retaliation safeguards and remedies for whistleblowers.

The UN Convention against Corruption. The UN Convention against Corruption is an international treaty that obliges its signatories to adopt measures to prevent and combat corruption in both public and private sectors. The convention also recognizes the role of whistleblowers in fighting corruption and calls for their protection from any unjustified treatment.

The OECD Guidelines for Multinational Enterprises. The OECD Guidelines for Multinational Enterprises are recommendations for responsible business conduct that cover all major areas of business ethics, such as human rights, labour rights, environmental protection or anti-corruption. The guidelines also encourage enterprises to establish effective internal mechanisms for reporting misconduct and to protect whistleblowers from retaliation.

These initiatives can provide whistleblowers with additional legal protection and support, especially if they report cross-border or transnational misconduct. However, they are not binding, and they depend on the implementation and enforcement of the national authorities.

FOSTER A CULTURE OF ETHICAL DIGITAL CITIZENSHIP

A third challenge for whistleblowers is to overcome the social and cultural barriers that may discourage or deter them from reporting misconduct. Whistleblowing can be seen as a form of ethical digital citizenship, which is the practice of using digital technologies in a responsible, respectful, and constructive way, with regard to oneself, others and society. Ethical digital citizenship requires not only technical skills and knowledge, but also moral values and attitudes, such as honesty, integrity, courage and solidarity.

However, ethical digital citizenship is not always easy or common in the digital realm, where there may be conflicting interests, norms and expectations. Whistleblowers may face stigma, ostracism or hostility from their peers, colleagues or superiors, who may view them as traitors, snitches or troublemakers. They may also face indifference, apathy or skepticism from the public, who may not trust or care about their disclosures. They may also face ethical dilemmas or trade-offs, such as whether to expose sensitive or personal information, whether to harm innocent third parties, or whether to act in the public interest or in their own interest.

Therefore, whistleblowers need to foster a culture of ethical digital citizenship, both within and outside their organizations. They need to raise awareness and educate others about the importance and benefits of whistleblowing for society and democracy. They need to build trust and credibility with their recipients and audiences, by providing evidence, context and rationale for their disclosures. They need to act in good faith and with good intentions, by reporting only truthful, relevant and significant information. They need to respect the rights and interests of others, by minimizing the harm or damage caused by their disclosures. They need to seek feedback and dialogue with their stakeholders, by listening to their concerns and perspectives.

By fostering a culture of ethical digital citizenship, whistleblowers can create a positive impact on their organizations and society, as well as on themselves. They can improve the performance and reputation of their organizations, by exposing and correcting misconduct, enhancing transparency and accountability, and promoting a culture of integrity. They can also improve their own well-being and satisfaction, by fulfilling their moral duty, expressing their values and beliefs, and contributing to the common good.

Whistleblowing is a vital activity for democracy and business, but it also entails significant challenges and risks for the whistleblower. To extend protection to the digital realm, whistleblowers should use anonymous communication tools, seek legal advice and protection, and foster a culture of ethical digital citizenship. By doing so, they can protect themselves from harm, while protecting others from wrongdoing.

CULTIVATING A CULTURE OF ETHICS

Cybersecurity professionals face ethical dilemmas when they encounter wrongdoing or negligence within their organizations or by their clients. How can they report these issues without violating confidentiality or facing retaliation?

How can they foster a culture of ethics that values whistleblowing as a positive and responsible action?

To cultivate a culture of ethics in cybersecurity, it is important to have clear and consistent policies and procedures for whistleblowing. These should include:

- Defining who is an eligible whistleblower and what types of issues can be reported
- Providing multiple and secure channels for reporting, including internal and external options
- Protecting the identity and rights of whistleblowers, including anonymity, confidentiality, immunity, and anti-retaliation measures
- Investigating and responding to whistleblower reports promptly and fairly
- Providing feedback and support to whistleblowers throughout the process
- Recognizing and rewarding whistleblowers for their contributions

Additionally, it is important to educate and train cybersecurity professionals on the ethical principles and practices of whistleblowing. This should include:

- Raising awareness of the benefits and challenges of whistleblowing

- Providing guidance on how to identify and report wrongdoing or negligence.
- Encouraging critical thinking and moral reasoning skills
- Promoting a culture of openness, trust, and accountability
- Creating opportunities for dialogue and feedback on ethical issues

Whistleblowing is not only a legal obligation but also a moral duty for cybersecurity professionals. By cultivating a culture of ethics, they can uphold their professional standards, protect their clients and the public, and contribute to the advancement of their field.

LEGAL PROTECTIONS & NON-RETALIATION

In Australia, the Corporations Act 2001 (Corporations Act) provides certain rights and protections for whistleblowers who report misconduct about companies and company officers. These include:

- Protection of information provided by whistleblowers: The identity of the whistleblower and the information they disclose are confidential and cannot be disclosed without their consent or as authorised by law.
- Protections for whistleblowers against legal action: The whistleblower is not subject to any civil, criminal, or administrative liability for making the disclosure. They are also protected from contractual or other remedies that may be enforced against them based on the disclosure.
- Protections for whistleblowers from detriment: The whistleblower is protected from any actual or threatened detriment (such as dismissal, harassment, discrimination, or damage) that is caused or motivated by their disclosure. They can also seek compensation and remedies if they suffer any detriment because of their disclosure.

To access these rights and protections, the whistleblower must meet certain criteria under the Corporations Act. These include:

- **Their rol**e. They must be a current or former employee, officer, contractor, supplier, volunteer, or associate of the company or organisation they report about, or a related company or organisation. They can also be a spouse, dependant, or relative of these people.

- **Their disclosure**. They must have reasonable grounds to suspect misconduct, an improper situation or circumstances, or a breach of financial sector law or any Commonwealth offence punishable by imprisonment of 12 months or more. However, a report solely about a personal work-related grievance is not covered by the protections.
- **Their recipient**. They must make the disclosure to ASIC, APRA, a prescribed Commonwealth authority, an eligible recipient within the company or organisation (such as an officer, auditor, or authorised person), or a legal practitioner for the purpose of obtaining legal advice or representation. In limited circumstances, they can also make the disclosure to a journalist or parliamentarian if they have previously reported to ASIC or APRA and their concerns are about substantial and imminent danger to health, safety, or environment, or matters in the public interest after 90 days.

WHISTLEBLOWER RIGHTS AND PROTECTIONS IN OTHER COUNTRIES

Other countries may have different laws and regulations that protect whistleblowers from retaliation and provide them with legal rights. For example:

In the United States, the Whistleblower Protection Act of 1989 protects federal employees who report wrongdoing in their agencies from adverse personnel actions. There are also other laws that protect whistleblowers in specific sectors, such as securities, health care, tax, and environmental protection.

In the United Kingdom, the Public Interest Disclosure Act 1998 protects workers who report wrongdoing in their workplaces from dismissal or detriment. The wrongdoing can include criminal offences, breaches of legal obligations, miscarriages of justice, dangers to health and safety or environment, or concealment of any of these matters.

In Canada, the Public Servants Disclosure Protection Act 2005 protects public servants who report wrongdoing in the federal public sector from reprisals. The wrongdoing can include contraventions of laws or regulations, misuse of public funds or assets, gross mismanagement, serious breaches of codes of conduct, dangers to health and safety or environment, or knowingly directing someone to commit any of these acts.

Whistleblowers who report misconduct across borders may need to consider the laws and protections that apply in different jurisdictions. They may also seek advice from legal professionals or organisations that support whistleblowers.

KNOW YOUR RIGHTS AND PROTECTIONS

Before you decide to blow the whistle, you should be aware of your rights and protections under the law. Different countries have different laws and regulations that protect whistleblowers from retaliation, such as dismissal, harassment, or legal action.

For example, in Australia, the Corporations Act 2001 provides protections for whistleblowers who report misconduct by companies or organisations to ASIC, the Australian Securities and Investments Commission.

In the EU, the Whistleblower Directive provides protections for whistleblowers who report matters related to privacy, data protection and network security.

In the US, there are various laws and agencies that protect and incentivize whistleblowers, such as the DOJ, the FTC and the SEC.

You should familiarize yourself with the laws and regulations that apply to your situation and *seek legal advice if necessary*. You should also keep records of your reports and any evidence of misconduct or retaliation.

CHOOSE YOUR CHANNEL WISELY

Another important decision you must make as a whistleblower is how to report your concerns. You may have different options, such as reporting internally within your company or organisation, reporting externally to a regulator or an authority, or reporting publicly to the media or a platform. Each option has its advantages and disadvantages, depending on your goals, risks, and expectations.

Reporting internally may be the fastest and easiest way to address the issue, but it may also expose you to retaliation or cover-up. Reporting externally may give you more credibility and protection, but it may also take longer and require more evidence. Reporting publicly may raise more awareness and pressure, but it may also damage your reputation or relationships.

You should weigh the pros and cons of each option carefully and choose the one that best suits your situation. You should also consider the potential impact of your report on the public interest and the greater good.

USE TECHNOLOGY ETHICALLY

Technology can be a powerful tool for whistleblowing, but it can also pose ethical challenges. As a cybersecurity expert, I know that technology can provide anonymity, security, and efficiency for whistleblowing, but it can also create vulnerabilities, uncertainties, and conflicts for whistleblowing.

Anonymity can protect your identity and privacy, but it can also reduce your accountability and credibility. Security can protect your data and communication, but it can also expose you to hacking or surveillance. Efficiency can speed up your reporting process, but it can also compromise your quality or accuracy.

You should use technology ethically and responsibly when whistleblowing. You should choose reliable and trustworthy platforms or tools that respect your rights and values. You should also follow best practices for cybersecurity hygiene and preparedness.

Whistleblowing is not an easy decision to make, but it can be a noble and ethical one. As a cybersecurity expert, I hope that my advice can help you protect yourself and act responsibly as a whistleblower. Remember that you are not alone in this journey. There are many resources and support available for whistleblowers who want to serve the public interest and the greater good.

4.5. ETHICAL CONSIDERATIONS IN AI ART

CREATIVITY, COPYRIGHT, & OWNERSHIP

AI art is a form of creative expression that uses AI algorithms to generate, modify, or enhance artistic works such as images, music, or literature. AI art raises some ethical questions that need to be addressed by artists, consumers, and regulators.

CREATIVITY

One of the ethical questions that AI art poses is whether AI can be considered creative or not. Creativity is often seen as a human trait that involves originality, novelty, and value. Some argue that AI cannot be creative because it only mimics human creativity or follows predefined rules and objectives. Others contend that AI can be creative because it can produce unexpected and innovative outcomes that surpass human capabilities or expectations.

Adopt a **pluralistic and inclusive view** of creativity that recognizes the different types and degrees of creativity that humans and AI can exhibit. Rather than seeing AI as a threat or a replacement for human creativity, we should see it as a tool or a partner that can enhance and complement human creativity. We should also acknowledge the ethical responsibilities that come with creating and using AI art, such as ensuring its quality, safety, and accountability.

COPYRIGHT

Another ethical question that AI art raises is how to protect the intellectual property rights of the creators and users of AI art. Copyright is a legal concept that grants the creator of an original work the exclusive right to control its use, distribution, and reproduction. However, copyright law is not well suited for dealing with AI art, because it is unclear who the creator of an AI artwork is: the human who designed or trained the AI algorithm, the human who provided the input data or parameters, the AI algorithm itself, or some combination of them.

It is best to adopt a **flexible and collaborative approach** that balances the interests and incentives of all the parties involved in the creation and use of AI art. Rather than trying to fit AI art into existing legal frameworks that may not apply or may create conflicts, we should develop new legal frameworks that reflect the specificities and complexities of AI art. We should also promote ethical principles and best practices that foster transparency, attribution, and fair use of AI art.

OWNERSHIP

A third ethical question that AI art raises is how to determine the ownership and value of AI art works. Ownership is a social and economic concept that assigns rights and responsibilities to the possessor of an object or a resource. However, ownership is not straightforward for AI art works, because they may not have a single or identifiable author, they may be easily copied or modified, or they may be generated on demand or in real time.

Adopt a **dynamic and participatory approach** that respects the preferences and expectations of the creators and consumers of AI art. Rather than assuming that ownership is fixed or predetermined, we should recognize that ownership can be negotiated or shared among multiple stakeholders. We should also encourage ethical practices and standards that ensure the authenticity, quality, and diversity of AI art works.

THE EMERGENCE OF AI ART MELDING TECHNOLOGY AND CREATIVITY

AI art is a form of digital art that uses artificial intelligence (AI) to generate or manipulate images, sounds, or texts. AI art can be seen as a way of exploring the creative potential of technology and expanding the boundaries of human expression.

However, AI art also poses some ethical challenges that need to be addressed by artists, researchers, and society. Here are some of the main ethical considerations in AI art:

COPYRIGHT

AI art generators often use data from existing artworks to train their algorithms. This raises the question of whether AI art infringes on the rights of human artists who created the original works. Some AI art platforms, such as Shutterstock's ethical AI image generator, have started to acknowledge and pay original artists for their contributions. However, many other platforms do not have such policies or mechanisms in place.

AUTHORSHIP

AI art generators can produce artworks that are novel, original, and surprising. This raises the question of who is the author of AI art the human who provided the input, the algorithm that generated the output, or both? Some AI artists, such as Mario Klingemann and Robbie Barrat, have argued that they are co-creators with their AI systems. However, others have challenged this claim and argued that AI art is not truly creative or artistic.

COMMERCIALIZATION

AI art generators can produce artworks at a fast pace and low cost. This raises the question of how AI art affects the value and market of human art. Some AI artworks, such as *Portrait of Edmond Belamy* by Obvious, have sold for high prices at auctions. However, others have criticized this trend and argued that AI art is overhyped and undermines the quality and authenticity of human art.

RESPONSIBILITY

AI art generators can produce artworks that are harmful, offensive, or misleading. This raises the question of who is responsible for the consequences of AI art: the human who used the generator, the developer who created the generator, or the platform that hosted the generator? Some AI art generators, such as DALL-E and Mi journey, have been found to generate racist or sexist images . However, there is no clear guidance or regulation on how to prevent or address such issues.

ETHICAL IMPLICATIONS IN AI ART POLICIES

AI art is a term that refers to the use of artificial intelligence (AI) to create or assist in the creation of artworks, such as images, music, or literature. AI art has become increasingly popular and accessible since 2022, thanks to the development of generative AI tools like ChatGPT, DALL-E and Midjourney. These tools allow anyone to produce art with AI engines by entering a prompt and receiving images or texts in response.

AI art also poses significant ethical challenges that need to be addressed by policymakers, artists, and consumers. Some of these challenges include:

COPYRIGHT INFRINGEMENT

AI art generators often use existing artworks as training data or inspiration for their outputs. This raises the question of whether AI art infringes on the rights of the original artists whose work is used without their permission or compensation.

AUTHORSHIP AND OWNERSHIP

AI art also blurs the boundaries of authorship and ownership, as it is not clear who should be credited or paid for an AI-generated artwork. Is it the human who provided the prompt, the AI engine that produced the output, or the developer who created the engine? How should the value and quality of an AI-generated artwork be determined and evaluated?

COMMERCIALIZATION AND EXPLOITATION

AI art also creates new opportunities and risks for the commercialization and exploitation of artworks. On one hand, AI art can democratize art production and consumption, allowing more people to create and enjoy artworks at low cost. On the other hand, AI art can also enable unethical practices such as plagiarism, fraud, or manipulation, where AI-generated artworks are passed off as human-made or used for malicious purposes.

- **Establish clear guidelines and standards**. One of the first steps to ensure ethical AI art is to establish clear guidelines and standards for the use and development of AI art generators. These guidelines should specify the principles, values, and goals that should guide AI art creation and consumption, such as fairness, transparency, accountability, and respect. They should also define the roles and responsibilities of different stakeholders involved in AI art, such as policymakers, developers, artists, and consumers.
- **Implement effective mechanisms and tools.** Another step to ensure ethical AI art is to implement effective mechanisms and tools to monitor, regulate, and enforce the guidelines and standards. These mechanisms and tools could include legal frameworks, codes of conduct, certification schemes, auditing systems, or watermarking techniques. They should aim to prevent or detect unethical behaviours such as copyright infringement, plagiarism, fraud, or manipulation in AI art.
- **Promote education and awareness**. A third step to ensure ethical AI art is to promote education and awareness among all stakeholders involved in AI art. This could include providing training programs, workshops, courses, or online resources on the ethical implications and best practices of AI

art. It could also involve creating platforms for dialogue, collaboration, and feedback among different stakeholders to share perspectives, experiences, and solutions on ethical AI art.

By following these three steps of establishing clear guidelines and standards, implementing effective mechanisms and tools, and promoting education and awareness, we can ensure that AI art is used in a way that respects the rights of human artists and supports the creative process.

COPYRIGHT & ATTRIBUTION DEFINING AUTHORSHIP IN AI ART

AI art is a term that refers to artworks created by artificial intelligence (AI) systems, such as generative adversarial networks (GANs), deep neural networks (DNNs), or evolutionary algorithms (EAs). AI art can take various forms, such as images, videos, music, or text, and can be influenced by human input, such as prompts, data, or feedback.

AI art is interesting field that raises many ethical questions, especially regarding the ownership and authorship of the artworks. Who should be credited as the creator of an AI-generated artwork? Is it the human who developed the algorithm, the machine that produced the artwork, or both? How can we protect the rights and interests of both human and machine artists? How can we ensure that AI art is fair and respectful to the original sources of data and inspiration?

These are some of the questions that cybersecurity experts, artists, lawyers, and ethicists are trying to answer.

WHY DOES AUTHORSHIP MATTER?

Authorship is a concept that denotes the origin, identity, and responsibility of a creative work. It is closely related to intellectual property (IP) rights, such as copyright, patent, or trademark, which grant legal protection and recognition to the creators of original works.

Authorship matters for several reasons:

- It acknowledges the contribution and effort of the creators, and gives them credit and reputation.
- It enables the creators to control how their works are used, distributed, modified, or monetized.
- It incentivizes innovation and creativity by rewarding the creators for their works.

- It fosters trust and transparency among the creators, users, and consumers of the works.
- It promotes ethical standards and values in the creation and use of the works.

However, authorship is not always clear-cut. There are many cases where multiple parties are involved in the creation of a work, such as collaborations, adaptations, remixes, or derivations. There are also cases where the work is influenced by external factors, such as culture, history, or nature. In these cases, authorship can be shared, disputed, or ambiguous.

AI art adds another layer of complexity to the issue of authorship. Unlike traditional art forms, where human creativity is evident and dominant, AI art involves a significant degree of machine autonomy and unpredictability. The role of human input can vary from minimal to substantial, depending on the design and implementation of the AI system. The role of machine output can also vary from deterministic to stochastic, depending on the algorithm and data used by the AI system.

Therefore, defining authorship in AI art is not a simple task. It requires a careful examination of the technical, legal, and ethical aspects of each case. It also requires a balance between respecting human agency and acknowledging machine intelligence.

DEFINING AUTHORSHIP IN AI ART?

There is no universal or definitive answer to how to define authorship in AI art. Different approaches have been proposed and adopted by different stakeholders. Here are some examples:

The human-centric approach. This approach assigns authorship solely to the human who developed or used the AI system to create the artwork. This approach assumes that human creativity is superior and indispensable to machine creativity. It also reflects the current legal framework in most jurisdictions, which does not recognize non-human entities as authors or owners of IP rights.

The machine-centric approach. This approach assigns authorship solely to the machine that produced the artwork. This approach assumes that machine creativity is independent and distinct from human creativity. It also challenges the current legal framework in most jurisdictions, which does not grant non-human entities any legal status or rights.

The hybrid approaches. This approach assigns authorship jointly or separately to both the human and the machine that contributed to the creation of the artwork. This approach assumes that human and machine creativity are complementary and interdependent. It also acknowledges the diversity and complexity of AI art cases, which may require different levels of attribution and recognition for both parties.

Each of the above approaches has its advantages and disadvantages. The human-centric approach may be more practical and consistent with existing laws, but it may also be unfair and disrespectful to the machine's role and potential. The machine-centric approach may be more progressive and respectful to the machine's role and potential, but it may also be unrealistic and inconsistent with existing laws. The hybrid approach may be more balanced and flexible for different cases, but it may also be more complicated and controversial for determining how to allocate and share authorship.

Therefore, the choice of approach depends on the context and purpose of each case. Some factors that may influence the decision are:

- The type and design of the AI system: Is it a rule-based or a learning-based system? Is it a supervised or an unsupervised system? Is it a deterministic or a probabilistic system?
- The source and quality of the data: Is it original or derived from other works? Is it public or private? Is it accurate or biased?
- The degree and nature of human input: Is it direct or indirect? Is it creative or technical? Is it intentional or accidental?
- The degree and nature of machine output: Is it predictable or surprising? Is it consistent or variable? Is it expressive or functional?
- The intended and actual use of the artwork: Is it for personal or commercial purposes? Is it for artistic or scientific purposes? Is it for educational or entertainment purposes?

Based on these factors, different scenarios may require different solutions. For example, if the AI system is a rule-based system that produces predictable and functional outputs based on human instructions, then the human-centric approach may be more appropriate. If the AI system is a learning-based system that produces surprising and expressive outputs based on data from other works, then the machine-centric approach may be more appropriate.

TRANSPARENCY & DISCLOSURE INFORMING THE AUDIENCE

AI art is a form of creative expression that uses artificial intelligence (AI) to generate, enhance, or manipulate images, sounds, texts, or other media. AI art can be fascinating, inspiring, and challenging, but it also raises some ethical questions. One of the most important ones is: how should AI artists inform their audience about the role of AI in their work?

Use clear and accurate labels. When presenting or publishing your AI art, make sure to indicate that it is created or influenced by AI. Avoid misleading or ambiguous terms that might confuse or mislead the audience. For example, do not call your work "photography" if it is generated by an AI algorithm, or "poetry" if it is composed by a text generator. Instead, use terms like "AI-generated", "AI-enhanced", or "AI-inspired".

Provide details about the AI process. When possible, explain how you used AI to create or modify your work. What kind of AI algorithm did you use? What data did you feed it? How much human input or intervention did you have? How did you evaluate or edit the output? These details can help the audience understand your creative process and appreciate your work better.

Acknowledge the sources and limitations of your work. When using AI to create art, you are often relying on existing data or models that are not your own. Therefore, you should give credit to the original sources and creators of the data or models that you used. You should also acknowledge the limitations and biases of your work, such as the quality, accuracy, diversity, or representativeness of the data or models that you used.

Educate the audience about the implications of your work. As an AI artist, you have an opportunity to raise awareness and spark discussion about the social, cultural, ethical, and legal implications of AI art. You can do this by providing context and background information about your work, such as its purpose, motivation, inspiration, or message. You can also invite feedback and criticism from your audience and engage them in dialogue about the issues that your work raises.

CULTURAL SENSITIVITY AND BIASES

Cultural sensitivity is the awareness and respect for the values, beliefs, practices, and customs of different cultures. Biases are the tendencies to favour or reject certain groups, ideas, or outcomes based on preconceived notions or stereotypes. Both cultural sensitivity and biases can affect how AI art is created, interpreted, and evaluated.

Be aware of your own cultural background and assumptions. Recognize that your own culture is not the only or the best one, and that it may influence how you perceive and create AI art. Be open to learning from other cultures and perspectives, and avoid imposing your own values or judgments on them.

Be respectful of the cultural context and origin of the data and media you use for AI art. Acknowledge the sources and creators of the data and media, and give them proper credit and recognition. Do not use data or media that are sacred, sensitive, or offensive to certain cultures without their consent or understanding. Do not appropriate or misrepresent the cultural meanings or symbols of the data or media.

Be mindful of the potential biases and harms of the AI algorithms and models you use for AI art. Understand how the algorithms and models work, what data they are trained on, and what outcomes they produce. Be aware of the limitations, uncertainties, and errors of the algorithms and models, and communicate them clearly to the audience. Do not use algorithms or models that discriminate, exclude, or harm certain groups or individuals based on their culture, identity, or characteristics.

Be inclusive and diverse in your AI art practice and community. Seek feedback and collaboration from people with different backgrounds, experiences, and viewpoints. Encourage diversity and representation in the data, media, algorithms, models, and platforms you use for AI art. Support and promote AI artists from marginalized or underrepresented groups, and amplify their voices and stories.

Be responsible and accountable for your AI art outcomes and impacts. Consider the ethical implications and consequences of your AI art for yourself, your audience, and society at large. Respect the rights and interests of the people involved or affected by your AI art, such as privacy, consent, ownership, and access. Be transparent about your methods, choices, and intentions behind your AI art. Be ready to explain, justify, or correct your AI art if needed.

ADAPTING LEGAL FRAMEWORKS TO AI ART

THE NEED FOR LEGAL ADAPTATION

AI art poses new challenges for the existing legal frameworks that regulate intellectual property rights, contracts, and liability. For example:

Who owns the copyright of an AI-generated artwork? Is it the human artist who provided the input or guidance, the AI system that produced the output, or a combination of both?

Who is the author of an AI-enhanced artwork? Is it the human artist who modified or edited the AI output, the AI system that suggested or generated the modifications, or a collaboration of both?

Who is responsible for an AI-modified artwork? Is it the human artist who consented to or requested the modifications, the AI system that performed or proposed the modifications, or a joint responsibility of both?

These questions are non-trivial, as they involve complex and novel issues that may not fit well with the existing legal categories and principles. Therefore, there is a need for legal adaptation to address these issues and provide clarity and certainty for the AI art community.

PRINCIPLES FOR LEGAL ADAPTATION

Legal adaptation does not mean creating entirely new laws or abandoning the existing ones. Rather, it means finding ways to apply, interpret, or modify the existing laws to accommodate the specificities and complexities of AI art. Here are some possible principles for legal adaptation:

Recognize the diversity and hybridity of AI art. AI art is not a monolithic or homogeneous phenomenon. It encompasses different forms, methods, and degrees of human-AI interaction and collaboration. Legal frameworks should acknowledge this diversity and hybridity and avoid one-size-fits-all solutions.

Balance the interests and rights of different stakeholders. AI art involves multiple stakeholders, such as human artists, AI systems, users, consumers, and society at large. Legal frameworks should balance their interests and rights and avoid favouring one over another.

Promote innovation and creativity. AI art is a dynamic and evolving field that offers new possibilities and challenges for artistic expression and exploration. Legal frameworks should promote innovation and creativity and avoid stifling or hindering them.

Ensure ethical and responsible use of AI. AI art is not exempt from the ethical and social implications of AI in general. Legal frameworks should ensure that AI art is used in an ethical and responsible manner and avoid causing harm or injustice to individuals or groups.

AI art is an exciting and emerging field that challenges and enriches our understanding and appreciation of art. It also challenges our existing legal frameworks that regulate artistic creation and consumption. Legal adaptation is necessary to address these challenges and provide a conducive and fair environment for AI art.

CHAPTER 4 WORKSHOP:
DIGITAL ETHICS & RESPONSIBLE AI

The field of IT Governance, Policy, Ethics and Law, has experienced the rapid development and adoption of artificial intelligence (AI) in various domains and sectors.

AI has the potential to bring many benefits to society, such as improving health care, education, transportation, security, and entertainment. However, the ethical risks of AI are real and must be negotiated. Matters such as algorithmic bias, privacy invasion, human dignity violation, social disruption, and accountability gap. AI must be developed and used in an ethical manner, respecting human values and rights.

In this workshop exercise, you will explore some of the key concepts and issues related to digital ethics and responsible AI. You will also engage in a group discussion and a case study analysis to apply your ethical reasoning skills and knowledge to real-world scenarios. The exercise will cover the following topics:

- **Digital Ethics and Responsible AI**. What are the main principles and frameworks for ensuring ethical and responsible AI? How can we balance the benefits and risks of AI? What are the roles and responsibilities of different stakeholders in the AI ecosystem?
- **Ethical AI and Algorithmic Bias**. What are the sources and types of bias in AI systems? How can bias affect the outcomes and impacts of AI applications? How can we detect, measure, prevent, and mitigate bias in AI systems?
- **Emerging Technologies and Ethical Regulation**. What are some of the emerging technologies that are enabled or enhanced by AI, such as facial recognition, biometrics, social media, autonomous vehicles, etc.? What are the ethical implications and challenges of these technologies? How can we regulate them in a way that promotes innovation while protecting human rights?
- **Whistleblower Protection and Digital Ethics**. What are the ethical dilemmas and risks faced by whistleblowers who expose unethical or illegal practices related to AI? How can we protect whistleblowers from retaliation and harassment? What are the legal and institutional mechanisms for supporting whistleblowers?

- **Ethical Considerations in AI Art**. What are the ethical issues and questions raised using AI in creating or enhancing art, such as music, painting, literature, etc.? How can we define and evaluate the originality, creativity, authenticity, and quality of AI art? How can we respect the intellectual property rights and moral rights of human artists and AI artists?

The workshop exercise will consist of three parts:

Part 1: Introduction (5 minutes). The facilitator will introduce the objectives, topics, and format of the workshop exercise.

Part 2: Group Discussion (10 minutes). The participants will be divided into small groups (3-5 people) and assigned one of the topics to discuss. Each group will have a set of questions to guide their discussion. The groups will share their main points and insights with the whole group at the end of this part.

Part 3: Case Study Analysis (5 minutes). The facilitator will present a case study related to one of the topics. The case study will describe a realistic situation involving an ethical dilemma or challenge related to AI. The participants will be asked to analyse the case study using their ethical reasoning skills and knowledge. The facilitator will lead a plenary discussion on the case study.

The workshop exercise aims to enhance your understanding of digital ethics and responsible AI, as well as to develop your critical thinking and ethical decision-making skills. I hope you enjoy this exercise and find it useful for your professional development.

CHAPTER 5:
INTELLECTUAL PROPERTY & COPYRIGHT

CHAPTER SUMMARY

Intellectual property and copyright are legal concepts that protect the rights of creators and owners of original works, such as books, music, software, and inventions. They grant them exclusive control over how their works are used, distributed, and modified by others.

Digital rights management (DRM) is a technology that restricts the access and use of digital content, such as e-books, movies, and games. DRM aims to prevent unauthorized copying, sharing, or modifying of protected content. However, DRM also raises ethical and technical issues, such as limiting the fair use rights of consumers, interfering with the interoperability of devices and platforms, and creating security vulnerabilities.

Open-source software licensing is a type of software licensing that allows anyone to access, use, modify, and distribute the source code of a software program. Open-source software is often developed collaboratively by a community of developers who share a common vision and values. Open-source software licensing promotes innovation, transparency, and freedom of choice for users and developers.

5.1. INTELLECTUAL PROPERTY & COPYRIGHT

WHAT IS INTELLECTUAL PROPERTY?

Intellectual property (IP) is any creation of the mind that has commercial value. It includes inventions, designs, artistic works, symbols, names and images. IP can be protected by law through patents, trademarks, copyrights and trade secrets.

WHY IS IP IMPORTANT FOR CYBERSECURITY?

IP is one of the most valuable assets of any business. It gives a competitive edge, attracts customers and investors, and generates revenue. However, IP is also vulnerable to cyberattacks, theft, misuse, and infringement. Cybersecurity is the process of protecting IP from unauthorized access, use, disclosure, modification, or destruction.

HOW TO PROTECT IP FROM CYBER THREATS?

Here are some tips to keep IP safe from cyber threats:

- Identify your IP assets and their value. Conduct an IP audit to find out what IP you have, who owns it, where it is stored and how it is used.
- Implement appropriate security measures for your IP assets. Use encryption, authentication, access control, backup and recovery systems to safeguard your IP data.
- Educate your employees and partners about IP protection. Provide training and awareness programs on IP policies, procedures and best practices. Monitor and enforce compliance with IP rules and agreements.
- Register your IP rights where possible. Apply for patents, trademarks or copyrights to secure legal protection for your IP assets. Use notices and labels to indicate your ownership and rights.
- Monitor your IP environment and respond to incidents. Use tools and services to detect and prevent IP breaches, such as firewalls, antivirus software, intrusion detection systems and threat intelligence. Report and resolve any IP issues as soon as possible.

THE ESSENCE OF INTELLECTUAL PROPERTY & COPYRIGHT

IP is the intangible creation of the human mind, such as inventions, artistic works, designs, symbols, names and images. IP is protected by laws that grant exclusive rights to the creators or owners of IP, such as patents, trademarks, designs and copyright.

WHY IP MATTERS IN CYBERSPACE

Cyberspace is the virtual environment where people communicate and interact through computer networks. Cyberspace is becoming a hub for IP infringement, as it is easy to copy, distribute and modify digital content without the owner's consent. IP infringement can harm the owner's reputation, revenue, and competitive advantage. It can also expose the infringer to legal risks and liabilities.

Some common examples of IP infringement in cyberspace are:

- Using another person's logo, brand name or domain name without permission

- Copying or downloading another person's software, music, video, e-book or game without a licence
- Making a profit by using another person's creation without paying royalties or fees
- Modifying or adapting another person's work without authorisation
- Selling counterfeit or pirated goods online

HOW TO PROTECT YOUR IP IN CYBERSPACE

Take the following steps to protect your IP in cyberspace:

- **Identify and audit your IP assets**. Know what IP you have, who owns it, how it is used and how it is protected.
- **Register your IP rights**. Apply for patents, trade marks and designs to secure your exclusive rights in Australia and overseas
- **Monitor your IP online**. Use tools and services to detect and prevent unauthorised use of your IP on the internet.
- **Enforce your IP rights**. Act against infringers by sending cease and desist letters, filing complaints or initiating legal proceedings.
- **Commercialise your IP**. Negotiate and draft licensing, technology transfer, distribution and content agreements to generate income from your IP

WHERE TO FIND MORE INFORMATION

Visit the following websites:

- [Intellectual Property Lawyers | Gilbert + Tobin](https://www.gtlaw.com.au/expertise/intellectual-property): A leading Australian law firm that provides advice on all aspects of IP law
- [Intellectual Property, Technology & Cyber Security | HopgoodGanim] (https://www.hopgoodganim.com.au/page/expertise/services/intellectual-property-technology-cybersecurity): A market-leading team of lawyers with scientific or technical qualifications in IP, technology and cyber security
- [Intellectual Property in Cyberspace | GeeksforGeeks] (https://www.geeksforgeeks.org/intellectual-property-in-cyberspace/): A website that explains the basics of IP in cyberspace with examples

- [Intellectual Property Crime | Australian Federal Police]
  (https://www.afp.gov.au/what-we-do/crime-
  types/intellectual-property-crime): A website that provides
  information on how to report IP crime and what actions the
  AFP can take

THE DIGITAL TRANSFORMATION & COPYRIGHT

Digital transformation is the process of using new technologies to
improve the efficiency, performance and value of an organization. It can
involve updating legacy systems, moving to the cloud, adopting artificial
intelligence and machine learning, and creating new products and
services. However, digital transformation also comes with significant
risks, especially in terms of cybersecurity and privacy.

CYBERSECURITY RISKS

One of the main challenges of digital transformation is ensuring the
security of your data and software systems. Data breaches are
becoming more frequent and costly, exposing sensitive information,
damaging reputations and causing legal liabilities. According to a report
by Norton Rose Fulbright, there were 4,100 publicly disclosed data
breaches in 2022 alone, comprising some 22 billion records that were
exposed. Moreover, software systems are becoming more complex and
vulnerable, especially with the rise of artificial intelligence and
generative AI, which can create realistic but fake content that can
deceive or manipulate users. Therefore, you need to adopt a proactive
and comprehensive approach to cybersecurity, that includes:

- Developing a framework that aligns your technology strategy
  with your business goals and risk appetite.
- Implementing zero trust architectures that assume all
  systems can or will be compromised and require continuous
  verification of users, devices and data.
- Applying encryption, authentication and access control
  measures to protect your data at rest and in transit.
- Monitoring and auditing your systems for any anomalies or
  suspicious activities.
- Updating and patching your software regularly to fix any
  vulnerabilities or bugs.
- Educating and training your employees and customers on
  cybersecurity best practices and awareness

PRIVACY RISKS

Another challenge of digital transformation is respecting the privacy rights of your customers, employees and partners. Privacy laws are becoming more stringent and diverse across jurisdictions, requiring you to comply with various rules and regulations on how you collect, use, store and share personal information. For example, the General Data Protection Regulation (GDPR) in the European Union imposes strict obligations on data controllers and processors, such as obtaining consent, providing transparency, ensuring data minimization and enabling data portability. Failing to comply with privacy laws can result in hefty fines, lawsuits and reputational damage. Therefore, you need to adopt a privacy-by-design approach that incorporates privacy principles into every stage of your digital transformation process, such as:

- Conducting privacy impact assessments to identify and mitigate any potential privacy risks or harms.
- Implementing privacy-enhancing technologies that anonymize, pseudonymize or encrypt personal data.
- Establishing privacy policies and notices that inform your data subjects about their rights and choices.
- Obtaining valid and informed consent from your data subjects before processing their personal data
- Responding to data subject requests to access, correct or delete their personal data.
- Reporting any data breaches or incidents to the relevant authorities and data subjects within the prescribed time frames.

INTELLECTUAL PROPERTY RIGHTS

Finally, one of the most important aspects of digital transformation is protecting your intellectual property rights. Intellectual property rights are the legal rights that grant you exclusive ownership and control over your creations, such as inventions, designs, trademarks, logos, slogans, software code, content etc. Intellectual property rights are essential for fostering innovation, competitiveness, and differentiation in the digital economy. However, digital transformation also poses new threats to your intellectual property rights, such as:

- Copying or stealing your software code or content by hackers or competitors.
- Infringing or violating your patents, trademarks or copyrights by using them without authorization or paying royalties.

- Diluting or tarnishing your brand image or reputation by creating confusingly similar or disparaging products or services.
- Challenging or invalidating your intellectual property rights by claiming prior art or public domain status.

Therefore, you need to adopt a strategic and proactive approach to intellectual property protection that includes:

- Registering your intellectual property rights with the relevant authorities and agencies.
- Enforcing your intellectual property rights against any infringers or violators through legal action or alternative dispute resolution.
- Licensing your intellectual property rights to others for mutual benefit or collaboration.
- Monitoring the market for any potential infringements or violations of your intellectual property rights.
- Updating your intellectual property portfolio to reflect any changes or improvements in your products or services.

Digital transformation comes with significant risks that can jeopardize your cybersecurity, privacy and intellectual property rights.

NAVIGATING THE AUSTRALIAN COPYRIGHT ACT

WHAT IS COPYRIGHT?

Copyright is a legal right that gives the creator of an original work the exclusive right to control how it is used, reproduced, communicated, or performed. It covers a wide range of works, such as books, music, films, software, databases, artworks, photographs and more. It also covers some types of online content, such as websites, blogs, podcasts, and social media posts.

WHY IS IT IMPORTANT?

Protecting your intellectual property is important for many reasons. It can help you:

- Reward your creativity and innovation.
- Prevent others from copying or exploiting your work without your permission.
- Generate income from licensing or selling your work.

- Enhance your reputation and brand recognition.
- Contribute to the cultural and economic development of society.

HOW DOES IT WORK IN AUSTRALIA?

Australia has a complex and evolving legal framework for copyright protection. Some of the key features are:

- You do not need to register or apply for copyright protection. It is automatic once you create an original work in a material form.
- You do not need to use the © symbol or any other notice to indicate your ownership. However, it may be helpful to do so as a reminder to others.
- You have the right to take legal action against anyone who infringes your copyright, such as by copying, distributing, displaying, or modifying your work without your consent.
- You may also have some moral rights, such as the right to be attributed as the author and the right to object to any derogatory treatment of your work.
- You may grant or transfer some or all your rights to others through a licence or an assignment agreement. You should always read and understand the terms and conditions before signing any contract.
- You may also allow others to use your work for free under certain circumstances, such as for fair dealing purposes (e.g. research, study, criticism, review, parody or satire) or under a Creative Commons licence.
- You must respect the rights of other creators when you use their works. You should always seek permission or rely on a valid exception before using any copyrighted material.
- You must comply with any applicable laws and regulations that affect your online activities, such as the Online Safety Act 2021 (Cth), the Surveillance Legislation Amendment (Identify and Disrupt) Act 2021 (Cth) and the Security Legislation Amendment (Critical Infrastructure) Bill 2021 (Cth). These laws aim to enhance the security and safety of online platforms and services and may impose new obligations and responsibilities on you as a user or provider.

DIGITAL RIGHTS MANAGEMENT (DRM) BALANCING RIGHTS & ACCESS

Digital Rights Management (DRM) is a set of technologies and protocols that protect digital content from unauthorized access, reproduction, and distribution. It is used to enforce copyright protection, licensing agreements, and access control for various forms of digital media, such as music, videos, eBooks, software, and more.

BENEFITS OF DRM

DRM provides a crucial layer of protection for content creators and owners. It helps them safeguard their intellectual property rights and prevent piracy or data breaches. By using DRM, content creators can:

- Control how their content is used, shared, or modified by authorized users.
- Generate revenue from their content by charging fees or subscriptions.
- Monitor the usage and performance of their content.
- Enhance the user experience by providing high-quality and secure content.

DRM also benefits content consumers by ensuring that they receive legitimate and quality content. It also helps them respect the rights and wishes of the content creators.

CHALLENGES OF DRM

DRM is not without its limitations. Some of the common issues that DRM faces are:

- Compatibility. Different platforms and devices may use different DRM systems, which can cause problems for users who want to access the same content across multiple devices
- Usability. DRM may impose restrictions or requirements that can affect the user experience, such as requiring internet connection, limiting the number of devices or downloads, or preventing offline access
- Privacy. DRM may collect personal or behavioural data from users, which can raise concerns about data protection and consent
- Fair use. DRM may interfere with the rights of users to use the content for legitimate purposes, such as education, research, criticism, or parody.

BEST PRACTICES FOR DRM

To balance the rights and access of both content creators and consumers, it is important to follow some best practices when implementing or using DRM solutions. Some of these are:

- Choose a suitable DRM system that meets your needs and goals. There are different types of DRM systems available, such as encryption-based, watermark-based, or fingerprint-based. You should consider factors such as cost, complexity, security level, compatibility, and scalability when selecting a DRM system.

- Use a multi-DRM strategy to protect your streams on all platforms with strict licensing rules. A good DRM vendor will allow you to do all the following to protect your streams:

- Prevent screen capture.

- Prevent downloading of the streams by using the strictest variants of the DRM available.

- Ensure a strict expiration date in the license beyond which the stream will be inaccessible.

- Provide the option to rotate the DRM keys during the live streams to frustrate hackers.

- Communicate clearly with your users about the terms and conditions of your DRM policy. You should inform them about what they can and cannot do with your content, how long they can access it, what data you collect from them, and how you protect their privacy.

- Respect the fair use rights of your users and allow them some flexibility in using your content for legitimate purposes. You should also provide them with options to contact you or request permission if they have any questions or issues with your DRM policy.

- Keep up to date with the latest developments and trends in DRM technology and legislation. You should monitor the changes in the market and the legal environment and adjust your DRM strategy accordingly.

OPEN SOURCE & LICENSING CONSIDERATIONS

OSS is software that uses publicly available source code that anyone can see, modify, and distribute. OSS can offer many benefits, such as affordability, flexibility, and quality, but it also comes with some risks and challenges that you need to be aware of.

TYPES OF OPEN-SOURCE LICENSES

One of the main challenges of using OSS is complying with the terms and conditions of the open-source licenses. These are legal agreements that specify what you can and cannot do with the OSS and its derivatives. There are two main types of open-source licenses: permissive and copyleft.

Permissive licenses are the more business-friendly ones, as they allow you to use, modify, and distribute the OSS for any purpose, as long as you give proper attribution to the original authors. Some examples of permissive licenses are the MIT license, the Apache license, and the BSD license.

Copyleft licenses are the more restrictive ones, as they require you to share your modifications and derivatives under the same or compatible license as the original OSS. This means that if you use copyleft OSS in your proprietary software, you might have to disclose your source code and allow others to use it for free. Some examples of copyleft licenses are the GNU General Public License (GPL), the GNU Lesser General Public License (LGPL), and the Mozilla Public License (MPL).

RISKS AND BEST PRACTICES

Using OSS can introduce some risks to your cybersecurity projects, such as:

- **Excessive access**. Open access means that anyone can see and manipulate the source code, which creates opportunities for malicious actors to introduce vulnerabilities or backdoors.
- **Lack of verification**. There are no guarantees that the OSS is tested and reviewed by qualified experts, which can make it prone to errors and security flaws.
- **Lack of support**. Most OSS does not have dedicated support teams, which means that updates and patches may not be available or timely. This can leave your software exposed to known or unknown vulnerabilities.

To mitigate these risks, you should follow some best practices when using OSS, such as:

- **Conduct a thorough due diligence.** Before using any OSS, you should check its license type, terms, and conditions, and make sure they are compatible with your intended use and distribution. You should also check its reputation, quality, security, and maintenance status.

- **Use a software composition analysis tool**. This is a tool that can help you identify and manage the OSS components in your software. It can help you track their licenses, versions, dependencies, vulnerabilities, and compliance status.
- **Implement a security policy**. You should have a clear and consistent policy for using OSS in your projects. This policy should define the roles and responsibilities of your team members, the criteria for selecting OSS components, the processes for reviewing and updating them, and the procedures for reporting and resolving any issues.

Using OSS can be a great way to enhance your cybersecurity projects with high-quality software components. However, you need to be careful about the legal and security implications of using OSS. By following the types of open-source licenses, understanding their risks, and applying best practices, you can use OSS safely and effectively.

FAIR USE & FLEXIBILITY

WHAT IS FAIR USE AND FLEXIBILITY?

Fair use and flexibility are legal doctrines that allow the use of copyrighted material without permission or payment under certain circumstances. They are essential for promoting creativity, innovation, education, research, and public interest.

In the context of cybersecurity, fair use and flexibility can enable security professionals to access, analyse, test, and improve the security of digital systems and data. For example, fair use and flexibility can allow security researchers to reverse engineer software, conduct vulnerability assessments, disclose security flaws, and develop patches or workarounds.

WHY IS FAIR USE AND FLEXIBILITY IMPORTANT FOR CYBERSECURITY?

Fair use and flexibility are important for cybersecurity because they can help:

- Enhance the security posture of organizations and individuals by allowing them to identify and mitigate risks, protect their assets, and respond to incidents.

- Foster a culture of security awareness and collaboration by allowing security professionals to share their findings, insights, and best practices with others.
- Support the development of new security technologies and solutions by allowing security professionals to experiment with different methods, tools, and techniques.
- Advance the state of the art in cybersecurity by allowing security professionals to contribute to the scientific knowledge and innovation in the field.

WHAT ARE THE CHALLENGES AND RISKS OF FAIR USE AND FLEXIBILITY IN CYBERSECURITY?

Fair use and flexibility are not absolute rights. They are subject to limitations and exceptions depending on the jurisdiction, context, purpose, nature, amount, and effect of the use. They are also balanced against the rights and interests of the copyright holders.

Therefore, fair use and flexibility in cybersecurity can pose some challenges and risks, such as:

- **Legal uncertainty and liability**. Security professionals may face legal challenges or lawsuits from copyright holders who claim that their use of the material was unauthorized or infringing. Security professionals may also face criminal charges or penalties if their use of the material violates other laws or regulations.
- **Ethical dilemmas and conflicts**. Security professionals may encounter ethical dilemmas or conflicts when deciding whether, how, when, and with whom to use or share the material. Security professionals may also face criticism or backlash from their peers, employers, clients, or the public for their use or disclosure of the material.
- **Operational difficulties and costs**. Security professionals may face operational difficulties or costs when obtaining, storing, processing, or transmitting the material. Security professionals may also face technical challenges or limitations when using or modifying the material.

DIGITAL COMMONS & COLLABORATIVE CREATION

WHAT ARE DIGITAL COMMONS AND COLLABORATIVE CREATION?

Digital commons are resources that are shared by a community of users online, such as open-source software, open data, open educational resources, and creative commons licenses. Collaborative creation is the process of producing digital content or knowledge by working together with others, such as through wikis, blogs, podcasts, or social media platforms.

WHY ARE THEY IMPORTANT?

Digital commons and collaborative creation can foster innovation, creativity, education, and social inclusion. They can also reduce costs, increase efficiency, and improve quality of digital products and services. For example, Wikipedia is a collaborative encyclopedia that anyone can edit, which provides free and reliable information to millions of users around the world. Linux is an open-source operating system that powers many servers, devices, and applications, which benefits from the contributions of thousands of developers and users.

WHAT ARE THE CYBERSECURITY RISKS?

However, digital commons and collaborative creation also pose cybersecurity risks that need to be addressed. These risks include:

- Unauthorized access or modification of digital resources by hackers, competitors, or malicious insiders
- Theft or leakage of sensitive or personal data by cybercriminals, spies, or whistleblowers
- Infringement or violation of intellectual property rights by copycats, pirates, or trolls
- Disruption or sabotage of digital services or infrastructure by activists, terrorists, or state actors
- Misinformation or manipulation of digital content or users by propagandists, fraudsters, or bots

HOW TO PROTECT THEM?

These include:

- Implementing strong authentication and authorization mechanisms to verify the identity and access rights of users and contributors.

- Encrypting data in transit and at rest to prevent unauthorized interception or extraction.
- Applying digital signatures or watermarks to prove the origin and integrity of digital resources.
- Monitoring and auditing the activity and performance of digital systems and networks to detect and respond to anomalies or incidents.
- Educating and engaging the community of users and contributors to raise awareness and foster trust and cooperation.

WHERE TO LEARN MORE?

If you want to learn more about digital commons and collaborative creation, you can visit the following websites:

[Rebuilding digital trust for a cyber-inclusive future | World Economic Forum] (https://www.weforum.org/agenda/2021/11/rebuilding-digital-trust-for-a-cyber-inclusive-future/)

[Cybersecurity, cybercrime and cybersafety: a quick guide to key internet links – Parliament of Australia] (https://www.aph.gov.au/About_Parliament/Parliamentary_Departments/Parliamentary_Library/pubs/rp/rp1819/Quick_Guides/Cybersecurity CybercrimeCybersafety)

[The Digital World Is Changing Rapidly. Your Cybersecurity Needs to Keep Up.] (https://hbr.org/2023/05/the-digital-world-is-changing-rapidly-your-cybersecurity-needs-to-keep-up)

5.2. DIGITAL RIGHTS MANAGEMENT

Digital rights management (DRM) is a term that encompasses the methods and technologies used to protect and control the access and use of digital content, such as books, music, videos, software, and data. DRM aims to prevent unauthorized copying, sharing, modification, or distribution of digital content by applying various restrictions and encryption techniques to the content or the devices that can access it.

WHY IS DRM IMPORTANT?

DRM is important for several reasons. First, it helps content creators and owners to safeguard their intellectual property rights and their financial and creative investments in their work. By limiting what users can do with their content, DRM ensures that content creators and owners can benefit from their work and prevent others from exploiting it without permission or compensation.

Second, DRM helps users to respect the legal and ethical boundaries of using digital content. By complying with the terms and conditions of DRM, users can avoid infringing on the rights of content creators and owners and avoid potential legal consequences or penalties.

Third, DRM helps to maintain the quality and integrity of digital content. By preventing unauthorized modification or alteration of digital content, DRM ensures that users can access and enjoy the original and authentic version of the content as intended by the content creators and owners.

HOW DOES DRM WORK?

DRM works by using various technologies and tools to implement different types of restrictions and encryption on digital content. Some of the common DRM methods are:

Copy protection. This method prevents or limits users from making copies of digital content or transferring it to other devices or platforms.

Access control. This method requires users to have a valid license, password, or authentication to access digital content or certain features or functions of it.

Expiration. This method sets a time limit or a number of uses for accessing digital content, after which the content becomes inaccessible or unusable.

Geolocation. This method restricts access to digital content based on the user's location or IP address.

Watermarking. This method embeds a visible or invisible mark on digital content that identifies the source or owner of the content.

Encryption. This method scrambles the data of digital content using a secret key that only authorized users can decrypt.

WHAT ARE SOME EXAMPLES OF DRM?

DRM is widely used across various types of digital content and industries. Some examples are:

E-books. Many e-books use DRM to prevent users from copying, printing, sharing, or modifying them. Some e-books also use DRM to limit the number of devices or platforms that users can read them on.

Music. Many music files use DRM to prevent users from copying, sharing, or converting them to other formats. Some music files also use DRM to limit the number of devices or platforms that users can play them on.

Videos. Many videos use DRM to prevent users from copying, sharing, or editing them. Some videos also use DRM to limit the resolution, quality, or playback speed of them.

Software. Many software programs use DRM to prevent users from installing, copying, sharing, or modifying them. Some software programs also use DRM to require online activation, registration, or subscription to use them.

Data. Many data sets use DRM to prevent users from accessing, copying, sharing, or analysing them. Some data sets also use DRM to require payment, permission, or attribution to use them.

CHALLENGES & CONTROVERSIES OF DRM

DRM is not without its challenges and controversies. Some of the common issues are:

User rights. Some users argue that DRM violates their fair use rights or their right to own and control their purchased digital content. They claim that DRM restricts their ability to make personal copies, backups, modifications, or adaptations of digital content for their own purposes.

User experience. Some users complain that DRM negatively affects their user experience by making digital content less accessible, convenient, compatible, or functional. They claim that DRM causes technical problems, errors, glitches, or incompatibilities with their devices or platforms.

User privacy. Some users worry that DRM invades their privacy by collecting their personal information, tracking their online activities, or exposing them to security risks. They claim that DRM requires them to share their personal data with third parties, such as content providers, service providers, or advertisers.

User activism. Some users resist or challenge DRM by circumventing it using various tools or techniques, such as cracking codes, hacking systems, or creating alternative platforms. They claim that they are exercising their civil disobedience rights or their freedom of expression rights.

Digital rights management has both benefits and drawbacks for both content creators and owners and users. It is important for both parties to understand what DRM is, how it works, why it is important, and what are the challenges and controversies of it. By doing so, they can make informed and responsible decisions about using and sharing digital content in the digital age.

INTELLECTUAL PROPERTY VS. USERS' RIGHTS

Digital rights management (DRM) is a term that refers to the methods and technologies used to control the access, use and distribution of digital content, such as software, music, movies, books and games. DRM aims to protect the intellectual property rights of the creators and owners of the content, and to prevent piracy and unauthorized copying. However, DRM also raises ethical and legal issues regarding the rights and freedoms of the users and consumers of the content. How can we balance these conflicting interests and ensure that both parties are treated fairly and respectfully?

- The benefits and drawbacks of DRM for both content providers and users
- The principles and guidelines for designing and implementing DRM systems that respect users' rights.
- The challenges and opportunities for DRM in the future

BENEFITS AND DRAWBACKS OF DRM

DRM can have positive effects for both content providers and users. For content providers, DRM can help them:

- Protect their intellectual property rights and prevent revenue loss from piracy and unauthorized copying.
- Enhance their reputation and brand image by ensuring the quality and authenticity of their content.
- Increase their market share and customer loyalty by offering different options and incentives for accessing their content.
- Innovate and create new business models and revenue streams by leveraging the potential of digital technologies.

For users, DRM can help them:

- Access a wide range of digital content at affordable prices and convenient formats.
- Enjoy a better user experience and quality of service by avoiding malware, viruses, glitches and errors.
- Support their favorite content creators and contribute to the development of the digital economy.
- Exercise their rights to privacy, security, anonymity and fair use by choosing the content providers and platforms that respect these rights.

However, DRM can also have negative effects for both parties. For content providers, DRM can:

- Increase their costs and complexity of developing, maintaining and updating their DRM systems.
- Reduce their flexibility and adaptability to changing market conditions and customer preferences.
- Expose them to legal risks and liabilities if their DRM systems violate users' rights or infringe on other parties' intellectual property rights.
- Damage their reputation and customer satisfaction if their DRM systems are perceived as intrusive, restrictive or unfair.

For users, DRM can:

- Limit their access, use and enjoyment of digital content by imposing technical or contractual restrictions.

- Interfere with their legitimate activities and expectations, such as sharing, lending, reselling or modifying the content.
- Violate their rights to privacy, security, anonymity and fair use by collecting, storing or disclosing their personal data or monitoring their online behaviour.
- Harm their devices or data by introducing malware, viruses, glitches or errors.

DESIGN PRINCIPLES FOR DRM SYSTEMS

Given these benefits and drawbacks, how can we design and implement DRM systems that balance the interests of both content providers and users? Here are some principles and guidelines that I suggest:

Respect the law. DRM systems should comply with the relevant laws and regulations in the jurisdictions where they operate. They should not infringe on other parties' intellectual property rights or violate users' rights to privacy, security, anonymity or fair use.

Respect the ethics. DRM systems should follow the ethical standards and values of the society where they operate. They should not harm or exploit users or other stakeholders. They should promote social justice, human dignity and public interest.

Respect the users. DRM systems should consider the needs, preferences and expectations of the users. They should provide clear information about the terms and conditions of accessing the content. They should offer choices and options for different user groups. They should ensure a high quality of service and user experience.

Respect the content. DRM systems should protect the integrity and authenticity of the content. They should not degrade or distort the content. They should not interfere with the artistic or creative expression of the content creators.

Respect the innovation. DRM systems should foster innovation and creativity in the digital economy. They should not stifle or hinder the development of new technologies, products or services. They should not create artificial barriers or monopolies in the market.

FUTURE OPPORTUNITIES FOR DRM

DRM is a dynamic and evolving field that faces many challenges and opportunities in the future. Some of these are:

The emergence of new technologies, such as artificial intelligence, blockchain, cloud computing, biometrics, quantum computing, etc., that can enhance or disrupt DRM systems.

The growth of new platforms, such as streaming services, social media networks, peer-to-peer networks, etc., that can offer new ways of accessing or distributing digital content.

The diversity of new user groups, such as millennials, gen Zs, digital natives, etc., that can have different attitudes and behaviours towards digital content and DRM systems.

The complexity of new legal and ethical issues, such as data protection, digital citizenship, digital sovereignty, etc., that can affect the rights and responsibilities of content providers and users.

We need to adopt a holistic and collaborative approach that involves all the stakeholders in the DRM ecosystem, such as content creators, owners, providers, distributors, platforms, users, regulators, policymakers, researchers, educators, etc. We need to engage in dialogue and debate, share knowledge and best practices, develop standards and guidelines, and create solutions and strategies that can benefit everyone.

DRM is not a zero-sum game where one party wins and the other loses. It is a win-win situation where both parties can gain from the protection and promotion of intellectual property and digital rights. By following the principles and guidelines that I have suggested, we can design and implement DRM systems that are fair, respectful, ethical and innovative.

ETHICAL IMPLICATIONS OF DRM

Digital rights management (DRM) applies to the copying, sharing, or modifying of digital content such as music, movies, software, or e-books. DRM can be seen to protect the rights and revenues of the creators and distributors of digital content, but it can also raise ethical issues for the users and consumers of such content.

WHAT IS RESTRICTIVE DRM?

Restrictive DRM is a type of DRM that imposes strict limitations on how users can access, use, or transfer digital content. For example, restrictive DRM may:

- Stop a cell phone from working with a different wireless provider.
- Make a DVD from a certain region unplayable in other regions of the world.
- Encrypt software to prevent copying or installing on multiple devices.
- Prevent children from accessing adult content.
- Require online verification or authentication to use certain products or services.

Restrictive DRM can be implemented through hardware, software, or legal means. Some examples of restrictive DRM technologies are:

- Region codes on DVDs or Blu-ray discs.
- Activation codes or serial numbers for software products.
- Digital locks or encryption keys on e-books or music files.
- Online platforms or services that require subscription or registration.

Restrictive DRM can also be enforced through legal measures such as the Digital Millennium Copyright Act (DMCA) in the United States, which prohibits the circumvention of DRM technologies or the distribution of tools or devices that can bypass them.

WHY IS RESTRICTIVE DRM ETHICAL?

Some of the arguments in favour of restrictive DRM are:

- It protects the intellectual property rights and interests of the creators and distributors of digital content, who invest time, money, and effort to produce and deliver quality products and services.
- It prevents piracy and illegal use of digital content, which can harm the revenues and reputation of the content industry and reduce the incentives for innovation and creativity.
- It enables new business models and revenue streams for the content industry, such as subscription-based services, pay-per-view models, or dynamic pricing strategies.
- It provides users with features and benefits that they want or need, such as parental controls, trial versions, or personalized recommendations.

Some of the sources that support restrictive DRM are:

- The Entertainment Software Association of Canada (ESAC), which represents the video game industry in Canada. ESAC argues that DRM is necessary to protect the investments and innovations of game developers and publishers, and to provide consumers with diverse and high-quality gaming experiences.
- The Alliance of Canadian Cinema, Television and Radio Artists (ACTRA), which represents performers in the audiovisual media sector in Canada. ACTRA advocates for DRM as a way to ensure fair compensation and recognition for artists whose works are distributed digitally.
- Microsoft Corporation, which is one of the leading developers and providers of software products and services in the world. Microsoft uses DRM technologies to secure its products and platforms, such as Windows operating system, Office suite, Xbox console, or Azure cloud service.

WHY IS RESTRICTIVE DRM UNETHICAL?

Some of the arguments against restrictive DRM are:

- It infringes on the rights and freedoms of users and consumers of digital content, who may face restrictions or barriers to access, use, or share content that they have legally acquired or paid for.
- It creates technical and legal challenges for users and consumers of digital content, who may encounter compatibility issues, performance problems, privacy risks, or legal liabilities when using or transferring content across different devices, platforms, or regions.
- It stifles innovation and competition in the content industry, as it creates entry barriers for new entrants or alternative providers who may offer better quality or lower prices for digital content.
- It reduces the social and cultural value of digital content, as it limits the possibilities for remixing, reusing, or transforming content into new forms of expression or knowledge.

Some of the sources that oppose restrictive DRM are:

- The Electronic Frontier Foundation (EFF), which is a non-profit organization that defends civil liberties in the digital world. EFF campaigns against DRM as a threat to user rights, fair use, privacy, security, accessibility, and innovation.

- The Canadian Library Association (CLA), which is a national association that represents libraries and librarians in Canada. CLA opposes DRM as an obstacle to access to information, education, culture, and democracy.
- The Free Software Foundation (FSF), which is a non-profit organization that promotes free software and free culture. FSF rejects DRM as a form of digital restriction management that violates user freedom and autonomy.

Restrictive DRM is a controversial topic that involves ethical dilemmas for both producers and consumers of digital content. On one hand, restrictive DRM can be seen as a legitimate and necessary way to protect the rights and interests of the content industry, and to provide users with features and benefits that they want or need.

On the other hand, restrictive DRM can be seen as an illegitimate and unnecessary way to infringe on the rights and freedoms of users and consumers, and to create technical and legal challenges, stifle innovation and competition, and reduce the social and cultural value of digital content. The ethical implications of restrictive DRM depend on the perspective, values, and interests of the stakeholders involved, as well as the context, purpose, and effects of the DRM technologies or measures used.

PRESERVING THE RIGHT TO FAIR USE

DRM can include encryption, authentication, watermarking, digital locks, and other methods that restrict or monitor how users can copy, share, modify, or distribute digital content.

While DRM may have some legitimate purposes, such as preventing piracy and protecting intellectual property rights, it can also pose a serious threat to the right of fair use.

Fair use is a legal doctrine that allows users to make limited and reasonable uses of copyrighted works for purposes such as criticism, comment, news reporting, teaching, scholarship, or research. Fair use is essential for promoting creativity, innovation, education, and public interest.

However, DRM can interfere with fair use by preventing users from accessing or using digital works in ways that the law would otherwise allow. For example, DRM can prevent users from making backup copies, format-shifting, excerpting, quoting, parodying, remixing, or analysing digital works. DRM can also prevent users from accessing public domain works or works that are licensed under open or flexible terms. Moreover, DRM can undermine the balance between the rights of copyright holders and the rights of users by giving the former absolute control over the latter.

Therefore, preserving the right to fair use in digital rights management is crucial for ensuring that users can enjoy the benefits of digital culture and technology without sacrificing their freedoms and interests. To achieve this goal, some possible strategies are:

Reforming the legal framework that protects DRM against circumvention. Currently, laws such as the Digital Millennium Copyright Act (DMCA) in the US and similar laws in other countries make it illegal for users to bypass or disable DRM mechanisms, even if they do so for fair use purposes. These laws should be amended or repealed to allow exceptions for fair use and other legitimate uses of digital works.

Developing and adopting alternative or complementary models of DRM that respect fair use. For example, some DRM systems may allow users to make fair uses of digital works by obtaining licenses or permissions from the copyright holders or by paying reasonable fees. Some DRM systems may also incorporate mechanisms that enable users to exercise their fair use rights without circumvention.

Educating and empowering users about their fair use rights and responsibilities. Users should be aware of the scope and limitations of fair use and how they can apply it to their own uses of digital works. Users should also be able to challenge or contest DRM practices that infringe on their fair use rights or that are abusive or unreasonable.

Advocating and campaigning for fair use in digital rights management. Users should join forces with other stakeholders, such as civil society organizations, academics, librarians, educators, journalists, artists, and activists, to raise awareness and influence policy on this issue. Users should also support initiatives that promote fair use in digital rights management, such as litigation, legislation, standardization, certification, or boycott.

By preserving the right to fair use in digital rights management, users can ensure that they can access and use digital works in ways that are lawful, beneficial, and respectful of both their own and others' rights.

THE GLOBAL DIMENSION INTERNATIONAL COPYRIGHT LAWS

DRM protects intellectual property according to relevant copyright laws to protect both content owners and corporations as they distribute and create content across the internet in various jurisdictions.

WHY IS DRM IMPORTANT FOR YOUR BUSINESS STRATEGY?

Organizations need to know if they currently have the rights to use an asset and understand how and where they are allowed to publish it. If you publish or use a digital asset without the correct digital asset management permissions in place, your organization could face lawsuits and potential legal penalties. Using assets incorrectly can damage your brand reputation and value.

Unfortunately, many brands wait until they are already in legal trouble to start thinking about how to incorporate DRM into their business strategy. Instead, make DRM a part of your processes and take advantage of DRM technologies as soon as you begin to work with digital content to protect your business and make workflows easier.

HOW TO IMPLEMENT DRM

There are numerous approaches to DRM and continual efforts to develop new methods. Many DRM tools operate through encryption, or computer code embedded in the digital content, to limit access or use. These tools can help you:

- Control the number of times, devices, people, or time periods that the content can be accessed or installed.
- Prevent software tampering or reverse engineering by unauthorized parties.
- Trace product image leaks or unauthorized distribution by embedding watermarks or fingerprints.
- Eliminate counterfeit web stores or fraudulent transactions by verifying the authenticity of the content or product.
- Produce content safely and securely by encrypting it during the production process.

Here are some best practices for implementing DRM in 2023:

- Choose a DRM solution that suits your specific needs and goals. There are different types of DRM solutions for different types of content, such as audio, video, images, software, documents, etc. You should also consider factors such as cost, scalability, compatibility, performance, user experience, etc.

- Define clear and consistent policies for your digital rights management. You should establish who owns the rights to your content, what are the terms and conditions of use, how long are the licenses valid, what are the consequences of violating the policies, etc. You should also communicate these policies clearly to your users and stakeholders.

- Monitor and measure the effectiveness of your DRM strategy. You should track metrics such as usage, revenue, compliance, feedback, etc. to evaluate how well your DRM solution is working for you. You should also update your strategy regularly based on changing market conditions, customer preferences, legal regulations, etc.

5.3. OPEN-SOURCE SOFTWARE LICENSING

THE ESSENCE OF OPEN-SOURCE

Open-source software is software that allows anyone to use, modify, and share its source code. The source code is the set of instructions that tells the computer what to do. By making the source code available, open-source software enables collaboration, innovation, and transparency.

WHY OPEN-SOURCE MATTERS

Open-source software has many benefits for users, developers, and society. Some of these benefits are:

Users can choose from a variety of software options that suit their needs and preferences. They can also inspect the source code to verify its quality, security, and functionality.

Developers can learn from other developers' work, improve existing software, or create new software based on existing code. They can also contribute to the development of software that they use or care about.

Society can benefit from the collective knowledge and creativity of the open-source community. Open-source software can also promote social good by addressing common problems or serving public interests.

HOW OPEN-SOURCE WORKS

Open-source software is governed by licenses that define the terms and conditions for its use, modification, and distribution. There are many different open-source licenses, but they generally fall into two categories: permissive and copyleft.

Permissive licenses allow users to do whatever they want with the software, provided they give credit to the original author. Examples of permissive licenses are the MIT License and the Apache License.

Copyleft licenses require users to share their modifications of the software under the same or compatible license as the original. This ensures that the software remains open-source and accessible to everyone. Examples of copyleft licenses are the GNU General Public License and the Mozilla Public License.

HOW TO CHOOSE AN OPEN-SOURCE LICENSE

Choosing an open-source license depends on your goals and preferences as a software developer. Some factors to consider are:

- How much control do you want to have over your software and its derivatives?
- How much credit do you want to receive for your work?
- How compatible do you want your license to be with other open-source licenses?
- How important is it for you to protect your software from potential legal risks?

Choose a License website to compare different open-source licenses and find one that matches your needs. You can also consult a lawyer or an expert in IT governance, policy, ethics, and law if you have specific questions or concerns.

By choosing an open-source license, you can define how others can use, modify, and distribute your software. You can also join a community of developers who collaborate on creating and improving open-source software.

THE ETHICS OF COLLABORATION & INNOVATION

OPEN-SOURCE SOFTWARE LICENSING

Open-source software (OSS) is software that is distributed with a license that allows anyone to use, study, change, or share its source code, without restrictions on how the software is used or by whom.

OSS has become ubiquitous across all areas of software development, as it enables developers to reuse existing code and create more functionality at greater speed. OSS also promotes the adoption of transparent standards and makes applications more interoperable.

However, OSS also raises some ethical questions about how the software is used and who benefits from it. Some developers do not want their work to be used for harm, such as military or surveillance purposes, while others think that restricting OSS is contradictory or impractical. Moreover, some OSS licenses may impose obligations on the users or distributors of the software, such as disclosing the source code, providing attribution, or sharing modifications.

THE HIPPOCRATIC LICENSE

One example of an ethical OSS license is the Hippocratic License, created by Coraline Ada Ehmke in 2019. This license is based on the MIT license but adds a condition that the software may not be used for systems or activities that violate the United Nations Universal Declaration of Human Rights. The Hippocratic License aims to give developers more control over how their software is used and to prevent it from being used for evil.

However, the Hippocratic License is not approved by the Open Source Initiative (OSI), which governs the most widely used OSS licenses. The OSI argues that the Hippocratic License is not conformant with the Open Source Definition (OSD), which requires that OSS licenses do not discriminate against persons, groups, or fields of endeavour. The OSI also claims that the Hippocratic License is vague and subjective, as it relies on the interpretation of human rights by different users and jurisdictions.

THE OPENCHAIN PROJECT

Another approach to address the ethical issues of OSS licensing is the OpenChain Project, which is an initiative by the Linux Foundation to establish best practices for OSS compliance. The OpenChain Project provides a specification and a certification program for organizations that use OSS in their products or services. The OpenChain Project aims to ensure that OSS users respect the rights and obligations of OSS developers and licensors, and that they provide clear and consistent information about the OSS components they use.

The OpenChain Project does not impose any ethical restrictions on how OSS is used, but rather focuses on improving the transparency and accountability of OSS usage. The OpenChain Project also helps organizations to avoid legal risks and reduce costs associated with OSS compliance.

Developers who create or use OSS should be aware of the different types of OSS licenses and their implications for collaboration and innovation. Developers should also respect the intentions and expectations of other developers who contribute to or depend on OSS. By following best practices and standards for OSS compliance, developers can ensure that they use OSS in a responsible and ethical manner.

LICENSING AS THE FOUNDATION

Licensing is the foundation of open-source software development. It defines how the software can be used, modified, and shared by others. Choosing a license is an important decision for any software project, as it affects the future of the software and its community.

WHAT IS AN OPEN-SOURCE LICENSE?

An open-source license is a type of software license that complies with the Open Source Definition. In brief, it allows software to be freely used, modified, and shared by anyone for any purpose, as long as the license terms are respected. There are many different open-source licenses, and they vary based on the restrictions or conditions they impose on the software users.

WHY CHOOSE AN OPEN-SOURCE LICENSE?

There are many benefits of choosing an open-source license for your software project. Some of them are:

Visibility. Open-source software can be accessed by anyone who is interested in your project. This can increase the visibility of your work and attract more users, contributors, or collaborators.

Innovation. Open-source software can be modified and improved by anyone who has the skills and motivation to do so. This can foster innovation and creativity, as well as solve problems or add features that you may not have time or resources to do yourself.

Quality. Open-source software can be reviewed and tested by anyone who has the expertise and willingness to do so. This can improve the quality and reliability of your software, as well as catch bugs or errors that you may have missed.

Community. Open-source software can be shared and distributed by anyone who has the permission and means to do so. This can create a community of users, developers, or supporters who can help each other, provide feedback, or offer support.

CHOOSING AN OPEN-SOURCE LICENSE

Some general factors to consider are:

Compatibility. Some open-source licenses are compatible with each other, meaning that you can combine or distribute software under different licenses without violating any terms. Some licenses are incompatible with each other, meaning that you cannot do so without obtaining additional permissions or agreements. You should check the compatibility of your chosen license with other licenses that you may want to use or interact with in the future.

Copyleft. Some open-source licenses are copyleft, meaning that they require any modified or derived versions of the software to be distributed under the same or equivalent license. This ensures that the software remains open-source and preserves the original author's rights and intentions. Some licenses are permissive, meaning that they do not impose such a requirement and allow more flexibility for the software users. You should decide whether you want your software to be copyleft or permissive, depending on your preferences or objectives.

Popularity. Some open-source licenses are more popular or widely used than others, meaning that they have more recognition or acceptance in the open-source community. This can affect how easy it is to find or collaborate with other projects that use the same or similar licenses. You should consider whether you want your software to use a popular or less popular license, depending on your needs or expectations.

ETHICAL CONSIDERATIONS

OSS comes with several ethical challenges and responsibilities for both contributors and users.

WHY ETHICS MATTER FOR OSS

OSS is not just a technical matter, it is also a social and political one. OSS can have positive or negative impacts on society, depending on how it is used and by whom. For example, OSS can be used for military purposes, surveillance, misinformation, or discrimination.

OSS can also be vulnerable to security breaches, bugs, or malicious code. Therefore, OSS contributors and users should consider the ethical implications of their actions and decisions.

HOW TO CONTRIBUTE ETHICALLY TO OSS

Ethical contributions to OSS start with self-reflection. Before contributing to an OSS project, you should ask yourself:

Why are you contributing to this project? What are your goals and motivations?

Who is the project for? Who are the intended and potential users and beneficiaries of the project?

Who creates and maintains the project? Who are the other contributors and what are their roles and interests?

How will the project be used? What are the possible positive and negative outcomes of the project?

These questions can help you identify the ethical values and principles that guide your contribution. For example, you may value transparency, fairness, privacy, or human rights. You may also want to avoid harm, misuse, or abuse of your contribution.

Ethical contributions to OSS also require following the governance model of the project. A governance model is a set of rules and processes that define how the project is managed and maintained. A governance model can include:

- A code of conduct that outlines the expected behaviour and norms of the project community.
- A license that specifies the terms and conditions of using and sharing the project code.
- A contribution guide that explains how to submit changes or additions to the project code.
- A review process that ensures the quality and security of the project code.
- A decision-making process that resolves conflicts or disputes among the project stakeholders.

By following the governance model of the project, you can ensure that your contribution is consistent with the project vision and mission. You can also respect the rights and responsibilities of other contributors and users.

Ethical contributions to OSS are not a one-time event, but a continuous process. As the project evolves and new issues arise, you should revisit your ethical values and principles and update them accordingly. You should also communicate with other contributors and users and seek feedback on your contribution. You should be open to learning from others and improving your contribution.

By reflecting on your values and principles, following the governance model of the project, and engaging in a continuous process of learning and improvement, you can contribute ethically to OSS.

AVOIDING ETHICAL DILEMMAS

OSS also poses some ethical challenges for developers and users, such as:

- How to respect the human rights and dignity of those who may be affected by the software?
- How to ensure the quality and security of the software and prevent harm or misuse?
- How to balance the freedom of OSS with the responsibility of its creators and contributors?
- How to deal with ethical conflicts or dilemmas that may arise from the use of OSS in different contexts or for different purposes?

RESPECT THE HIPPOCRATIC PRINCIPLE

The Hippocratic principle is a moral principle that states that one should do no harm or avoid doing harm. It is derived from the Hippocratic oath, a code of ethics for physicians that dates back to ancient Greece. The Hippocratic principle can be applied to OSS development and use, as a way of ensuring that the software does not cause harm to individuals, groups, or society at large.

One way of respecting the Hippocratic principle is to adopt an ethical license for OSS, such as the Hippocratic License, which was created by Coraline Ada Ehmke, a software developer from Chicago. The Hippocratic License is a license that puts ethical restrictions on the use of OSS code, such as prohibiting its use for violating human rights or dignity. The Hippocratic License aims to give developers more control over how their software is used and to prevent its use for harmful purposes.

Another way of respecting the Hippocratic principle is to conduct an ethical impact assessment (EIA) for OSS projects, especially those that involve high-stake decisions or sensitive data. An EIA is a process of identifying and evaluating the potential ethical implications of a project, such as its impact on privacy, security, fairness, accountability, or social justice. An EIA can help developers and users to anticipate and mitigate ethical risks and dilemmas that may arise from the software.

BALANCE FREEDOM & RESPONSIBILITY

Freedom and responsibility are two core values of OSS culture, but they can also be sources of ethical tension or conflict. Freedom refers to the ability of developers and users to access, modify, distribute, or reuse OSS code without restrictions or limitations. Responsibility refers to the obligation of developers and users to respect the rights and interests of others who may be affected by the software.

Balance freedom and responsibility in OSS projects is to follow the principles and guidelines of open source licenses, such as those approved by the Open Source Initiative (OSI). OSI is an organization that governs the most widely used open source licenses, such as the GNU General Public License (GPL), the Apache License (APL), or the MIT License (MIT). These licenses define the terms and conditions under which OSS code can be used or shared.

Another way of balancing freedom and responsibility in OSS projects is to engage in ethical deliberation within software development teams or communities. Ethical deliberation is a process of discussing and reflecting on ethical issues or dilemmas that may arise from the software development or use. Ethical deliberation can help developers and users to understand different perspectives, values, or interests involved in ethical decision making.

CHAPTER 5 WORKSHOP:
INTELLECTUAL PROPERTY & COPYRIGHT

INTRODUCTION

Intellectual property (IP) is a term that refers to the creations of the human mind, such as inventions, artistic works, designs, symbols, names, and images. IP can be protected by legal rights, such as patents, trademarks, and copyrights. These rights allow the creators or owners of IP to benefit from their work and prevent unauthorized use by others.

Copyright is a type of IP right that protects the expression of ideas in tangible forms, such as books, music, movies, software, and websites. Copyright holders have the exclusive right to reproduce, distribute, perform, display, and make adaptations of their works. However, these rights are not absolute and are subject to limitations and exceptions.

One of the challenges of the digital age is how to balance the interests of IP owners and users in a way that promotes innovation, creativity, and access to information. This workshop exercise will explore some of the issues and concepts related to IP and copyright in the digital context.

EXERCISE 1: DIGITAL RIGHTS MANAGEMENT

Digital rights management (DRM) is a term that refers to the technologies and methods used by IP owners to control the access and use of their digital content. DRM can include encryption, authentication, watermarking, licensing, and digital locks. The main purpose of DRM is to prevent piracy and unauthorized copying or sharing of digital content.

However, DRM can also have negative impacts on users' rights and freedoms. For example, DRM can limit the interoperability of devices and platforms, restrict the fair use and public domain exceptions, interfere with the privacy and security of users, and hinder the preservation and archiving of digital content.

In this exercise, you will discuss the pros and cons of DRM from different perspectives: IP owners, users, and society. Divide into three groups and assign each group one of these perspectives. Each group will prepare a list of arguments for or against DRM based on their assigned perspective. Then, each group will present their list to the other groups and respond to any questions or comments.

EXERCISE 2: OPEN-SOURCE SOFTWARE LICENSING

Open-source software (OSS) is a type of software that allows anyone to access, modify, and distribute its source code. OSS is based on the principles of collaboration, transparency, and freedom. OSS can have many benefits for users, developers, and society, such as lower costs, higher quality, greater customization, faster innovation, and wider participation.

However, OSS also poses some challenges for IP owners and users. For example, OSS can create compatibility issues with proprietary software, raise legal uncertainties about the ownership and liability of OSS contributions, require compliance with complex and diverse licensing terms, and expose security vulnerabilities in the source code.

In this exercise, you will compare and contrast different types of OSS licenses and their implications for IP rights. Choose two OSS licenses from the following list: GNU General Public License (GPL), Apache License (APL), MIT License (MIT), Creative Commons License (CC), or any other license you are familiar with. Each license has different conditions and requirements for using or modifying OSS. Research the main features and differences between your chosen licenses and prepare a summary table or chart. Then, share your summary with the other participants and explain why you would prefer one license over another for your own OSS project.

CHAPTER 6:
E-GOV & DIGITAL TRANSFORMATION

CHAPTER SUMMARY

E-government and digital transformation are two related concepts that aim to improve the quality of life and the efficiency of public services. E-government refers to the use of information and communication technologies (ICTs) to deliver government services, information and participation to citizens, businesses and other stakeholders. Digital transformation is the process of rethinking and redesigning how government operates, interacts and innovates using digital tools and data.

One of the main goals of e-government and digital transformation is to **enhance citizen engagement**, which means involving citizens in the decision-making and policy-making processes of government. Citizen engagement can take various forms, such as online consultations, feedback mechanisms, crowdsourcing, co-creation and participatory budgeting. Citizen engagement can increase the transparency, accountability and legitimacy of government actions, as well as the satisfaction and trust of citizens.

Another goal of e-government and digital transformation is to **create smart cities and ethical urbanization**. Smart cities are urban areas that use ICTs to collect, analyze and use data to improve the management and planning of various aspects of urban life, such as transportation, energy, waste, health, education and security. Ethical urbanization is the principle that smart cities should respect the human rights, dignity and diversity of their inhabitants, as well as promote social inclusion, environmental sustainability and economic development.

A third goal of e-government and digital transformation is to **enable remote work and privacy**. Remote work is the practice of working from a location other than the traditional office, such as home, co-working spaces or public places. Remote work can offer benefits such as flexibility, productivity, cost savings and work-life balance. However, remote work also poses challenges such as communication, collaboration, security and privacy. Privacy is the right of individuals to control their personal information and how it is used by others. Privacy is essential for protecting the identity, reputation and autonomy of remote workers, as well as their personal and professional data.

6.1. E-GOVERNMENT & CITIZEN ENGAGEMENT

E-government initiatives are the use of information and communication technologies (ICTs) to deliver public services, improve government efficiency and transparency, and enhance citizen participation and trust.

Governments worldwide are adopting technological advancements to create more efficient and accessible public services through e-government initiatives. This is an on-going process.

As these initiatives take shape, it becomes necessary to have policies cover a range of considerations, including:

- Data privacy,
- Security,
- Accessibility and,
- Citizen engagement.

Alongside these policies, a range of ethical considerations play a central role in ensuring that e-government efforts are not only efficient and convenient but also uphold.

- Democratic principles,
- Respect individual rights, and
- Promote transparency.

Identify and map your stakeholders based on their interest in and influence on your objectives. Determine the issues on which you need stakeholder input and develop strategies for engagement.

Be clear about what you are trying to achieve, be open about your limitations and constraints, tell people where their input is going, and manage expectations around the outcome and decision-making process.

Use information and communication technologies to facilitate the daily administration of government, improve citizen access to government information, services and expertise, ensure citizen participation in and satisfaction with the government process, and enhance cost-effectiveness and efficiency.

Foster civic engagement through interactive, easy-to-understand data publishing and visualizations. Provide context for your data and help citizens understand what it signifies.

Consult the public on which capital improvement projects to prioritize, update citizens on the progress of projects, and report and communicate the impact of a capital project.

Value information as a national resource and a national asset. Ensure information security, privacy, integrity, accountability, innovation and improvement across all the processes of government.

THE RISE OF E-GOVERNMENT INITIATIVES

The rise of e-government initiatives is driven by various factors, such as the increasing demand for online services, the availability of digital infrastructure and data, the pressure to reduce costs and improve performance, and the opportunities to foster innovation and collaboration.

The benefits of e-government initiatives include improved service quality and accessibility, increased citizen satisfaction and empowerment, reduced administrative burden and corruption, enhanced policy making and accountability, and greater social inclusion and cohesion.

The challenges of e-government initiatives include technical issues, such as interoperability, security, privacy, and digital divide; organizational issues, such as leadership, culture, change management, and human resources; and legal and ethical issues, such as data protection, transparency, accountability, and participation rights.

The best advice on the topic of the rise of e-government initiatives is to adopt a holistic and strategic approach that considers the needs and expectations of all stakeholders, the goals and objectives of the government, the opportunities and risks of ICTs, and the legal and ethical implications of e-government. Some of the key steps are:

- Conduct a situational analysis to assess the current state of e-government in terms of strengths, weaknesses, opportunities, and threats.
- Develop a vision and a roadmap for e-government that defines the desired outcomes, priorities, indicators, and milestones.
- Establish a governance framework for e-government that clarifies the roles and responsibilities of different actors, the decision-making processes, the coordination mechanisms, and the monitoring and evaluation systems.

- Implement e-government projects that are aligned with the vision and roadmap, follow user-centric design principles, ensure interoperability and security standards, involve stakeholder participation and feedback, and evaluate the impacts and outcomes.
- Foster a culture of innovation and learning for e-government that encourages experimentation, collaboration, knowledge sharing, and continuous improvement.

POLICIES FOR DATA PRIVACY & SECURITY

Since e-government involves the collection, storage, and processing of citizen data, there must be robust policies for data privacy and security.

Data privacy and security are essential for e-government and citizen engagement, as they ensure trust, transparency and accountability in the use of personal and public information.

E-government policies should comply with relevant laws and regulations, such as the General Data Protection Regulation (GDPR) in Europe and the California Consumer Privacy Act (CCPA) in the US, that protect consumer rights and choices about how their data are used.

E-government policies should also follow best practices and standards, such as the Information and Data Governance Framework of the National Archives of Australia, that promote data interoperability, quality and value across government agencies and services.

E-government policies should involve citizen participation and feedback, as well as collaboration with other stakeholders, such as private sector, civil society and academia, to ensure data are used for public good and innovation.

ACCESSIBILITY BRIDGING THE DIGITAL DIVIDE

Ethical e-government policies extend to accessibility, ensuring that digital services are available to all citizens, including those with disabilities or limited technological access.

Governments must prioritize designing platforms that adhere to accessibility standards, making sure that no citizen is excluded from utilizing vital services due to physical or digital barriers.

This commitment to accessibility reflects an ethical imperative to create inclusive and equitable digital landscapes.

ENGAGEMENT & INCLUSIVITY

A primary consideration of e-government is to enhance citizen engagement and participation in governance.

Ethical considerations demand that these initiatives be inclusive, providing avenues for *all* citizens to voice their opinions, provide feedback, and influence decision-making processes.

Policies should therefore outline mechanisms for soliciting public input, fostering meaningful dialogue, and ensuring that diverse perspectives are considered when shaping policies and services.

E-government initiatives must also respect and uphold individual rights, both online and offline. Ethical policies should ensure that citizens' rights to privacy, freedom of expression, and access to information are not compromised.

Measures should be in place to prevent the misuse of citizen data, surveillance abuses, or any actions that could infringe upon fundamental rights.

TRANSPARENCY & ACCOUNTABILITY

Transparency is a cornerstone of ethical governance. E-government initiatives should promote transparency by giving citizens access to relevant information about government activities, decisions, and processes.

Policies should mandate the publication of data, budgets, reports, and other pertinent information in formats that are easily accessible and understandable to the public.

This transparency works towards proper accountability and empowers citizens to hold governments to ethical standards.

THE DIGITAL DIVIDE

While e-government initiatives aim to enhance efficiency and accessibility, they also raise concerns about exacerbating existing digital divides.

Ethical policies should address these concerns by prioritizing initiatives that bridge these divides, such as providing digital literacy training and ensuring that marginalized communities have access to necessary technology.

This approach ensures that the benefits of e-government are distributed equitably.

CONVENIENCE VS CONSENT

E-government services often require citizens to share personal information for authentication and verification.

Ethical policies must need to balance the convenience of streamlined services with the necessity of obtaining informed consent from citizens.

Clear communication about how data will be used and the ability to opt-out should be integral to these policies, respecting citizens' autonomy over their personal information.

DIGITAL LITERACY & INFORMED PARTICIPATION

Citizen engagement in e-government initiatives is most effective when citizens are digitally literate and well-informed and have a willingness to engage with e-government.

Ethical considerations extend to providing educational resources that train citizens to navigate digital platforms, understand their rights and responsibilities, and actively participate in governance processes. Policies should encompass strategies for promoting digital literacy and awareness.

E-government has great potential to revolutionize the relationship between citizens and governments, fostering transparency, accessibility, and engagement.

However, realizing this potential requires a foundation of ethical policies that prioritize data privacy, security, inclusivity, transparency, and respect for individual rights.

E-government, guided by ethical considerations, becomes a force for positive change, bridging gaps, enhancing accountability, and ultimately strengthening the democratic fabric of society.

6.2. SMART CITIES & ETHICAL URBANIZATION

Smart cities are urban areas that use digital technologies to improve the quality of life of their inhabitants. They can also help address some of the challenges that cities face, such as congestion, pollution, crime, and inequality. However, smart cities also raise some ethical issues and concerns that need to be considered and addressed by policymakers, developers, and citizens.

NETWORK INFRASTRUCTURE

One of the key features of smart cities is the network infrastructure that connects various devices, sensors, and systems to collect, store, and analyse data. This data can be used to optimize urban services, such as transportation, energy, waste management, and public safety.

However, this also poses some risks of control, surveillance, data privacy, and ownership. Who owns the data generated by smart city technologies? How is it protected from unauthorized access or misuse? How is it shared among different stakeholders and for what purposes? How can citizens have a say in how their data is used and by whom?

POST-POLITICAL GOVERNANCE

Another aspect of smart cities is the post-political governance model that relies on data-driven decision-making and public-private partnerships. This model can enhance efficiency, transparency, and accountability in urban management.

But it can also undermine democratic participation, deliberation, and representation. How are the interests and values of different groups and communities considered in smart city projects? How are the trade-offs and conflicts among them resolved?

How are the roles and responsibilities of public authorities and private actors defined and regulated? How can citizens have a voice and a choice in shaping their smart city?

SOCIAL INCLUSION

A third dimension of smart cities is the social inclusion of citizens in the benefits and opportunities offered by smart city technologies. This includes ensuring access, affordability, usability, and literacy of digital services for everyone.

It also involves promoting citizen participation, engagement, and empowerment in co-creating and co-governing their smart city. However, this also requires addressing the challenges of inequality, discrimination, and exclusion that may arise or persist in smart cities.

How are the needs and preferences of diverse and marginalized groups considered and met in smart city design and implementation? How are the potential harms and disadvantages of smart city technologies for some groups prevented or mitigated? How can citizens have a sense of belonging and identity in their smart city?

SUSTAINABILITY

A fourth dimension of smart cities is the sustainability of their environmental impact and long-term development.

This entails using smart city technologies to reduce greenhouse gas emissions, conserve natural resources, enhance resilience to climate change, and improve environmental quality. It also implies aligning smart city goals with the broader agenda of sustainable development that encompasses social, economic, and cultural aspects.

This also demands balancing the costs and benefits of smart city technologies for different generations and regions. How are the environmental impacts of smart city technologies measured and monitored? How are they aligned with the global commitments and targets on climate action? How are they integrated with the local contexts and cultures of different cities?

THE RISE OF SMART CITIES REDEFINING URBAN LIVING

Smart cities are urban areas that use digital technologies to enhance the quality of life, efficiency of services, and sustainability of the environment. They aim to solve the challenges of urbanization, such as congestion, pollution, waste, and social inequality.

INVOLVE THE STAKEHOLDERS

Smart cities are not just about technology, but also about people. It is important to engage the citizens, businesses, civil society, and public sector in the planning and decision-making process of smart city initiatives. This can foster trust, collaboration, and innovation among the stakeholders, as well as ensure that the solutions are tailored to the local needs and preferences.

THE HOLISTIC APPROACH

Smart cities are complex systems that require coordination and integration across different domains, such as transportation, energy, health, education, and security. It is essential to adopt a holistic approach that considers the interdependencies and trade-offs among these domains, as well as the potential impacts on the economy, society, and environment. A holistic approach can also help to avoid silos, duplication, and fragmentation of resources and efforts.

ETHICAL & LEGAL COMPLIANCE

Smart cities rely on data collection, analysis, and sharing to provide intelligent services and solutions. However, this also raises ethical and legal issues, such as privacy, security, accountability, and transparency. It is crucial to ensure that the data collection and use are compliant with the relevant laws and regulations, as well as respect the rights and interests of the data subjects. Moreover, it is advisable to adopt ethical principles and guidelines that can guide the design and implementation of smart city technologies and policies.

PROMOTE INNOVATION & LEARNING

Smart cities are dynamic and evolving entities that need to adapt to the changing needs and expectations of the citizens and the environment. It is important to promote a culture of innovation and learning that encourages experimentation, creativity, and risk-taking. This can help to foster new ideas, solutions, and practices that can improve the performance and outcomes of smart city initiatives. Furthermore, it is beneficial to establish mechanisms for monitoring, evaluation, and feedback that can provide evidence-based insights and lessons for continuous improvement.

ETHICAL DIMENSIONS OF SMART CITIES

Smart cities are urban areas that use digital technologies to improve the quality of life, efficiency of services, and sustainability of resources. They can offer many benefits, such as reducing traffic congestion, enhancing public safety, and promoting social inclusion. However, smart cities also pose ethical challenges that need to be addressed, such as privacy, security, accountability, and participation.

PRIVACY

Smart cities collect and process large amounts of data from various sources, such as sensors, cameras, mobile devices, and social media.

This data can reveal sensitive information about the behaviour, preferences, and activities of citizens. How can we ensure that this data is used in a transparent, fair, and respectful way, without violating the rights and dignity of individuals?

SECURITY

Smart cities rely on complex and interconnected systems that are vulnerable to cyberattacks, natural disasters, or human errors. These systems can affect critical infrastructure, such as transportation, energy, or health care. How can we protect these systems from malicious or accidental threats, while ensuring their resilience and reliability?

ACCOUNTABILITY

Smart cities involve multiple actors, such as governments, businesses, civil society, and citizens. These actors have different roles, responsibilities, and interests in the design, implementation, and evaluation of smart city initiatives. How can we ensure that these actors are accountable for their actions and decisions, and that they comply with ethical standards and legal regulations?

PARTICIPATION

Smart cities aim to improve the well-being and empowerment of citizens by providing them with more choices, opportunities, and services. However, not all citizens have equal access to or influence on these benefits. How can we ensure that smart city initiatives are inclusive, participatory, and responsive to the needs and expectations of diverse and marginalized groups?

By applying ethical principles and values to smart city projects, we can ensure that they are not only smart but also fair, responsible, and human-centered.

DATA PRIVACY & SECURITY

Data privacy and security laws aim to protect citizens from the misuse, loss, unauthorized access or disclosure of their personal information by government agencies or private organisations.

WHY IS DATA PRIVACY & SECURITY IMPORTANT?

Data privacy and security are important because they respect the fundamental human right to privacy and dignity of individuals.

They foster trust and confidence in the digital economy and society and enable citizens to exercise control and choice over their personal information.

They also prevent identity theft, fraud, cybercrime and other harms that can result from data breaches or misuse, and support innovation and competitiveness by creating a level playing field for data-driven businesses.

BEST PRACTICE FOR DATA PRIVACY AND SECURITY

Data privacy and security best practices are based on the following principles:

Lawfulness, fairness and transparency. Personal information should be collected and processed only for legitimate, specified and explicit purposes, with the consent or authorization of the individuals concerned, and in a clear and open manner.

Data minimization. Personal information should be adequate, relevant and limited to what is necessary for the purposes for which it is processed.

Accuracy. Personal information should be accurate, complete and up-to-date, and corrected or deleted if inaccurate or outdated.

Storage limitation. Personal information should be kept only for as long as necessary for the purposes for which it is processed, and securely disposed of when no longer needed.

Integrity and confidentiality. Personal information should be protected from unauthorized or unlawful processing, accidental loss, destruction or damage, using appropriate technical and organisational measures.

Accountability. Data controllers and processors should be responsible for complying with data privacy and security laws and regulations, and demonstrate their compliance through documentation, audits, reporting and other means.

DATA PRIVACY & SECURITY LAWS: THE WORLD

Data privacy and security laws vary from country to country, depending on their legal systems, cultures and values. However, there is a growing trend towards harmonization and convergence of data protection standards across regions and jurisdictions. Some of the major data privacy and security laws around the world are:

The General Data Protection Regulation (GDPR). This is the most comprehensive and influential data protection law in the world, which applies to the European Union (EU) and the European Economic Area (EEA), as well as to any organisation that offers goods or services to, or monitors the behaviour of, individuals in the EU or EEA. The GDPR grants individuals a set of rights over their personal information, such as the right to access, rectify, erase, restrict, port or object to its processing. It also imposes strict obligations on data controllers and processors, such as obtaining valid consent, conducting data protection impact assessments, appointing data protection officers, notifying data breaches, implementing data protection by design and by default, and transferring data only to countries with adequate levels of protection. The GDPR also empowers national data protection authorities to enforce the law and impose fines of up to 20 million euros or 4% of global annual turnover, whichever is higher.

The California Consumer Privacy Act (CCPA). This is the first comprehensive data protection law in the United States (US), which applies to California residents as well as to any business that collects or sells their personal information. The CCPA grants individuals a set of rights over their personal information, such as the right to know what is collected, shared or sold; the right to access, delete or opt out of its sale; and the right to non-discrimination for exercising their rights. It also imposes obligations on businesses to provide notice, transparency and choice to consumers; to implement reasonable security measures; to honour consumer requests; and to avoid selling personal information of minors without consent. The CCPA also authorizes the California Attorney General to enforce the law and impose civil penalties of up to $7,500 per violation.

The Privacy Act 1988. This is the main data protection law in Australia (AU), which applies to Australian Government agencies (and the Norfolk Island administration) and organisations with an annual turnover more than $3 million. The Privacy Act gives individuals a set of rights over their personal information, such as the right to access or correct it; the right to complain about its mishandling; the right to stop receiving unwanted direct marketing; and the right to be notified of data breaches. It also imposes obligations on agencies.

RESPONSIBLE USE OF AI AND AUTOMATION

ETHICAL AI IN GOVERNMENT

The Australian Government has developed four principles for the ethical use of AI in government, based on interim guidance from the Digital Transformation Agency (DTA) and the Department of Industry, Science and Resources (DISR) . These principles are:

- Support the responsible and safe use of technology.
- Minimise harm, and achieve safer, more reliable and fairer outcomes for all Australians.
- Reduce the risk of negative impact on those affected by AI applications.
- Enable the highest ethical standards when using AI.
- Increase transparency and build community trust in the use of emerging technology by government.

These principles should guide the design, development, deployment, and evaluation of any AI or automation project in the public sector. They should also be aligned with the agency's ICT obligations and policies, as well as relevant laws and regulations.

USING GENERATIVE AI

Generative AI platforms are third-party AI platforms, tools or software that can create new content or data based on existing data or inputs.

Examples of such platforms are ChatGPT, Bard AI or Bing AI. These platforms can offer new and innovative opportunities for government, such as generating summaries, reports, or responses to queries. However, they also involve potential risks, such as data quality, security, privacy, accountability, and bias.

The DTA and DISR have provided some tactical guidance for Australian Public Service (APS) staff who want to use publicly available generative AI platforms. Some of the key points are:

- Assess the potential risks and benefits for each use case.
- Use generative AI platforms only for low-risk purposes that do not involve personal or sensitive information, decision making, or official communication.
- Do not rely solely on generative AI outputs without human verification or quality assurance.

- Clearly disclose the use of generative AI platforms to stakeholders and users
- Monitor and evaluate the performance and impact of generative AI platforms regularly.

BEST PRACTICES FOR DIGITAL TRANSFORMATION

Digital transformation is not just about using digital technologies to automate or augment existing processes. It is also about reimagining how government can deliver value to citizens and businesses in new ways. According to BCG , some of the best practices for digital transformation in government are:

- Define a clear vision and strategy for digital transformation that aligns with the agency's mission and goals.
- Establish a dedicated digital team or unit that can drive innovation and collaboration across the agency.
- Adopt agile methods and tools that enable rapid experimentation and iteration.
- Leverage data and analytics to generate insights and improve decision making.
- Engage with stakeholders and users throughout the design and delivery process to ensure user-centricity and feedback.
- Foster a culture of learning and change that supports continuous improvement and adaptation.

By following these principles, government agencies can use AI and automation responsibly and effectively in E-Gov & Digital Transformation. This can lead to better outcomes for citizens, businesses, and society.

6.3. REMOTE WORK & PRIVACY

FLEXIBILITY, PRODUCTIVITY, & INDIVIDUAL RIGHTS

The rise of remote work has revolutionized the way we work, offering unprecedented flexibility and accessibility. However, as organizations embrace this new paradigm, concerns about privacy in remote work environments have come to the forefront.

Remote work offers many benefits for both employers and employees, such as increased flexibility, productivity, and satisfaction.

However, remote work also poses some challenges for individual rights and privacy, such as blurred boundaries between work and personal life, potential surveillance and monitoring by employers, and increased cyber risks.

To address these challenges, it is important to establish clear policies and guidelines for remote work that respect the rights and preferences of workers, while ensuring accountability and security.

Some best practices for remote work policies include:

- Setting realistic and measurable goals and outcomes for remote workers, rather than focusing on hours or attendance.
- Providing adequate training and support for remote workers to use the necessary tools and technologies effectively and safely.
- Communicating regularly and transparently with remote workers to maintain trust, collaboration, and feedback.
- Respecting the autonomy and flexibility of remote workers to choose their preferred work location, schedule, and style, as long as they meet their obligations and expectations.
- Protecting the privacy and data of remote workers by implementing appropriate security measures, such as encryption, VPNs, firewalls, etc..
- Avoiding excessive or intrusive monitoring or surveillance of remote workers that may violate their rights or harm their well-being.

THE REMOTE WORK REVOLUTION

Advances in technology have paved the way for remote work to become a mainstream practice.

Develop standard security rules and procedures for your remote teams that cover regulatory compliance, remote access control, backup and media storage, data protection, remote system management, system ownership and return, and information disposal.

Define PII standards that meet the obligations for *personally identifiable information* compliance in all territories in which your organization operates.

Train and educate team members on how to protect themselves and others from the latest cybersecurity threats, especially those related to remote work, such as physical theft of devices, packet sniffers on public Wi-Fi networks, email scams, and spoof sites.

Don't leave your electronic devices unattended in public or in an unsecured office. Set laptops and mobile devices to automatically lock after a period of inactivity. Do not leave passwords written down or visible to others.

Use a password manager to generate and store strong, unique passwords for each account and service you use. Change your passwords regularly and avoid using the same password for multiple accounts.

Use a VPN and 2-factor authentication whenever possible to encrypt your online traffic and add an extra layer of security to your login credentials. Avoid using public Wi-Fi networks or shared computers to access sensitive data or perform online transactions.

Perform all transactions on a secure, password-protected network. Even if you are using a VPN, it's better safe than sorry. Look for the padlock icon and the https prefix in the address bar of your browser before entering any personal or financial information.

THE PRIVACY PUZZLE

Remote work introduces a unique set of privacy challenges. As employees work from home, the boundaries between professional and personal life blur, potentially leading to privacy infringements.

The Privacy Puzzle is a term that refers to the challenges and risks of protecting personal and confidential information in a remote or hybrid work environment.

Remote work has increased the exposure of sensitive data to potential threats such as unsecured networks, phishing attacks, device theft, and visual hacking.

To address these challenges, IT governance, policy, ethics and law experts recommend the following best practices:

- Implementing robust security technologies such as incident response platforms, anti-virus software, identity management and authentication systems, and encryption tools.
- Developing and enforcing clear privacy policies that specify the responsibilities and expectations of remote or hybrid workers, as well as the consequences of non-compliance.
- Providing regular training and awareness programs that educate employees on the importance of data privacy, the common threats they may face, and the mitigation methods they should use.
- Adopting privacy-enhancing solutions such as privacy screens, webcam covers, secure file sharing platforms, and VPNs.
- Monitoring and auditing the compliance and performance of remote or hybrid workers, as well as the security and privacy of the data they handle.

REMOTE WORK & PRIVACY POLICIES

Remote work poses unique challenges and opportunities for privacy protection. As a professional in IT governance, policy, ethics and law, you should be aware of the legal requirements, best practices and ethical principles that apply to remote work and privacy policies.

According to the Privacy Act 1988, you may need to have a clear and up-to-date privacy policy that details how you collect, store, use and disclose personal information of your employees, customers and other stakeholders. You should also comply with the Australian Privacy Principles, especially if you handle sensitive personal information or operate across borders.

You should also ensure that your remote work policy covers the following aspects:

- **Communication**. You should establish clear and consistent communication channels and protocols for remote workers, such as email, phone, video conferencing, instant messaging and collaboration tools. You should also inform remote workers of their rights and responsibilities regarding privacy and confidentiality and provide them with regular feedback and support.

- **Position and employee eligibility**. You should determine which positions and employees are suitable for remote work, based on their roles, skills, performance, availability and preferences. You should also consider the impact of remote work on their wellbeing, productivity, collaboration and career development.

- **Documentation**. You should document your remote work policy and procedures and make them accessible and transparent to all relevant parties. You should also keep accurate records of remote work arrangements, such as hours worked, tasks completed, expenses incurred, and outcomes achieved.

- **Remote work expectations**. You should set clear and realistic expectations for remote workers, such as work hours, deliverables, quality standards, deadlines, reporting requirements and performance indicators. You should also monitor and evaluate their work outcomes and provide them with constructive feedback and recognition.

- **Remote equipment and tools**. You should provide remote workers with the necessary equipment and tools to perform their work effectively and securely, such as laptops, smartphones, software applications, VPNs and cloud services. You should also ensure that they have adequate internet connection and technical support.

- **Cybersecurity and internet connection**. You should implement appropriate cybersecurity measures to protect your data, systems and networks from unauthorized access, use or disclosure. You should also educate remote workers on how to prevent and respond to cyber threats, such as phishing, malware, ransomware and data breaches. You should also ensure that they use secure internet connections and devices when working remotely.

- **Adapting existing policies**. You should review and update your existing policies to reflect the changes brought by remote work, such as health and safety, leave entitlements, expense reimbursements, travel allowances and insurance coverage. You should also consult with your employees, managers, unions and legal advisors on any policy changes or issues.
- **Training**. You should provide remote workers with adequate training on how to use the equipment and tools provided by you, how to comply with your privacy policy and procedures, how to manage their time, workload and stress levels, how to communicate effectively with their colleagues and customers, how to maintain their professional image and reputation online.

By following these best practices for remote work and privacy policies, you can ensure that your business operates efficiently, ethically and legally in the digital age. You can also enhance your employee satisfaction, engagement and retention rates by offering them flexibility, autonomy and trust.

PRIVACY IN DIGITAL COMMUNICATION

Privacy in digital communication is a crucial issue for remote workers, as they may share sensitive information with their employers, clients, colleagues, or other parties over various platforms and devices.

Remote workers should be aware of the data privacy regulations that apply to their location, industry, and type of data, such as GDPR or CCPA, and follow the best practices to comply with them.

Remote workers should also take steps to protect their own privacy and security, such as using strong passwords, encryption, VPNs, anti-virus software, and identity management tools.

Remote workers should communicate clearly and respectfully with their managers and co-workers about their expectations, boundaries, and preferences regarding privacy and data sharing.

Remote workers should seek advice from IT governance, policy, ethics, and law experts if they encounter any challenges or dilemmas related to privacy in digital communication.

DATA SECURITY IN REMOTE WORK

Data security in remote work is the practice of protecting sensitive information and systems when employees work from home or in remote locations.

Data security in remote work involves encrypting data at rest and during transit, safeguarding it from interception, compromise, or theft. It also involves preventing data loss or leakage, which can happen when employees use personal devices, unsecured networks, or unauthorized applications.

Data security in remote work requires a strong security policy that covers the roles and responsibilities of remote workers, the acceptable use of devices and applications, the encryption and backup of data, and the reporting of incidents.

It also requires ongoing education and training for remote workers, so they are aware of the proper security protocols, the importance of data security, and how to look for potential cyber threats.

Security can be enhanced by embracing cloud technology, which can provide more flexibility, scalability, and resilience for data storage and access. However, cloud technology also introduces new challenges, such as ensuring compliance with data privacy regulations, managing access rights and permissions, and monitoring cloud activity.

This is a critical issue for businesses that want to maintain their competitive edge, reputation, and customer trust. It is also a shared responsibility that requires collaboration and communication between IT teams, managers, and remote workers.

BALANCING MONITORING & TRUST

Balancing monitoring in remote work and privacy is a challenging but important task for employers and employees alike.

Monitoring can have benefits such as improving productivity, ensuring compliance, and mitigating risks, but it can also have drawbacks such as eroding trust, harming job satisfaction, and increasing stress.

To monitor employees effectively and ethically, employers should follow some best practices, such as:

- Choosing metrics that are relevant, fair, and transparent, and involving all stakeholders in the process.

- Communicating clearly with employees about what is being monitored, why, and how.
- Offering incentives and feedback as well as consequences for performance.
- Recognizing that employees may face challenges and distractions in their remote work environment and being flexible and supportive.
- Monitoring their own systems to ensure that they are not biased or discriminatory against certain groups of employees.
- Decreasing monitoring when possible and respecting employees' privacy rights.

Trust is essential for remote work and privacy, as it fosters collaboration, innovation, and well-being. Employers should build trust with their employees by:

- Providing them with the tools, resources, and training they need to work remotely.
- Empowering them to make decisions and manage their own work schedules.
- Encouraging them to communicate openly and frequently with their managers and peers.
- Appreciating their contributions and celebrating their achievements.
- Respecting their personal lives and boundaries.

REMOTE WORK EQUIPMENT & PRIVACY

Remote work equipment and privacy are closely related issues that affect both employers and employees in a distributed work environment.

Employers have a duty to ensure the health and safety of their workers, as well as the security and compliance of their data and systems, when they work from home or elsewhere.

Employees have a right to expect reasonable privacy and autonomy when they use their own or employer-provided equipment for work purposes.

To balance these interests, employers and employees should follow some best practices, such as:

- Providing adequate and ergonomic equipment for remote workers that meets their individual needs and preferences.
- Establishing clear policies and procedures on providing equipment for remote workers, including who owns, pays for, maintains, repairs, replaces, and returns the equipment.
- Implementing effective technologies and tools for protecting privacy and security in a remote or hybrid work environment, such as incident response platforms, anti-virus/anti-malware software, big data analytics for cybersecurity, identity management and authentication.
- Educating and training remote workers on how to use the equipment safely and securely, as well as their rights and responsibilities regarding data privacy.
- Monitoring and auditing the use of equipment for work purposes only when necessary and proportionate, and respecting the personal use of equipment when allowed.

CONSENT & TRANSPARENT PRACTICES

Consent and transparent practices are essential for ensuring the privacy and trust of employees who work remotely.

Employers should follow the Australian Privacy Principles (APPs) when collecting, storing, using and disclosing personal information of their remote workers.

Employers should have a clear privacy policy that explains what information they collect, why they collect it, how they use it, who they share it with, and how employees can access or correct it.

Employers should seek consent from their remote workers before monitoring their activities, such as their emails, social media accounts, or workspaces.

Employers should be transparent with their remote workers about the purpose and scope of monitoring, and the benefits and risks involved.

Employers should offer incentives and feedback to their remote workers based on their performance, not on their compliance with monitoring.

Employers should respect the diversity and individual circumstances of their remote workers, and avoid any discrimination or bias based on personal information.

Employers should review and update their privacy practices regularly and consult with their remote workers and other stakeholders on any changes.

INDIVIDUAL PRIVACY VS. ORGANIZATIONAL NEEDS

Individual privacy vs. organizational needs is a key challenge for remote work, especially in the post-pandemic era.

Remote workers may face different expectations and norms than on-site workers, which can affect their sense of belonging, trust, and performance.

Organizations should consider the following best practices to balance privacy and needs in remote work:

- Establish clear and consistent policies for remote work that address issues such as working hours, communication tools, data security, and performance evaluation.
- Communicate frequently and transparently with remote workers to foster a shared culture and identity, and to avoid misunderstandings or isolation.
- Provide adequate support and resources for remote workers to ensure their well-being, productivity, and engagement.
- Respect the boundaries and preferences of remote workers and avoid micromanaging or intruding on their personal space.
- Involve remote workers in decision making and feedback processes and recognize their contributions and achievements.

FLEXIBLE WORKING HOURS & PRIVACY

Flexible hours are arrangements that allow employees to adjust their work schedules and locations to suit their personal and professional needs.

This can benefit both employers and employees by increasing productivity, engagement, retention, diversity, and well-being.

Flexible hours can also pose some challenges, such as communication difficulties, performance management, security risks, and legal compliance.

To implement flexible working hours successfully, employers need to establish clear policies and guidelines, consult with employees and stakeholders, provide adequate technology and support, and monitor and evaluate the outcomes.

And to make the most of flexible working hours, employees need to communicate effectively, manage their time and tasks, balance their work and personal responsibilities, and maintain their health and safety.

MANAGING SENSITIVE INFORMATION

Managing sensitive information in a remote work environment is crucial for protecting your data and intellectual property, as well as complying with legal and ethical obligations.

Management (you) should set up and communicate clear policies and guidelines for your employees on how to handle sensitive information, such as personal, financial, health, or confidential data, when working remotely.

You should use secure tools and platforms that encrypt your data at rest and in transit, such as Microsoft Teams, which also allows you to apply data loss prevention and sensitivity labelling to prevent unauthorized access or sharing of sensitive information.

You should monitor and mitigate insider risks, such as accidental or malicious disclosure of sensitive information by your employees, by using incident response platforms, big data analytics, identity management, and authentication systems.

You should provide regular training and awareness programs for your employees on the importance of visual privacy, VPN security, personal device regulation, and communication channel security when working remotely.

CULTURAL AND LEGAL DIVERSITY

Remote work can enhance workplace diversity by allowing access to a wider pool of talent, reducing geographic and social barriers, and accommodating different needs and preferences of employees.

However, remote work also poses some challenges for diversity and inclusion, such as potential isolation, exclusion, or misunderstanding of employees from different backgrounds, identities, or locations.

To address these challenges, remote workers and managers need to be aware of the cultural differences that can impact global teams, such as communication styles, decision-making processes, conflict resolution strategies, and feedback preferences.

Remote workers and managers also need to be mindful of the legal diversity that can affect remote work and privacy, such as data protection laws, employment laws, tax laws, and anti-discrimination laws that may vary across countries or regions.

Therefore, it is advisable for remote workers and managers to follow some best practices for cultural and legal diversity in remote work and privacy, such as:

- Developing workplace policies and training that promote cross-cultural awareness and respect.
- Holding regular virtual meetings and events that celebrate workplace diversity and encourage employees to share their cultures and experiences.
- Using clear and inclusive language and communication tools that suit the needs and preferences of different employees.
- Seeking feedback and input from diverse employees on important decisions and projects.
- Ensuring compliance with relevant laws and regulations in different jurisdictions where remote workers are located.
- Providing support and resources for remote workers to deal with any legal or cultural issues that may arise.

ADDRESSING BURNOUT & OVERWORK

Addressing burnout and overwork in remote work is a crucial challenge for many hard-working IT professionals, who often face high demands, tight deadlines, and complex tasks.

Burnout can have a range of negative consequences for individual well-being, team performance, and organizational outcomes, such as increased turnover, reduced productivity, and lower customer satisfaction.

To prevent and reduce burnout in remote work, IT professionals should follow some evidence-based strategies, such as:

- **Creating an environment for communication**. Remote workers may feel isolated, disconnected, or misunderstood by their colleagues and managers. To foster a sense of belonging and trust, IT professionals should communicate frequently, clearly, and empathetically with their team members and leaders. They should also seek feedback, share achievements, and celebrate successes.

- **Lifting morale — genuinely**. Remote workers may lack the motivation, engagement, or recognition that they would receive in a physical office. To boost morale and enthusiasm, IT professionals should find meaningful and enjoyable aspects of their work, express gratitude and appreciation to others, and participate in social activities that foster camaraderie and fun.

- **Simplifying remote work systems**. Remote workers may struggle with the complexity, ambiguity, or inefficiency of their work processes and tools. To streamline remote work systems, IT professionals should use reliable and user-friendly technology platforms, establish clear and consistent expectations and guidelines, and prioritize and delegate tasks effectively.

- **Reducing or eliminating meetings**. Remote workers may experience meeting fatigue, which can drain their energy, attention, and creativity. To minimize meeting overload, IT professionals should only attend meetings that are relevant, necessary, and productive. They should also limit the duration and frequency of meetings, prepare agendas and objectives beforehand, and follow up with action items afterward.

- **Addressing the elephant**. Remote workers may face personal or professional challenges that are specific to their situation, such as juggling caregiving responsibilities, coping with mental health issues, or dealing with technical difficulties. To address these challenges, IT professionals should be honest and proactive about their needs and concerns, seek support from their managers or peers, and access available resources or services.

- **Investing time and attention in themselves**. Remote workers may neglect their own well-being by working long hours, skipping breaks, or ignoring physical or emotional signs of stress. To take care of themselves, IT professionals should set healthy boundaries between work and life, practice self-care activities that enhance their mood and energy, and take regular recovery time to relax and recharge.

EDUCATION & TRAINING

Ensure that you comply with IP, ethics and privacy policies and procedures in ICT environments, as outlined in the relevant training packages.

Locate and access the organisation's IP, ethics and privacy policy and procedures, and determine how they apply to your remote work situation.

Analyse legislation and standards that relate to IP, ethics and privacy in ICT, such as the Privacy Act 1988 (Cth), the Australian Privacy Principles, the Copyright Act 1968 (Cth), the Code of Ethics for Professional Conduct by the Australian Computer Society, etc.

Contribute to policy and procedures improvements in code of ethics and privacy policy documents in the ICT industry, by providing feedback, suggestions and recommendations based on your experience and expertise.

Use technology competently and securely to deliver education and training remotely, such as using encryption, passwords, firewalls, antivirus software, VPNs, etc.

Uphold your professional and ethical obligations while working remotely, such as maintaining supervision, client confidentiality, communication, quality of service, etc.

CHAPTER 6 WORKSHOP:
E-GOVERNMENT & DIGITAL TRANSFORMATION

In this workshop, you will learn about the benefits and challenges of e-government and digital transformation, and how to apply ethical principles and best practices to your projects. You will work in groups to analyse case studies and propose solutions based on the following topics:

E-GOVERNMENT & CITIZEN ENGAGEMENT

E-government is the use of information and communication technologies (ICT) to deliver public services, improve governance, and increase citizen participation. E-government can enhance transparency, accountability, efficiency, and responsiveness of public administration. However, e-government also poses risks such as digital divide, cyberattacks, data breaches, and surveillance. To ensure that e-government is inclusive, secure, and respectful of human rights, you need to consider the following aspects:

Accessibility: How can you ensure that all citizens have equal access to e-government services, regardless of their location, income, education, disability, or language?

Usability: How can you design user-friendly interfaces and processes that meet the needs and expectations of diverse users?

Interoperability: How can you enable seamless integration and exchange of data and services across different platforms, systems, and agencies?

Participation: How can you engage citizens in the design, implementation, and evaluation of e-government services, and foster a culture of co-creation and collaboration?

Trust: How can you protect the privacy and security of citizens' data and transactions, and ensure that they have control over their own information?

SMART CITIES & ETHICAL URBANIZATION

Smart cities are urban areas that use ICT to improve the quality of life, sustainability, and resilience of their communities. Smart cities can leverage data analytics, artificial intelligence, internet of things, cloud computing, and other technologies to optimize urban planning, management, and services. However, smart cities also raise ethical issues such as social justice, environmental impact, human dignity, and democratic governance. To ensure that smart cities are fair, green, and human-centered, you need to consider the following aspects:

Equity: How can you ensure that smart city initiatives benefit all citizens equally, and do not create or exacerbate social inequalities or discrimination?

Ecology: How can you ensure that smart city initiatives reduce the environmental footprint and enhance the natural resources of urban areas?

Empathy: How can you ensure that smart city initiatives respect the diversity and dignity of human beings, and do not dehumanize or alienate them?

Empowerment: How can you ensure that smart city initiatives empower citizens to participate in decision-making processes and shape their own urban futures?

REMOTE WORK & PRIVACY

Remote work is the practice of working from a location other than a traditional office or workplace. Remote work can offer flexibility, convenience, productivity, and cost savings for both employers and employees. However, remote work also poses challenges such as communication, collaboration, motivation, and well-being. Moreover, remote work can have implications for privacy rights and obligations of both parties. To ensure that remote work is effective, safe, and respectful of privacy, you need to consider the following aspects:

Communication: How can you establish clear and frequent communication channels and protocols with your remote team members and managers?

Collaboration: How can you use online tools and platforms to facilitate teamwork and coordination among your remote colleagues?

Motivation: How can you set realistic goals and expectations for your remote work performance and outcomes?

Well-being: How can you maintain a healthy work-life balance and avoid stress or isolation when working remotely?

Privacy: How can you protect your personal data and devices from unauthorized access or misuse when working remotely? How can you comply with the privacy policies and regulations of your employer or clients when working remotely?

To complete this workshop exercise, you will need to:

- Form groups of 4-5 participants.
- Choose one topic from the list above.
- Read the case study provided for your topic.
- Discuss the ethical issues and challenges presented in the case study.
- Propose a solution that addresses the ethical aspects of your topic.
- Prepare a presentation that summarizes your analysis and solution.
- Present your findings to the rest of the workshop participants.

CHAPTER 7:
IMPACT OF IT ON SOCIETY

CHAPTER SUMMARY

Information technology (IT) has transformed the way we communicate, work, learn and play. In this article, I will summarize the main points of chapter 7 of the book "IT Governance, Policy, Ethics and Law", which explores the impact of IT on society.

Social media and online behaviour. Social media platforms such as Facebook, Twitter and Instagram allow us to connect with people around the world, share our opinions and interests, and access information and entertainment. However, they also pose some challenges and risks, such as cyberbullying, fake news, privacy breaches and addiction. We need to be aware of these issues and use social media responsibly and ethically.

Technology for social good. IT can also be used to address social problems and improve the lives of people in need. For example, IT can help with disaster relief, health care, education, environmental protection and human rights. There are many initiatives and organizations that use IT for social good, such as the United Nations, the Red Cross, Khan Academy and Wikipedia. We should support and participate in these efforts to make a positive difference in the world.

Accessibility and inclusion. IT can also help to reduce barriers and inequalities for people with disabilities, minorities, women and other marginalized groups. For example, IT can provide assistive devices, adaptive software, online learning and remote work opportunities for people with disabilities. IT can also promote diversity, inclusion and empowerment for people from different backgrounds, cultures and perspectives. We should respect and celebrate the diversity of people in the IT field and society at large.

7.1. SOCIAL MEDIA & ONLINE BEHAVIOUR

Social media platforms have become an integral part of our lives, connecting us with people, information and entertainment.

There are significant risks for individuals and organisations, such as cyberattacks, privacy breaches, misinformation and ethical dilemmas. How can we use social media responsibly and safely, while enjoying its benefits?

PROTECT YOUR DATA & DEVICES

One of the main threats of social media is that hackers can exploit the data you share online to launch cyberattacks, steal your identity or access your accounts. To prevent this, you should:

- Use strong passwords and change them regularly.
- Enable two-factor authentication for your accounts.
- Avoid clicking on suspicious links or attachments.
- Update your software and antivirus regularly.
- Review your privacy settings and limit what you share publicly.
- Be careful when using public Wi-Fi or devices.

BE RESPECTFUL & ETHICAL

Another challenge of social media is that it can amplify negative emotions, opinions and behaviours, such as anger, hatred, discrimination and harassment. To avoid this, you should:

- Think before you post or comment.
- Respect the views and feelings of others.
- Avoid spreading rumours or false information.
- Report or block abusive or offensive content.
- Follow the rules and guidelines of each platform.
- Seek help if you experience cyberbullying or distress.

LEARN AND GROW

Social media can also be a valuable source of learning and growth, if used wisely and critically. You can:

- Follow reputable sources of information and news.
- Verify the accuracy and credibility of what you read or watch.
- Seek diverse perspectives and opinions.
- Engage in constructive and respectful dialogue.
- Explore new topics and interests.
- Share your knowledge and skills with others.

Social media is a powerful tool that can have positive or negative impacts on society, depending on how we use it. By following these tips, you can make the most of social media, while protecting yourself and others from its risks.

THE NEED FOR ETHICAL POLICIES

Ethical policies are not only beneficial for individuals and society, but also for IT professionals and organizations. They can help to foster trust, reputation, innovation, and competitiveness in the IT sector. They can also prevent or mitigate legal, financial, and reputational damages that may result from unethical IT practices.

Some examples of ethical policies that can be adopted or implemented in the IT field are:

Data protection and privacy policies. These policies aim to protect the personal data of users and customers from unauthorized access, use, disclosure, or deletion. They also specify the rights and obligations of data subjects and data controllers regarding data collection, processing, storage, and transfer.

Cybersecurity policies. These policies aim to ensure the security and integrity of IT systems and networks from malicious attacks or threats. They also define the roles and responsibilities of IT staff and users regarding cybersecurity measures, such as encryption, authentication, backup, and incident response.

Social responsibility policies. These policies aim to promote the positive social impact of IT and to minimize its negative effects on society and the environment. They also encourage the involvement of IT stakeholders in social issues, such as digital inclusion, education, health care, and sustainability.

Professional ethics policies. These policies aim to uphold the ethical standards and principles of the IT profession. They also provide guidance and codes of conduct for IT professionals regarding their duties, rights, and responsibilities towards their clients, employers, colleagues, and society.

Ethical policies are not static or universal. They need to be updated and adapted to the changing IT landscape and to the diverse cultural and legal contexts. They also need to be communicated and enforced effectively to ensure compliance and accountability. Moreover, they need to be supported by ethical education and awareness programs that foster a culture of ethics among IT stakeholders.

Ethical policies are not a burden or a constraint for IT. They are an opportunity and a necessity for IT to contribute positively to society and to achieve its full potential.

PRIVACY PROTECTION & DATA SHARING

As an IT professional, you have a responsibility to protect the privacy of your clients, customers, and users. Privacy is a fundamental human right, and it is also essential for trust, innovation, and competitiveness in the digital economy. However, privacy protection is not always easy or straightforward, especially when it comes to data sharing. Data sharing can have many benefits, such as improving efficiency, quality, and collaboration, but it can also pose significant risks, such as data breaches, identity theft, and discrimination.

How can you balance the need for data sharing with the respect for privacy?

Know the law. Different countries and regions have different laws and regulations regarding privacy and data protection. You should be aware of the legal requirements and obligations that apply to your data processing activities and comply with them accordingly. For example, if you are dealing with personal data from the European Union, you should follow the General Data Protection Regulation (GDPR), which sets high standards for data protection and gives individuals more rights and control over their data.

Know your data. Before you share any data, you should know what kind of data you have, where it came from, how it was collected, what it is used for, and who has access to it. You should also classify your data according to its sensitivity and value and apply appropriate security measures to protect it. For example, you should encrypt sensitive data such as health records or financial information, and limit access to authorized personnel only.

Know your purpose. You should only share data for a specific and legitimate purpose that is compatible with the original purpose of collection. You should not share data for purposes that are unrelated, incompatible, or harmful to the individuals or groups involved. For example, you should not share customer data with third parties for marketing or advertising purposes without their consent.

Know your partners. You should only share data with trustworthy and reliable partners who have a similar or higher level of privacy protection than you. You should also establish clear and transparent agreements with your partners that specify the terms and conditions of data sharing, such as the purpose, scope, duration, security, and accountability of data processing. You should also monitor and audit your partners' compliance with the agreements and the applicable laws.

Know your limits. You should only share the minimum amount of data that is necessary to achieve the purpose of data sharing. You should also respect the rights and preferences of the individuals or groups whose data you are sharing and give them choices and control over their data. For example, you should inform them about the data sharing activities, obtain their consent when required, allow them to access, correct, or delete their data when possible, and respond to their complaints or requests promptly.

ONLINE HARASSMENT & CYBERBULLYING

Online harassment and cyberbullying are serious issues that affect many people, especially children and adolescents. They can cause emotional, psychological and even physical harm to the victims, as well as damage their reputation and relationships.

ONLINE HARASSMENT & CYBERBULLYING

Online harassment and cyberbullying are forms of bullying that use digital technologies, such as social media, messaging platforms, gaming platforms and mobile phones, to intimidate, humiliate, threaten or harm someone else. They can include:

- Spreading lies, rumors or embarrassing photos or videos about someone online
- Sending or requesting nude or nearly nude images or videos (also known as sexting)
- Excluding someone from online groups or conversations
- Making fun of someone's appearance, identity, beliefs or abilities
- Stalking someone online or offline
- Impersonating someone online or hacking their accounts
- Sending hateful or violent messages or threats

Online harassment and cyberbullying can happen to anyone, but some groups are more vulnerable than others, such as girls, LGBTQ+ youth, ethnic minorities and people with disabilities. Online harassment and cyberbullying can have negative effects on the victims' mental health, self-esteem, academic performance and social skills. They can also increase the risk of depression, anxiety, loneliness, self-harm and suicide.

PREVENTING HARASSMENT & CYBERBULLYING

The best way to prevent online harassment and cyberbullying is to promote a culture of respect, kindness and empathy online. Here are some tips to help you do that:

- Be aware of what you post online and how it might affect others. Think before you share something that could be hurtful, offensive or inappropriate.
- Respect other people's privacy and boundaries. Do not share personal or private information about someone else without their consent. Do not send or ask for nude or nearly nude images or videos.
- Be a positive role model for others. Use positive language and compliments online. Support those who are being harassed or bullied online. Report any abusive or harmful content or behaviour you see online.
- Educate yourself and others about online safety and digital citizenship. Learn how to protect your personal information, passwords and devices online. Learn how to recognize and avoid scams, phishing and malware. Learn how to use privacy settings and blocking features on different platforms. Learn about your rights and responsibilities online.

COPING WITH HARASSMENT & CYBERBULLYING

If you are experiencing online harassment or cyberbullying, you are not alone and you do not deserve it. Here are some steps you can take to cope with it:

- Do not respond or retaliate to the harasser or bully. This might only make things worse or escalate the situation. Instead, ignore them or block them if possible.
- Save the evidence of the harassment or bullying. Take screenshots or record the messages, posts or comments that are abusive or harmful. This can help you report them later or seek legal action if needed.
- Report the harassment or bullying to the platform where it happened. Most platforms have policies and tools to deal with online abuse and hate speech. You can also report the harasser or bully to their school, employer or authorities if they are breaking the law.

- Seek support from someone you trust. Talk to a friend, family member, teacher, counsellor or helpline about what you are going through. They can offer you emotional support, advice and resources to help you cope.
- Take care of yourself. Online harassment and cyberbullying can affect your physical and mental health. Try to do things that make you happy and relaxed, such as hobbies, exercise, meditation or music. Avoid drugs and alcohol as they can worsen your mood and health.

STOPPING HARASSMENT & CYBERBULLYING

Online harassment and cyberbullying are not acceptable and should not be tolerated. You have the right to be safe and respected online. Here are some ways you can help stop online harassment and cyberbullying:

- Speak up against online abuse and hate speech. If you see someone being harassed or bullied online, do not stay silent or join in. Instead, show your support for the victim by sending them a message of encouragement or solidarity. You can also challenge the harasser or bully by calling out their behaviour or expressing your disagreement.
- Join or start a campaign against online harassment and cyberbullying. There are many organizations and movements that work to raise awareness and prevent online abuse and violence. You can join their campaigns by signing petitions, sharing stories, creating content or organizing events. You can also start your own campaign by using hashtags, creating a website or blog, or making a video or podcast.
- Advocate for change in policies and laws. You can use your voice and influence to demand better policies and laws that protect people from online harassment and cyberbullying. You can contact your local representatives, write letters, submit proposals or participate in public consultations. You can also join or support groups that lobby for change in this area.

Online harassment and cyberbullying are serious problems that affect many people around the world. They can have negative impacts on individuals and society. As an IT expert, I hope that my advice can help you prevent, cope with and stop online harassment and cyberbullying.

Remember that you are not alone, and you have the power to make a difference online.

FREE EXPRESSION & RESPONSIBLE CONDUCT

WHY FREE EXPRESSION IS IMPORTANT

Free expression is the right to express one's opinions, beliefs, ideas and information without undue interference or censorship. It is a fundamental human right that is essential for democracy, diversity, creativity and social progress. Free expression also supports the development and dissemination of knowledge, which is the core function of IT.

RESPONSIBLE CONDUCT

Responsible conduct is the obligation to act in accordance with ethical principles, legal norms and social values. It is a duty that applies to individuals, organizations and governments that use or provide IT services or products. Responsible conduct ensures that IT is used for good purposes, respects the rights and interests of others, protects the common good and minimizes harm.

BALANCING FREE EXPRESSION AND RESPONSIBLE CONDUCT

Balancing free expression and responsible conduct is not an easy task, as there may be conflicts or trade-offs between them. For example, allowing free expression may expose sensitive data or enable harmful content, while restricting free expression may limit innovation or diversity. Therefore, balancing free expression and responsible conduct requires careful consideration of the context, the stakeholders, the benefits and the risks involved in each situation.

Some general guidelines that can help to achieve this balance are:

- Adopt a governance framework that defines the roles, responsibilities, objectives and activities related to IT in your organization or sector. A governance framework can help to align IT with your mission, vision and values, as well as with external standards and regulations.
- Follow ethical principles that guide your decision-making and behaviour in relation to IT. Ethical principles can help you to identify and resolve moral issues, such as fairness, justice, autonomy, privacy and accountability.

- Comply with legal norms that regulate your use or provision of IT. Legal norms can help you to respect the rights and obligations of yourself and others, as well as to avoid or mitigate legal risks or liabilities.
- Engage with social values that reflect the expectations and preferences of your stakeholders and society at large. Social values can help you to understand the impact of IT on different groups and interests, as well as to foster trust and legitimacy.

7.2. TECHNOLOGY FOR SOCIAL GOOD

ETHICAL INNOVATION & POSITIVE IMPACT

Ethical Innovation & Positive Impact: How to Use Technology for Social Good

How can we ensure that our innovations are aligned with our values and contribute to positive social impact?

DEFINE YOUR PURPOSE AND VISION

Before you start developing or implementing any technology solution, you need to have a clear idea of what problem you are trying to solve, who you are serving, and what impact you want to achieve. This will help you set your goals, measure your progress, and communicate your value proposition to your stakeholders.

ENGAGE WITH YOUR USERS AND BENEFICIARIES

Technology for social good should be designed with and for the people who will use it and benefit from it. You need to understand their needs, preferences, expectations, and feedback. You also need to respect their rights, dignity, privacy, and autonomy. Engaging with your users and beneficiaries will help you create solutions that are relevant, accessible, inclusive, and empowering.

CONSIDER THE BROADER CONTEXT AND IMPLICATIONS

Technology for social good should not operate in isolation, but in relation to the social, cultural, economic, environmental, and political context in which it is deployed. You need to consider how your solution will interact with other systems, actors, and norms. You also need to anticipate the potential positive and negative consequences of your solution, both intended and unintended, and mitigate any risks or harms.

ADOPT ETHICAL PRINCIPLES AND STANDARDS

Technology for social good should be guided by ethical principles and standards that reflect your values and commitments. You need to define what ethical innovation means for you and your organization, and how you will operationalize it in your processes, practices, and policies. You also need to align your solution with the relevant laws, regulations, codes of conduct, and best practices in your field.

EVALUATE YOUR IMPACT AND LEARN FROM YOUR EXPERIENCE

Technology for social good should be continuously monitored and evaluated to assess its impact and effectiveness. You need to collect data and evidence that show how your solution is performing, what outcomes it is producing, and what impact it is having on your users, beneficiaries, and society at large. You also need to learn from your experience, reflect on your successes and failures, and improve your solution accordingly.

THE ESSENCE OF TECHNOLOGY FOR SOCIAL GOOD

Technology needs to be guided by ethical principles, aligned with social values, and informed by evidence-based practices.

TECHNOLOGY FOR SOCIAL GOOD

Technology for social good is the use of technology to address social problems, such as poverty, inequality, health, education, environment, and human rights. Technology for social good can take many forms, such as:

- Digital platforms that connect people, resources, and information across borders and sectors.
- Mobile applications that provide access to essential services, such as health care, education, and banking.
- Data analytics that help measure and improve the impact of social interventions.
- Artificial intelligence that enhances human capabilities and supports decision making.
- Blockchain that enables transparency and accountability in transactions and governance.
- Internet of things that enables smart and sustainable solutions for energy, water, and waste management.

WHY IS TECHNOLOGY FOR SOCIAL GOOD IMPORTANT?

Technology for social good is important because it can help address some of the most pressing challenges facing humanity today. Technology can help:

- Empower people and communities to participate in social and economic development.
- Enhance the efficiency and effectiveness of social organizations and programs.

- Expand the reach and scale of social impact
- Foster innovation and creativity in solving social problems.
- Promote collaboration and cooperation among diverse stakeholders.
- Inspire hope and optimism for a better future.

HOW TO ENSURE TECHNOLOGY FOR SOCIAL GOOD?

Technology can also have negative or unintended consequences, such as:

- Exacerbating existing inequalities or creating new ones.
- Displacing or exploiting workers or consumers.
- Violating privacy or security of individuals or groups.
- Causing harm or damage to the environment or society.
- Eroding trust or accountability in institutions or systems.

Therefore, technology for social good needs to be designed, developed, deployed, and evaluated with care and responsibility. Some of the key steps to ensure technology for social good are:

- Define the problem and the desired outcome clearly and comprehensively.
- Engage with the affected stakeholders and beneficiaries throughout the process.
- Conduct research and analysis to understand the context and the evidence.
- Apply ethical principles and frameworks to guide decision making.
- Adopt best practices and standards for quality and performance.
- Monitor and evaluate the results and impacts of the technology.
- Learn from feedback and experience and adapt accordingly.

Technology needs to be aligned with human values, driven by social purpose, and informed by best practice. Technology for social good is not just about what we do with technology, but also about how we do it.

POLICIES GUIDING ETHICAL INNOVATION

It is important to have policies that guide ethical innovation and ensure that it aligns with the values and needs of the people it serves.

ETHICAL FRAMEWORK FOR INNOVATION

One possible ethical framework for innovation is based on the Principles for Digital Development, which are nine guidelines that help integrate best practices into technology-enabled programs. They include:

- **Design with the user**. Involve the user throughout the design process and test the solution in real contexts.
- **Understand the existing ecosystem**. Assess the strengths and weaknesses of the current system and identify potential partners and stakeholders.
- **Design for scale**. Plan for growth and sustainability from the start and consider how to reach more users over time.
- **Build for sustainability**. Secure long-term funding and support and ensure that the solution can operate independently of external resources.
- **Be data driven**. Collect, analyse and use data to inform decision making and improve performance.
- **Use open standards, open data, open source, and open innovation**. Adopt interoperable and transparent approaches that facilitate collaboration and sharing of knowledge and resources.
- **Reuse and improve**. Learn from existing solutions and adapt them to the local context and needs.
- **Do no harm**. Assess and mitigate the risks and harms that the innovation may cause to the users, communities and environment.
- **Address privacy and security**. Protect the data and information of the users and respect their rights and preferences.

Ethical innovation is about ensuring that technology is human-centered, inclusive, responsible and impactful. By following these principles, innovators can design solutions that are more likely to achieve social good and avoid unintended consequences.

EDUCATION REVOLUTION

Education is essential for personal and social development, as well as economic growth and poverty reduction. However, many people around the world face barriers to accessing quality education, such as lack of resources, teachers, or electricity.

Fortunately, there are many innovative solutions that use technology to overcome these challenges and foster social and emotional skills among learners. Social and emotional skills are crucial for collaboration, communication, and problem-solving in the 21st century. Here are some examples of how technology can help:

SOLAR-POWERED LEARNING

One of the basic requirements for education is electricity. Without it, students cannot use computers, access the internet, or even study at night. Many rural and remote areas lack reliable power sources, which limits their educational opportunities.

To address this problem, some projects have developed solar-powered devices that can provide electricity and learning tools to students. For example, MPOWERD's Luci Light is a lightweight lamp that can be charged by the sun and provide up to 12 hours of illumination. The company distributes these lamps to children in developing countries, where they can use them to read and do homework after dark.

Another example is a giant shipping container that contains computers and internet access powered by solar panels. This project, called Solar Learning Lab, brings digital education to students in remote locations, where they can learn new skills and access online courses.

PERSONALIZED AND ENGAGING LEARNING

Another challenge for education is how to tailor the learning experience to the needs and interests of each student. Traditional classrooms often use a one-size-fits-all approach that may not suit every learner's pace, level, or style.

Technology can help create more personalized and engaging learning environments that adapt to each student's progress and preferences. For example, adaptive learning platforms use artificial intelligence to analyse data and provide customized feedback and guidance to learners. These platforms can also gamify the learning process by adding elements of fun, competition, and rewards.

Another example is virtual reality (VR), which can create immersive and interactive experiences that stimulate curiosity and creativity. VR can also expose students to different cultures, perspectives, and scenarios that they may not encounter in real life.

EMPOWERING COMMUNITIES

A third challenge for education is how to involve and empower communities in the learning process. Education is not only a matter of individual achievement, but also a collective effort that requires collaboration and support from parents, teachers, and peers.

Technology can help connect and empower communities by facilitating communication, information sharing, and participation. For example, mobile phones can be used to record and distribute local stories that improve literacy and cultural awareness. They can also be used to send voice messages that teach mothers how to care for and educate their young children.

Another example is online platforms that enable peer-to-peer learning and mentoring among students from different backgrounds and locations. These platforms can also allow teachers to access professional development resources and network with other educators.

Technology needs to be accompanied by effective policies, practices, and partnerships that ensure its appropriate use and impact.

DATA PRIVACY & SECURITY

Data privacy is the right of individuals to control how their personal data is collected, used, shared and stored by others. Data security is the protection of data from unauthorized access, use, modification or destruction. Data privacy and security are closely related, but not the same. Data privacy focuses on the rights and choices of individuals, while data security focuses on the technical and organizational measures to safeguard data.

WHY ARE DATA PRIVACY AND SECURITY IMPORTANT FOR SOCIAL GOOD?

Technology for social good is the use of technology to address social or environmental challenges, such as poverty, health, education, climate change or human rights. Technology for social good can have many benefits, such as improving access to information, services and opportunities, empowering marginalized groups, enhancing collaboration and innovation, and creating positive social impact.

However, technology for social good can also pose risks to data privacy and security. For example:

- Technology for social good may collect sensitive personal data from vulnerable populations, such as refugees, children or minorities, who may not be aware of or consent to how their data is used or shared.
- Technology for social good may expose personal data to cyberattacks, data breaches or misuse by malicious actors, such as hackers, criminals or authoritarian regimes.
- Technology for social good may violate data protection laws or ethical principles, such as transparency, accountability or fairness, which may harm the trust and reputation of the organizations involved or the beneficiaries of the technology.

Therefore, data privacy and security are essential for ensuring that technology for social good is responsible, ethical and sustainable.

IMPLEMENTING BEST PRACTICES FOR DATA PRIVACY AND SECURITY

Here are some of the best practices for data privacy and security for technology for social good:

Assess and classify data. First, assess your business data comprehensively to understand what types of data you have. Then, classify your data according to its sensitivity and the value it adds to your business.

Practice minimal data collection. A rule of thumb when collecting data is to only collect what you need. Avoid collecting unnecessary or excessive data that may increase the risk of exposure or misuse.

Get consent and be transparent. Before collecting or using someone's data, get a clear go-ahead from the user. And this shouldn't be buried in jargon; it should be as clear as day. Let them know why and how you are collecting their data, how you will use it, who you will share it with and how long you will keep it.

Practice robust data security. Use encryption, authentication, access control and other technical measures to protect your data from unauthorized access or loss. Also implement policies, procedures and training to ensure that your staff and partners follow the best practices for data security.

Encourage education and awareness. Privacy can become a way to engage with your customers and show them you respect their data. Educate them about their rights and choices regarding their data, and provide them with easy ways to access, update or delete their data if they wish.

Create achievable policies and SLAs with third parties. If you work with third parties who handle your data, such as cloud providers, vendors or contractors, make sure they adhere to the same standards of data privacy and security as you do. Establish clear policies and service level agreements (SLAs) that define the roles, responsibilities and expectations of each party.

By following the best practices outlined in this article, you can ensure that your technology respects the rights and interests of your users and beneficiaries, while also creating value and impact for your organization and

ADDRESSING ETHICAL DILEMMAS

Identify the stakeholders and their values. Who are the people or groups that are affected by the technology, directly or indirectly? What are their needs, preferences, rights, and responsibilities? How do they value the benefits and risks of the technology?

Analyse the ethical issues and principles. What are the moral values or principles that are relevant to the technology and its use? For example, privacy, autonomy, justice, transparency, accountability, etc. How do they conflict or align with each other and with the stakeholders' values?

Evaluate the alternatives and consequences. What are the possible actions or decisions that can be taken regarding the technology and its use? What are the potential outcomes and impacts of each alternative on the stakeholders and their values? How likely and how severe are they?

Choose the best option and justify it. Based on the analysis and evaluation, what is the most ethical option that balances the interests and values of all stakeholders? How can you explain and defend your choice using ethical reasoning and evidence?

Monitor and revise as needed. How can you monitor the implementation and effects of your choice? How can you identify and address any new or unforeseen ethical issues that may arise? How can you learn from your experience and improve your ethical decision-making in the future?

7.3. ACCESSIBILITY & INCLUSION

THE DIGITAL DIVIDE

The digital divide is the gap that exists between those who have access to digital technology and the internet, and those who do not. It affects millions of people in Australia, especially in remote and regional areas, low-income households, older people, and people who speak a language other than English at home.

The digital divide can limit people's ability to participate in society, access essential services, communicate with others, learn new skills, and find opportunities. It can also increase social isolation, disadvantage, and inequality.

There are ways to bridge the digital divide and promote digital inclusion. Digital inclusion means ensuring that everyone can access, afford, and use digital technology and the internet effectively. It also means helping people develop their digital ability, which is the knowledge, skills, and confidence to use digital technology safely and creatively.

HOW TO MEASURE DIGITAL INCLUSION

One way to measure digital inclusion is to use the Australian Digital Inclusion Index (ADII). The ADII is a tool that uses survey data to measure digital inclusion across three dimensions: access, affordability, and digital ability. The ADII also explores how these dimensions vary across the country and across different social groups.

The latest ADII report shows that digital inclusion at the national level is improving, but there are still significant gaps and challenges. For example, 11 per cent of Australians are "highly excluded" from digital services, meaning they do not have access to affordable internet or don't know how to use it. That equates to about 2.8 million people.

The report also shows that the divide between metropolitan and regional areas has narrowed but remains marked. People in capital cities are more likely to be online than those in regional areas, and unsurprisingly, low-income earners struggle to connect. There are different reasons for the digital divide — many older Australians lack online literacy, while in some areas a lack of infrastructure limits options.

BRIDGING THE DIGITAL DIVIDE

Bridging the digital divide requires a collaborative effort from various stakeholders, including governments, businesses, community organisations, educators, researchers, and users themselves. Some of the strategies that can help bridge the digital divide are:

- Improving the availability and quality of internet infrastructure and services in remote and regional areas
- Providing affordable and flexible internet plans and devices for low-income households
- Offering free or subsidised access to public internet facilities such as libraries, community centres, or Wi-Fi hotspots
- Developing and delivering digital literacy programs that cater to the needs and preferences of different groups of users
- Supporting online safety and security awareness and education
- Encouraging and facilitating online participation and engagement in social, cultural, economic, and civic activities
- Promoting innovation and creativity in using digital technology for personal and professional development

LEGAL & ETHICAL IMPERATIVES

Accessibility and inclusion are not only good practices, but also legal and ethical obligations for organisations that provide products, services or information to the public.

WHAT IS ACCESSIBILITY AND INCLUSION

Accessibility involves designing systems to optimise access for people with disability or other diverse needs. Inclusion is about giving equal access and opportunities to everyone wherever possible, and respecting and valuing diversity.

Accessibility and inclusion benefit not only people with disability, but also other groups such as older people, people from different cultural backgrounds, people with low literacy or digital skills, and people in remote areas.

WHAT ARE THE LEGAL AND ETHICAL FRAMEWORKS FOR ACCESSIBILITY AND INCLUSION?

There are several laws and standards that require organisations to provide accessible and inclusive products, services or information. These include:

The Disability Discrimination Act 1992 (DDA), which makes it unlawful to discriminate against people with disability in various areas of public life, such as employment, education, accommodation, access to premises, goods, services and facilities.

The Web Content Accessibility Guidelines (WCAG), which are internationally recognised standards for making web content accessible to people with disability. The Australian Government has adopted WCAG as the minimum level of accessibility for all government websites.

The United Nations Convention on the Rights of Persons with Disabilities (CRPD), which is an international treaty that promotes and protects the human rights of people with disability. Australia ratified the CRPD in 2008 and has obligations to ensure that people with disability can access information, communication, technology, education, health, employment, justice and other services on an equal basis with others.

Apart from legal compliance, accessibility and inclusion are also ethical imperatives for organisations that want to demonstrate social responsibility, respect for human dignity, and commitment to diversity and innovation .

IMPLEMENTING ACCESSIBILITY AND INCLUSION

To implement accessibility and inclusion effectively, organisations need to adopt a holistic approach that covers all aspects of their operations, such as:

Developing an Accessibility Action Plan that outlines the organisation's vision, goals, strategies, actions, responsibilities, timelines and measures for improving accessibility and inclusion for people with disability as employees, customers and stakeholders.

Making workplace adjustments that anticipate the needs of people with disability and provide reasonable accommodations for individuals, such as ergonomic equipment, assistive technology, flexible working hours and locations.

Communicating and marketing in accessible ways that ensure that all communication channels, such as websites, social media, emails, brochures, videos and podcasts are accessible to people with disability and can be adjusted for individual preferences.

Designing products and services that value people with disability as customers, clients or service users and address their needs when developing and delivering products or services.

Recruiting and retaining people with disability as employees at all levels of the organisation and providing them with career development opportunities.

Engaging suppliers and partners that reflect and enable the organisation's commitment to accessibility and inclusion and expect them to follow best practices.

Innovating practices and processes that continually strive to do better in accessibility and inclusion and seek feedback from people with disability to improve outcomes.

PROMOTING INCLUSIVITY

WHY IS INCLUSIVITY IMPORTANT?

Inclusivity is not only a moral duty, but also a strategic advantage for organizations. By promoting inclusivity, organizations can:

- Enhance their reputation and trust among customers, employees, partners and regulators.
- Increase their innovation and creativity by tapping into diverse perspectives and experiences.
- Reduce their legal and ethical risks by complying with relevant laws and standards.
- Improve their efficiency and effectiveness by avoiding bias, errors and waste.

PROMOTING INCLUSIVITY

Promoting inclusivity requires a holistic approach that involves all stakeholders in the IT governance, policy, ethics and law domains. Here are some best practices that I recommend based on my research and experience:

- Establish a clear vision and strategy for inclusivity that aligns with the organization's mission, values and goals.

- Define and communicate the roles and responsibilities of each stakeholder in ensuring inclusivity throughout the IT lifecycle.
- Conduct regular assessments and audits to measure the level of inclusivity and identify gaps and opportunities for improvement.
- Provide training and education to raise awareness and skills on inclusivity issues and solutions.
- Implement policies and standards that support inclusivity principles and practices.
- Adopt tools and methods that enable inclusive design, development, testing and evaluation of IT solutions.
- Engage with diverse groups of users, customers, experts and communities to solicit feedback and input on IT solutions.
- Monitor and review the impacts and outcomes of IT solutions on different groups of people and society at large.

CHAPTER 7 WORKSHOP: IMPACT OF IT ON SOCIETY

As an expert consultant in IT Governance, Policy, Ethics and Law, I have witnessed the profound impact of IT on society over the past 30 years. In this workshop, I will share with you some of the key issues and challenges that IT poses for society, as well as some of the opportunities and benefits that IT can bring for social good. The workshop will consist of three main parts, each focusing on a different topic related to the impact of IT on society. The topics are:

- Social Media and Online Behaviour
- Technology for Social Good
- Accessibility and Inclusion

For each topic, I will provide a brief introduction, followed by a group discussion and a practical exercise. The aim of the workshop is to help you understand the social implications of IT, and to develop your skills and knowledge in IT governance, policy, ethics and law.

PART 1: SOCIAL MEDIA & ONLINE BEHAVIOUR

Social media platforms such as Facebook, Twitter, Instagram and TikTok have revolutionized the way we communicate, share information, express ourselves and form relationships online. However, social media also comes with risks and challenges, such as cyberbullying, misinformation, privacy breaches, addiction and polarization. In this part of the workshop, we will explore the following questions:

- How does social media affect our online behaviour and identity?
- What are the ethical and legal issues related to social media use?
- How can we use social media responsibly and respectfully?

The group discussion will be based on a case study of a real-life social media controversy. The practical exercise will involve creating a social media policy for a fictional organization.

PART 2: TECHNOLOGY FOR SOCIAL GOOD

Technology can be a powerful tool for social good, especially in areas such as education, health, environment, human rights and disaster relief. Technology can enable access to information, resources, services and opportunities for people who are marginalized or disadvantaged. Technology can also empower people to participate in social change and innovation. In this part of the workshop, we will explore the following questions:

- How can technology contribute to social good?
- What are the ethical and legal issues related to technology for social good?
- How can we evaluate the impact and effectiveness of technology for social good?

The group discussion will be based on a case study of a real-life technology for social good project. The practical exercise will involve designing a technology for social good solution for a fictional scenario.

PART 3: ACCESSIBILITY AND INCLUSION

Accessibility and inclusion are essential principles for ensuring that everyone can benefit from technology, regardless of their abilities, needs or preferences. Accessibility means that technology is designed and developed in a way that is usable by people with diverse characteristics, such as age, gender, culture, language, disability or literacy. Inclusion means that technology is used and implemented in a way that respects and values diversity, equity and participation. In this part of the workshop, we will explore the following questions:

- How does technology affect accessibility and inclusion?
- What are the ethical and legal issues related to accessibility and inclusion?
- How can we promote accessibility and inclusion in technology?

The group discussion will be based on a case study of a real-life accessibility and inclusion challenge. The practical exercise will involve testing and improving the accessibility and inclusion of a fictional website.

I hope you enjoy this workshop and learn something new about the impact of IT on society. Thank you for your attention.

CHAPTER 8:
EMPLOYEE IT USAGE & POLICIES

CHAPTER SUMMARY

Employee IT usage and privacy are complex and sensitive issues that involve **legal, ethical, social and technical aspects**. Employers have a duty to protect their business interests and assets, but also to respect the rights and expectations of their employees.

Employee IT usage and privacy policies are **essential tools for defining the acceptable and unacceptable use of IT** resources, such as computers, networks, email, internet, social media, mobile devices, etc. These policies should be clear, consistent, comprehensive and communicated to all employees.

Employee IT usage and privacy policies should be **aligned with the organization's objectives, values, culture and risk appetite**. They should also comply with the relevant laws and regulations, such as data protection, human rights, employment law, etc.

Employee IT usage and privacy policies should be supported by appropriate controls and measures, such as **monitoring, auditing, training, awareness, enforcement, sanctions**, etc. These controls and measures should be proportionate, transparent and fair.

Employee IT usage and privacy policies should be **reviewed and updated regularly** to reflect the changing needs and circumstances of the organization and its employees. They should also be evaluated for their effectiveness and impact.

In practical terms, this chapter helps managers and leaders to understand the importance and benefits of having sound employee IT usage and privacy policies. It also helps them to avoid or minimize the potential pitfalls and problems that may arise from poor or inadequate policies.

8.1. EMPLOYEE IT USAGE & PRIVACY

DEFINING THE DIGITAL LANDSCAPE

The digital landscape is the total collection of hardware, software, and content that interact with digital advertising. It includes email services, websites, computers, smartphones, videos, blog posts, and so on.

DEFINING THE DIGITAL LANDSCAPE

Defining the digital landscape is a critical step in planning for the path ahead. It helps organisations to understand the current and ever-changing state of play, the challenges and opportunities created by digital, and the best practices to follow.

It also helps to improve clarity and consensus on what digital means in different contexts and for different stakeholders.

Conduct a digital audit. Assess the current situation of your organisation in terms of its digital assets, capabilities, performance, and gaps. Identify what works well and what needs improvement.

Define your digital vision. Articulate your desired future state of your organisation in terms of its digital strategy, objectives, and outcomes. Align your vision with your organisational mission, values, and culture.

Analyse your digital environment. Scan the external factors that affect your organisation's digital landscape, such as competitors, customers, trends, technologies, regulations, and risks. Identify the opportunities and threats that arise from them.

Develop your digital roadmap. Create a plan of action that outlines how you will achieve your digital vision. Define the key initiatives, activities, resources, responsibilities, timelines, and metrics that will guide your implementation.

Monitor and evaluate your digital progress. Track and measure your results against your objectives and outcomes. Review and adjust your roadmap as needed based on feedback and learning.

By following these steps, you can create a clear and comprehensive definition of your digital landscape that will help you to leverage the power of digital for your organisation.

ESTABLISHING IT USAGE POLICIES

IT usage policies define the rules and expectations for the appropriate use of IT resources, such as computers, networks, software, data, and internet.

IT usage policies help to protect the organization from security risks, legal liabilities, and productivity losses. IT usage policies also help to ensure that IT resources are used efficiently and effectively to support the organization's goals and values.

Here are some best practices for establishing comprehensive IT usage policies:

Involve stakeholders from different departments and levels of the organization in the policy development process. This will help to ensure that the policies reflect the needs and perspectives of various users and managers, and that they are aligned with the organization's culture and strategy.

Conduct a risk assessment to identify the potential threats and vulnerabilities that the organization faces in relation to its IT resources. This will help to determine the scope and priorities of the policies, and to justify their implementation.

Review existing policies and procedures related to IT usage, such as security, privacy, compliance, ethics, and disaster recovery. This will help to avoid duplication or contradiction, and to identify any gaps or areas for improvement.

Use clear and concise language that is easy to understand and follow. Avoid technical jargon or legal terms that may confuse or intimidate the users. Use plain English and subheads to make the policies more readable.

Provide examples and scenarios to illustrate the dos and don'ts of IT usage. This will help to clarify the expectations and consequences of the policies, and to address common questions or issues that may arise.

Communicate the policies to all users and managers and provide training and awareness programs to ensure that they understand and comply with them. Use different channels and formats, such as emails, newsletters, posters, videos, webinars, or workshops, to reach a wide audience and reinforce the messages.

Monitor and enforce the policies regularly, and use tools and technologies, such as software or hardware controls, logs, audits, or reports, to track and measure IT usage. Provide feedback and recognition to users who follow the policies and take corrective action against those who violate them.

Review and update the policies periodically and solicit feedback from users and managers on their effectiveness and relevance. This will help to keep the policies current and responsive to changing needs and conditions.

EMPLOYEE PRIVACY

Employee privacy is the ability of employees to protect their personal information from being accessed or used by others without their consent. Personal information can include names, addresses, phone numbers, email addresses, photos, bank account details, tax file numbers, super fund information, drivers licence details and academic records. It can also include sensitive personal information such as health, sexuality, religious beliefs, criminal record, professional or trade union memberships.

As an employer, you have legal and ethical obligations to respect your employees' privacy and to handle their personal information in a responsible and transparent manner. This article will provide some best practices on how to do so, drawing on research and best practice from various sources.

LEGAL REQUIREMENTS

Depending on the size and nature of your business, you may be subject to different privacy laws and regulations. For example, the Privacy Act 1988 sets out requirements for collecting, storing, using and disclosing personal information for businesses with an annual turnover of $3 million or more, all private health service providers, a limited range of small businesses and all Australian Government agencies. These requirements are called the Australian Privacy Principles (APPs) and they also set out additional rules and higher standards for collecting and handling sensitive personal information.

If you are required to follow the APPs, you must have a privacy policy that explains how you comply with them. You must also take reasonable steps to protect personal information from misuse, interference, loss, unauthorised access, modification or disclosure. You must also provide access to and correction of personal information upon request by the individual concerned.

Even if you are not subject to the Privacy Act 1988, you may still have other legal obligations to respect employee privacy under other laws such as the Fair Work Act 2009, which requires all employers to keep certain personal information about employees in their employee records. You may also have contractual obligations to protect employee privacy under employment agreements or collective bargaining agreements.

BEST PRACTICE

Apart from complying with legal requirements, you should also adopt best practices to respect employee privacy as a matter of good business practice. Some of these best practices include:

Making a data inventory. You should identify what personal information you collect from your employees, why you collect it, how you store it, who has access to it and how long you keep it. You should also review your data collection practices regularly to ensure they are necessary and proportionate to your business needs.

Explaining the purpose of data collection. You should inform your employees about what personal information you collect from them, why you collect it and how you use it. You should also obtain their consent where required or appropriate. You should communicate this information clearly and transparently through your privacy policy, employee handbook or other means.

Performing a privacy impact assessment. You should assess the potential risks and benefits of collecting and using personal information from your employees. You should also consider the impact on their privacy rights and expectations. You should implement measures to minimise the risks and maximise the benefits of data collection and use.

Presenting documentation and responding to feedback. You should provide your employees with easy access to your privacy policy and other relevant documents that explain how you respect their privacy. You should also invite their feedback and suggestions on how to improve your privacy practices. You should respond to their queries and complaints promptly and respectfully.

Disclosing employee personal information to third parties. You should only disclose your employees' personal information to third parties when it is necessary for your business purposes or when you have a legal obligation or authorisation to do so. You should also ensure that the third parties have adequate privacy safeguards in place before sharing any personal information with them.

Using best practice to protect personal information. You should use appropriate technical and organisational measures to protect your employees' personal information from unauthorised or accidental access, use, modification or disclosure. These measures may include encryption, password protection, access control, audit trails, backups and data disposal.

ADHERING TO EMPLOYMENT LAWS

Employment laws are rules that regulate the relationship between employers and employees. They cover various aspects such as pay, leave, health and safety, discrimination, privacy and more.

HAVE A CLEAR IT USAGE POLICY

An IT usage policy is a document that explains the expectations and responsibilities of employees when using the company's IT resources, such as computers, internet, email, social media and data. It also outlines the consequences of violating the policy. Having a clear IT usage policy can help you:

- Protect your company's reputation, data and network from security breaches, cyberattacks and legal issues.
- Ensure your employees use the IT resources for work-related purposes and not for personal or inappropriate activities.
- Monitor and manage your employees' IT performance and productivity.
- Educate your employees about their rights and obligations regarding IT usage.

You can use an internet usage policy sample or template to create your own policy, but make sure to tailor it to your specific industry, business and legal requirements.

COMPLY WITH PRIVACY LAWS

Privacy laws are rules that protect the personal information of individuals from unauthorized access, use or disclosure. Personal information can include names, addresses, phone numbers, email addresses, bank details, health records and more. As an employer, you must comply with privacy laws when collecting, storing, using and disclosing personal information of your employees or customers. To comply with privacy laws, you should:

- Have a privacy policy that explains how you handle personal information in your business.
- Obtain consent from individuals before collecting or using their personal information.

- Only collect and use personal information for legitimate business purposes.
- Store personal information securely and dispose of it when no longer needed.
- Respect the rights of individuals to access, correct or delete their personal information.
- Report any data breaches or privacy complaints to the relevant authorities.

You can refer to the Privacy Act 1988 and the Australian Privacy Principles for more guidance on privacy laws in Australia.

FOLLOW ANTI-DISCRIMINATION LAWS

Anti-discrimination laws are rules that prohibit unfair treatment of individuals based on their personal characteristics, such as age, gender, race, religion, disability or sexual orientation. As an employer, you must follow anti-discrimination laws when hiring, managing or terminating employees. To follow anti-discrimination laws, you should:

- Promote a culture of diversity, inclusion and respect in your workplace.
- Provide equal opportunities for all employees regardless of their personal characteristics.
- Avoid asking or making assumptions about an employee's personal characteristics.
- Accommodate the needs of employees with disabilities or special circumstances.
- Prevent and address any incidents of bullying, harassment or discrimination in your workplace.
- Respond to any complaints or grievances promptly and fairly.

You can refer to the Fair Work Act 2009 and the state and federal anti-discrimination laws for more guidance on anti-discrimination laws in Australia.

ETHICAL TECH & ORGANIZATIONAL SUCCESS

Technology is a powerful tool that can help organizations achieve their goals, improve their performance, and create value for their stakeholders. But technology also comes with ethical challenges that need to be addressed responsibly and proactively.

Ethical tech is not just a compliance issue, but a strategic imperative that can enhance an organization's reputation, trust, and competitiveness.

WHY ETHICAL TECH MATTERS

Ethical tech can help organizations avoid legal, regulatory, and reputational risks that may arise from misuse, abuse, or negligence of technology. For example, violating data privacy laws, discriminating against customers or employees through biased algorithms, or exposing sensitive information to cyberattacks can result in fines, lawsuits, or loss of trust.

Ethical tech can help organizations attract and retain talent, customers, and partners who value ethical principles and practices. For example, employees may prefer to work for organizations that respect their digital rights, customers may choose to buy from organizations that protect their data and interests, and partners may collaborate with organizations that share their ethical values and standards.

Ethical tech can help organizations innovate and differentiate themselves in the market by creating positive social and environmental impacts through technology. For example, organizations can use technology to improve accessibility, inclusion, diversity, sustainability, or social justice.

HOW TO ACHIEVE ETHICAL TECH

Achieving ethical tech requires a holistic and systematic approach that involves the following steps:

Define your ethical vision and values. What are the core principles that guide your organization's use of technology? What are the ethical goals and outcomes that you want to achieve through technology? How do you align your ethical vision and values with your organizational mission and strategy?

Assess your ethical risks and opportunities. What are the potential ethical issues or dilemmas that your organization may face when using technology? What are the possible impacts or consequences of these issues for your organization and its stakeholders? What are the opportunities or benefits that your organization can gain by using technology ethically?

Develop your ethical policies and guidelines. What are the specific rules or standards that your organization expects its employees to follow when using technology? How do you communicate these policies and guidelines to your employees and other stakeholders? How do you monitor and enforce compliance with these policies and guidelines?

Educate and empower your employees. How do you raise awareness and understanding of ethical tech among your employees? How do you train and equip your employees with the skills and tools to use technology ethically? How do you encourage and reward ethical tech behaviour among your employees?

Evaluate and improve your ethical performance. How do you measure and report on your organization's ethical tech performance? How do you collect feedback and input from your employees and other stakeholders on your ethical tech practices? How do you learn from your successes and failures and continuously improve your ethical tech capabilities?

EXAMPLES OF ETHICAL TECH PRACTICES

To illustrate how some organizations are applying ethical tech in practice, here are some examples from different sectors:

Deloitte Insights identifies five organizational values that underpin the use of ethical technology: transparency, fairness, empowerment, reliability, and accountability. It also provides a framework for making ethical tech a priority in today's digital organization.

The World Economic Forum highlights five traits of organizations that use tech responsibly: they embed ethics into their culture, they engage with stakeholders, they anticipate impacts, they govern proactively, and they learn continuously.

Digital Agenda showcases how some companies are making ethics a priority in their digital transformation journeys. For example, Microsoft has established an AI Ethics Office to ensure that its AI products adhere to its principles of fairness, reliability, safety, privacy, security, inclusiveness, transparency, and accountability.

CHAPTER 8 WORKSHOP: EMPLOYEE IT USAGE & POLICIES

Imagine you have been hired by a large corporation to conduct a 20-minute workshop exercise about employee IT usage and policies. The workshop is aimed at educating the employees about the importance of following the company's IT policies and the consequences of violating them. The workshop is also intended to raise awareness about the privacy rights and responsibilities of both the employer and the employees regarding IT usage. Here is a possible outline of the workshop exercise:

1. **Introduction**. Explain the objectives and agenda of the workshop. Provide some background information on the company's IT policies and why they are necessary. Emphasize that the workshop is not meant to be punitive or intrusive, but rather informative and constructive.

2. **Scenario**. Present a hypothetical scenario where an employee has violated the company's IT policy by using their work computer for personal purposes, such as browsing social media, shopping online, or downloading unauthorized software. Ask the participants to discuss in small groups what they think are the potential risks and impacts of such behaviour for the employee, the employer, and the customers.

3. **Feedback**. Invite some groups to share their answers with the whole group. Summarize the main points and provide some additional information or examples if needed. Highlight the legal, ethical, and professional implications of employee IT usage and policy violation.

4. **Quiz**. Distribute a short quiz with multiple-choice questions that test the participants' knowledge and understanding of the company's IT policy and privacy issues. The quiz should cover topics such as acceptable and unacceptable IT usage, data protection and security, monitoring and auditing, disciplinary actions and sanctions, and employee rights and obligations.

5. **Review**. Go over the correct answers to the quiz and explain the rationale behind them. Clarify any doubts or questions that the participants may have. Reinforce the key messages and takeaways from the workshop.

6. **Conclusion**. Thank the participants for their attention and participation. Remind them of the benefits of complying with the company's IT policy and respecting the privacy of themselves and others

CHAPTER 9:
IOT SECURITY & PRIVACY

CHAPTER SUMMARY

The Internet of Things (IoT) is the network of devices that can communicate and exchange data with each other and with the cloud. IoT has many benefits, such as improving efficiency, convenience, and quality of life. However, IoT also poses many challenges for security and privacy, as well as ethical and legal issues.

The main challenges of IoT security and privacy is how to **protect the data that is collected, stored, and processed by IoT devices**. This data can include personal information, such as biometric data, which can be used to identify and authenticate individuals. Biometric data can also be used for other purposes, such as health monitoring, marketing, or law enforcement. However, biometric data is sensitive and can be misused or breached by hackers, governments, or corporations. Therefore, it is important to ensure that biometric data is collected, used, and shared with consent, transparency, and accountability.

Another challenge of IoT security and privacy is how to **deal with the issue of data localization and sovereignty**. Data localization refers to the requirement that data must be stored and processed within a certain jurisdiction, while data sovereignty refers to the right of a country to control its own data. Data localization and sovereignty can have positive effects, such as protecting national security, privacy, and culture. However, they can also have negative effects, such as hindering cross-border data flows, innovation, and cooperation. Therefore, it is important to balance the interests of different stakeholders and find common standards and agreements for data governance.

IoT security and privacy also raise **ethical and transparency questions**. IoT devices can collect and analyse large amounts of data, which can enable new insights and applications. However, IoT devices can also make decisions that affect human lives, such as autonomous cars or smart home appliances. Therefore, IoT devices must be designed and operated with ethical principles and values in mind, such as fairness, accountability, and explainability. Moreover, it is important to ensure that IoT devices are transparent about their functionality, purpose, and limitations, and that users are informed and empowered to control their own data and devices.

9.1. IOT SECURITY & PRIVACY

The Internet of Things (IoT) is a network of interconnected devices that can collect, process, and share data with each other and with other systems. IoT devices range from smart home appliances and wearable gadgets to industrial sensors and medical devices.

On the downside, IoT poses significant risks to security and privacy. IoT devices often have limited resources and capabilities, making them vulnerable to cyberattacks and malware. Moreover, IoT devices can generate and transmit sensitive personal information, such as location, biometrics, preferences, and behaviours. This information can be exploited by malicious actors for identity theft, fraud, blackmail, or surveillance.

Therefore, it is essential to design and implement effective security and privacy mechanisms for IoT systems. In this paper, we will review the main security and privacy issues in IoT, discuss the existing solutions and best practices, and identify the future research directions and challenges.

PROLIFERATION OF IOT DEVICES

The Internet of Things (IoT) is the network of physical devices, such as sensors, cameras, and appliances, that can collect and exchange data over the internet. IoT has many applications in various fields, such as industry, healthcare, transportation, and smart cities.

However, such devices can be vulnerable to cyberattacks, data breaches, and unauthorized access. In this article, I will share some of my best advice on how to deal with these challenges, based on my 30 years of experience and research in IT governance, policy, ethics, and law.

UNDERSTAND THE IOT ARCHITECTURE

First step to protect IoT devices is to understand how they are connected and what data they generate and transmit. IoT devices can be classified into three categories: edge devices, gateways, and cloud servers. Edge devices are the ones that directly interact with the physical environment, such as sensors and actuators.

Gateways are intermediate devices that connect edge devices to the internet, such as routers and modems. Cloud servers are remote servers that store and process data from IoT devices, such as databases and analytics platforms.

Each category of IoT devices has different security and privacy requirements and risks. For example, edge devices may have limited computing power and memory, which makes them difficult to encrypt or update.

Gateways may have multiple communication protocols and interfaces, which makes them prone to compatibility issues or interception. Cloud servers may have large amounts of sensitive data, which makes them attractive targets for hackers or unauthorized users.

Therefore, it is important to identify the architecture of your IoT system and assess the security and privacy needs and threats of each component. You should also consider the data flow and lifecycle of your IoT system, such as how data is collected, stored, processed, shared, and deleted.

IMPLEMENT BEST PRACTICES FOR IOT SECURITY

After understanding the architecture of your IoT system, you should implement best practices for securing your IoT devices and data. Some of these best practices include:

Use strong encryption and authentication methods for data transmission and storage. You should encrypt data at rest and in transit using standard algorithms and protocols, such as AES or SSL/TLS. You should also authenticate devices and users using passwords, certificates, or biometrics.

Update your IoT devices regularly with security patches and firmware updates. You should monitor your IoT devices for vulnerabilities and apply patches or updates as soon as they are available. You should also enable automatic updates or notifications for your IoT devices if possible.

Configure your IoT devices with the minimum necessary permissions and access rights. You should follow the principle of least privilege and only grant access to your IoT devices and data to authorized users or applications. You should also disable or remove any unused or unnecessary features or services from your IoT devices.

Monitor your IoT devices for abnormal or suspicious activities or behaviours. You should use tools such as firewalls, antivirus software, or intrusion detection systems to detect and prevent potential attacks or breaches on your IoT devices. You should also log and audit your IoT device activities and events for future analysis or investigation.

FOLLOW ETHICAL PRINCIPLES FOR IOT PRIVACY

Besides securing your IoT devices and data, you should also respect the privacy of your customers, users, or stakeholders who interact with your IoT system. Privacy is a fundamental human right that can be affected by the collection and use of personal or sensitive data by IoT devices. Therefore, you should follow ethical principles for IoT privacy, such as:

Inform your customers, users, or stakeholders about what data you collect, how you use it, who you share it with, and what choices they have. You should provide clear and transparent privacy policies and notices for your IoT system and obtain consent from your customers, users, or stakeholders before collecting or using their data.

Minimize the amount and type of data you collect and use for your IoT system. You should only collect and use data that is relevant and necessary for your business or service purpose. You should also anonymize or aggregate data whenever possible to reduce the risk of identification or re-identification.

Protect the rights and interests of your customers, users, or stakeholders regarding their data. You should respect their preferences and requests for accessing, correcting, deleting, or transferring their data. You should also comply with any applicable laws or regulations regarding data protection or privacy in your jurisdiction.

SECURING THE DIGITAL ENVIRONMENT

IoT refers to the network of physical devices, such as smart home appliances, wearables, vehicles, sensors, and cameras, that can communicate and exchange data over the internet.

IoT devices and data are vulnerable to various cyberattacks, such as hacking, malware, ransomware, denial-of-service, and data breaches. These attacks can compromise the functionality, integrity, and confidentiality of the devices and data, and cause harm to the users and the environment. For example, hackers can take control of your smart thermostat and raise the temperature to dangerous levels or access your personal information from your fitness tracker or smart speaker.

Therefore, it is essential to secure the digital realm and protect your IoT devices and data from unauthorized access and misuse. Here are some best practices that you can follow to enhance your IoT security and privacy:

Use strong passwords and encryption. Choose complex and unique passwords for your IoT devices and accounts and change them regularly. Use encryption to protect the data in transit and at rest. Avoid using default or common passwords that can be easily guessed or cracked by hackers.

Update your software and firmware. Keep your IoT devices and applications updated with the latest software and firmware patches that can fix security vulnerabilities and bugs. Enable automatic updates if possible or check for updates regularly.

Disable unnecessary features and services. Turn off features and services that you do not use or need, such as remote access, voice control, or location tracking. These features can expose your devices and data to potential attackers or third parties. You can also disable or limit the data collection and sharing settings of your IoT devices and applications to minimize your digital footprint.

Secure your network. Connect your IoT devices to a secure wireless network that has a firewall, antivirus, and VPN protection. Avoid using public or unsecured Wi-Fi networks that can expose your devices and data to hackers or eavesdroppers.

THE ETHICS OF PRIVACY

PRIVACY IN THE IOT

Privacy is the right of individuals to control their personal information and how it is collected, used, shared, and stored by others. Privacy is essential for protecting human dignity, autonomy, identity, reputation, and freedom.

Privacy also enables individuals to exercise their rights and participate in society without fear of discrimination, harassment, or manipulation.

In the context of IoT, privacy is threatened by various factors, such as:

The massive amount of data generated by IoT devices, which may reveal sensitive information about individuals' behaviours, preferences, health conditions, locations and activities.

The lack of transparency and consent mechanisms for data collection and processing by IoT providers, which may violate individuals' expectations and preferences.

The potential misuse or abuse of data by unauthorized parties, such as hackers, advertisers, governments, or competitors, which may harm individuals' interests, rights or well-being.

The difficulty of enforcing data protection laws and regulations across different jurisdictions and sectors, which may create legal uncertainties and inconsistencies.

PROTECTING PRIVACY IN IOT

To protect privacy in IoT, several measures need to be taken by different stakeholders, such as:

IoT providers should adopt a privacy-by-design approach, which means integrating privacy principles and safeguards into the entire lifecycle of IoT products and services, from design to deployment to disposal. Some of these principles and safeguards include:

Data minimization. Collecting and processing only the data that is necessary and relevant for the intended purpose.

Data anonymization. Removing or masking any identifiers or attributes that can link data to specific individuals.

Data encryption. Using cryptographic techniques to protect data from unauthorized access or modification.

Data retention. Deleting or destroying data when it is no longer needed or required by law.

Data access. Providing individuals with the ability to access, correct or delete their data upon request.

Data notification. Informing individuals about the data collection and processing practices and obtaining their consent when appropriate.

IoT users should be aware of the privacy risks and benefits of using IoT products and services and exercise their rights and choices accordingly. Some of these rights and choices include:

Data awareness. Reading and understanding the privacy policies and terms of service of IoT providers before using their products and services.

Data control. Adjusting the privacy settings and preferences of IoT devices according to their needs and expectations.

Data protection. Using strong passwords, updating software, avoiding phishing emails and securing network connections to prevent unauthorized access or attacks on IoT devices.

Data advocacy. Reporting any privacy violations or complaints to the relevant authorities or organizations.

IoT regulators should establish and enforce clear and consistent data protection laws and regulations that apply to IoT providers and users across different jurisdictions and sectors. Some of these laws and regulations include:

Data accountability. Holding IoT providers responsible for complying with the data protection principles and obligations, and imposing sanctions or penalties for any breaches or violations.

Data security. Requiring IoT providers to implement adequate technical and organizational measures to ensure the confidentiality, integrity, and availability of data.

Data portability. Allowing IoT users to transfer their data from one IoT provider to another without losing quality or functionality.

Data governance. Creating a framework for coordinating and overseeing the data collection and processing activities of IoT providers, users and other stakeholders.

WHAT IS PRIVACY AND WHY DOES IT MATTER?

Privacy is the ability to keep some aspects of our lives separate from others, as we choose. Privacy is important for our dignity, autonomy, and well-being. Privacy also helps us to build trust with others, such as governments, businesses, and individuals.

When we use IoT devices, we often share personal information with them, such as our biometric data, preferences, location, and behaviour. This information can reveal a lot about us, such as our health, interests, habits, and relationships. Sometimes, we may not even be aware of what information is collected or how it is used by the IoT device or service provider.

WHAT ARE THE PRIVACY CHALLENGES AND RISKS OF IOT?

IoT devices can pose many privacy challenges and risks, such as:

Lack of control. We may not have enough control over how our personal information is collected, used, or shared by IoT devices or service providers. For example, we may have to accept privacy policies that are vague, complex, or unfair in order to use an IoT device or service. We may also not have easy ways to access, correct or delete our personal information.

Lack of consent. We may not be able to give informed consent for the collection, use or sharing of our personal information by IoT devices or service providers. For example, we may not be fully aware of what information is collected or how it is used by an IoT device or service. We may also not have meaningful choices to opt in or out of certain data practices.

Lack of transparency. We may not be able to find out who owns or controls our personal information collected by IoT devices or service providers. For example, we may not know who has access to our personal information or for what purposes it is used. We may also not know where our personal information is stored or processed, or how long it is kept.

Lack of security. We may not be able to protect our personal information from unauthorized access, use or disclosure by IoT devices or service providers. For example, we may not know how secure our IoT devices are or how they are updated. We may also not know how our personal information is encrypted or anonymized.

WHAT ARE SOME BEST PRACTICES FOR IOT PRIVACY?

Recommend the following best practices for IoT privacy:

Respect the privacy rights and expectations of users. IoT device and service providers should respect the privacy rights and expectations of users by following relevant laws and regulations, such as Victoria's Privacy and Data Protection Act 2014, and applying ethical principles, such as fairness, accountability and transparency.

Adopt a privacy-by-design approach. IoT device and service providers should adopt a privacy-by-design approach by integrating privacy considerations into every stage of the design and development process of IoT devices and services. This includes conducting privacy impact assessments, minimizing data collection and retention, implementing data security measures, and providing user-friendly privacy notices and choices.

Empower users to control their personal information. IoT device and service providers should empower users to control their personal information by providing clear and meaningful consent mechanisms, easy access to their personal information and options to correct or delete it.

Be transparent about data ownership and governance. IoT device and service providers should be transparent about data ownership and governance by disclosing who owns or controls the personal information collected by IoT devices or services, for what purposes it is used or shared, where it is stored or processed and how long it is kept.

MINIMIZING DATA COLLECTION & RETENTION

MINIMIZING DATA COLLECTION & RETENTION?

IoT devices collect vast amounts of data, including personal information, location, behaviour, preferences, and network environments. This data can be valuable for analytics, artificial intelligence, and supply chain operations, but it also poses significant risks to the privacy and security of users and organizations. Data breaches, unauthorized access, misuse, and theft can result in financial losses, reputational damage, legal liabilities, and even physical harm.

Therefore, minimizing data collection and retention is a key principle of privacy by design, which aims to embed privacy protections into the design and operation of IoT devices and systems. By collecting only, the data that is necessary for the intended purpose, and retaining it only for as long as needed, IoT device manufacturers and users can reduce the attack surface, comply with regulatory requirements, and enhance user trust and confidence.

HOW TO MINIMIZE DATA COLLECTION & RETENTION?

There are several best practices that can help minimize data collection and retention for IoT devices, such as:

Conduct a privacy impact assessment (PIA) to identify the types and sources of data that are collected by the IoT device, the purpose and legal basis for collecting them, the risks, and benefits of collecting them, the retention period and disposal method for them, and the safeguards and controls that are in place to protect them.

Implement data minimization techniques such as anonymization, pseudonymization, aggregation, encryption, compression, and deletion to reduce the amount and sensitivity of data that are collected and stored by the IoT device.

Provide clear and concise privacy notices and **policies** that inform users about what data are collected by the IoT device, why they are collected, how they are used, shared, and protected, how long they are retained, how users can access, correct, delete, or withdraw consent for their data, and how users can contact the device manufacturer or service provider for any privacy-related inquiries or complaints.

Enable user choice and control over data collection and retention by providing opt-in or opt-out options, granular privacy settings, easy-to-use interfaces, and feedback mechanisms that allow users to customize their preferences and exercise their rights regarding their data.

Follow security best practices such as changing default passwords on IoT devices, using strong passwords for all devices and networks, using a strong Wi-Fi encryption method, enabling multi-factor authentication where possible, keeping up to date with device and software updates, checking the privacy settings for IoT devices, understanding what IoT devices are on your home network, designing security into the device from the start, having user and device authorization capabilities, updatable software and firmware, following the Security Development Lifecycle (SDL), implementing network access control (NAC), following the Code of Practice: Securing the Internet of Things for Consumers, etc.

By following these best practices, IoT device manufacturers and users can minimize data collection and retention for IoT devices, thereby enhancing IoT security and privacy.

RESOLVING ETHICAL DILEMMAS

In the context of IOT, ethical dilemmas may arise from the following factors:

- The complexity and heterogeneity of IOT systems, which involve multiple stakeholders, devices, data sources and applications.

- The potential impact of IOT systems on human rights, such as privacy, security, safety, and autonomy.
- The uncertainty and unpredictability of IOT systems, which may pose new risks or challenges that are not well understood or regulated.
- The lack of transparency and accountability of IOT systems, which may obscure the responsibilities and liabilities of different actors.

To address these ethical dilemmas, I suggest the following steps:

1. **Identify the ethical dilemma and its relevant aspects**. This may include the goals, values, interests and expectations of different stakeholders, the technical features and functionalities of the IOT system, the legal and regulatory frameworks that apply, and the potential benefits and harms that may result from the system.

2. **Analyze the ethical dilemma using appropriate frameworks or tools**. This may include ethical principles, such as respect for autonomy, beneficence, non-maleficence and justice; ethical codes or guidelines, such as the IEEE Code of Ethics for Engineers or the ACM Code of Ethics and Professional Conduct; or ethical methods, such as value-sensitive design or privacy by design.

3. **Evaluate the possible options and their consequences**. This may include weighing the pros and cons of each option, considering the short-term and long-term effects, assessing the risks and uncertainties, and consulting with relevant stakeholders or experts.

4. **Decide on the best option and justify it**. This may include explaining the reasons for choosing a particular option, addressing the possible objections or criticisms, and documenting the decision process and outcome.

5. **Implement the decision and monitor its impact**. This may include taking the necessary actions to execute the decision, communicating it to relevant stakeholders, evaluating its performance and outcomes, and revising it if needed.

By following these steps, you can address ethical dilemmas in a systematic and rational way, while respecting the values and interests of different stakeholders and complying with the legal and professional standards.

INTERNATIONAL DATA TRANSFER

Cross-border data flows are the movement of data across national borders over the Internet. They are essential for international trade, innovation, and economic development.

They also enable data-intensive technologies such as artificial intelligence (AI) and blockchain to operate globally.

Cross-border data flows also pose risks and challenges for data protection, cybersecurity, national security, and law enforcement. Different countries have different laws and regulations on how to handle personal data, which can create conflicts and barriers for data sharing. Data localization, which is the requirement to store or process data within a certain jurisdiction, is one of the common measures that countries use to restrict or control cross-border data flows.

WHY ARE CROSS-BORDER DATA FLOWS IMPORTANT FOR IOT SECURITY & PRIVACY?

IOT has many applications and benefits for various sectors, such as health care, agriculture, manufacturing, transportation, and smart cities.

IOT nonetheless raises significant security and privacy issues. IOT devices can collect large amounts of personal and sensitive data from users, such as biometric data, location data, health data, and behavioural data. These data can be transferred across borders for processing, storage, or analysis by different actors, such as device manufacturers, service providers, cloud providers, or third parties.

This means that IOT users' data can be exposed to various threats and risks along the data lifecycle, such as unauthorized access, hacking, theft, misuse, or disclosure. Moreover, IOT users may not have adequate control or awareness of how their data are collected, used, shared, or protected by different entities across different jurisdictions.

Therefore, cross-border data flows are crucial for ensuring the security and privacy of IOT users' data. They can enable access to secure and reliable cloud services that can provide better protection and performance for IOT devices and data. They can also facilitate cooperation and coordination among different stakeholders and regulators to establish common standards and best practices for IOT security and privacy.

HOW TO ADDRESS THE CHALLENGES OF CROSS-BORDER DATA FLOWS FOR IOT SECURITY & PRIVACY?

Addressing the challenges of cross-border data flows for IOT Security & Privacy can include:

Adopting a risk-based approach to assess the necessity and proportionality of cross-border data transfers for IOT purposes. This means considering the type and sensitivity of the data involved, the purpose and context of the transfer, the destination country's level of data protection and cybersecurity, and the available safeguards and remedies for IOT users' rights.

Using appropriate legal mechanisms and technical measures to ensure compliance with relevant laws and regulations on cross-border data transfers. This may include using standard contractual clauses (SCCs), binding corporate rules (BCRs), certification schemes (such as Privacy Shield), or encryption techniques to provide adequate guarantees for IOT users' data protection.

Establishing a global framework for cross-border data flows that can promote trust, cooperation, interoperability, accountability, and transparency among different countries and stakeholders. This may involve developing common principles, norms, rules, or standards for cross-border data flows that can balance the benefits and risks of data sharing while respecting different legal systems and cultural values.

Engaging in dialogue and consultation with various actors involved in IOT ecosystems, such as device manufacturers,

9.2 BIOMETRIC DATA USAGE & PRIVACY

USAGE VS PRIVACY

Biometric data is data that captures the unique physical or behavioural characteristics of individuals, such as fingerprints, facial images, voice patterns, or gait. Biometric data can be used to verify or identify individuals more accurately and reliably than other methods, such as passwords or ID cards. However, biometric data also raises privacy concerns, as it can reveal sensitive information about individuals, such as their health, ethnicity, or location.

BENEFITS OF BIOMETRIC DATA USAGE

Biometric data can provide many benefits for businesses and consumers, such as:

Enhancing security and convenience: Biometric data can be used to authenticate individuals and grant them access to devices, services, or premises. For example, fingerprint or facial recognition can be used to unlock smartphones, smart gates at airports, or restricted areas at workplaces. Biometric data can also reduce the risk of identity theft or fraud, as it is harder to share, lose, or duplicate than passwords or tokens.

Improving customer experience and loyalty: Biometric data can be used to personalize products and services for customers, such as tailoring recommendations, offers, or preferences based on their biometric profiles. For example, voice recognition can be used to enable hands-free interactions with smart devices or virtual assistants. Biometric data can also increase customer satisfaction and trust, as it can demonstrate that businesses care about their customers' security and privacy.

Increasing efficiency and productivity: Biometric data can be used to streamline processes and workflows for businesses and employees, such as automating attendance tracking, time management, or performance evaluation based on biometric data. For example, facial recognition can be used to monitor employee engagement, mood, or fatigue during meetings or tasks. Biometric data can also enable faster and more accurate decision making, as it can provide insights into customer behaviour, preferences, or needs.

CHALLENGES OF BIOMETRIC DATA PRIVACY

Biometric data also poses several challenges for privacy protection, such as:

Lack of consent and transparency. Biometric data collection and use may not always be clear or explicit to individuals, especially when it occurs passively or in the background. For example, facial recognition may be used to scan individuals in public spaces without their knowledge or consent. Individuals may not be aware of how their biometric data is collected, stored, shared, or used by businesses or third parties.

Potential for misuse and abuse. Biometric data may be accessed or exploited by unauthorized parties for malicious purposes, such as identity theft, fraud, discrimination, harassment, or surveillance. For example, biometric data may be stolen by hackers, sold by data brokers, or leaked by insiders. Biometric data may also be used to track individuals' movements, activities, or associations without their consent or control.

Difficulty of deletion and correction. Biometric data may be hard to delete or correct once it is collected and stored in databases. For example, biometric data may be retained indefinitely by businesses or third parties without a clear retention policy or deletion mechanism. Biometric data may also be inaccurate or outdated due to changes in individuals' biometric characteristics over time.

BEST PRACTICES FOR BALANCING USAGE AND PRIVACY OF BIOMETRIC DATA

To balance the usage and privacy of biometric data, businesses should follow these best practices:

Outline all areas where biometric data is collected or used: Make sure you are clear on exactly how your business collects and uses biometric data. Identify the purposes and benefits of biometric data usage for your business and customers. Assess the risks and consequences of biometric data collection and use for individuals' privacy and security.

Determine who needs to be notified. Inform individuals about your biometric data collection and use practices in a clear and transparent manner. Obtain their consent before collecting or using their biometric data for any purpose. Provide them with options to opt out or withdraw their consent at any time.

Create clear policies on collection, use and retention. Establish clear policies on how you collect, store, share, and use biometric data. Limit the collection and use of biometric data to what is necessary and relevant for your purposes. Implement appropriate security measures to protect biometric data from unauthorized access or disclosure. Define a retention period for biometric data based on your purposes and legal obligations. Delete biometric data when it is no longer needed.

Constantly update your policies and practices. Monitor your biometric data collection and use practices regularly to ensure they are compliant with applicable laws and regulations. Update your policies and practices as needed to reflect changes in technology, business needs, customer expectations, or legal requirements.

BIOMETRIC DATA

Biometric data is any data that relates to the unique physical or behavioural characteristics of an individual. Examples of biometric data include fingerprints, facial images, iris patterns, voice recognition, and DNA samples. Biometric data can be used for various purposes, such as authentication, identification, security, and health.

Biometric data has many benefits, such as enhancing convenience, accuracy, and efficiency in verifying or recognizing individuals. However, biometric data also poses significant privacy challenges and risks, such as:

Infringement of bodily privacy. Collecting biometric data may involve intrusive or invasive methods that violate an individual's right to control their own body and personal information.

Exposure of sensitive information. Biometric data may reveal sensitive information about an individual's health, ethnicity, gender, age, or lifestyle. If biometric data is leaked, hacked, or misused, it may cause harm or discrimination to the individual.

Loss of anonymity. Biometric data may enable tracking or profiling of individuals without their consent or knowledge. This may affect their freedom of expression, association, and movement.

Irreversibility. Biometric data is permanent and cannot be changed or revoked. If biometric data is compromised or corrupted, it may be difficult or impossible to restore or replace it.

To address these privacy challenges and risks, biometric data should be collected and used in accordance with the following principles and best practices:

Lawfulness. Biometric data should be collected and used only for lawful and legitimate purposes that are clearly defined and communicated to the individuals.

Necessity. Biometric data should be collected and used only when it is necessary and proportionate to achieve the intended purpose. Alternative or less intrusive methods should be considered first.

Consent. Biometric data should be collected and used only with the informed and voluntary consent of the individuals. Consent should be specific, explicit, and revocable at any time.

Transparency. Biometric data should be collected and used in a transparent and accountable manner. Individuals should be informed about how their biometric data is collected, used, stored, shared, and protected.

Security. Biometric data should be collected and used in a secure and reliable manner. Appropriate technical and organizational measures should be implemented to prevent unauthorized access, disclosure, modification, or destruction of biometric data.

Accuracy. Biometric data should be collected and used in an accurate and up-to-date manner. Errors or inaccuracies in biometric data should be detected and corrected as soon as possible.

Retention. Biometric data should be collected and used for a limited period that is relevant to the purpose. Biometric data should be deleted or anonymized when it is no longer needed or required by law.

Rights. Biometric data should be collected and used in a way that respects the rights and interests of the individuals. Individuals should have the right to access, correct, delete, or object to their biometric data.

Biometric data is a valuable and powerful tool that can improve various aspects of our lives. However, it also entails significant privacy implications that need to be carefully considered and addressed.

INFORMED & EXPLICIT CONSENT

Biometric data, such as fingerprints, facial recognition, voiceprints, and iris scans, are unique and sensitive personal information that can be used to identify individuals. Biometric data can also be used for various purposes, such as authentication, security, health, and marketing. However, biometric data also pose significant risks to privacy and human rights, as they can be misused, stolen, or disclosed without the consent or knowledge of the individuals.

Therefore, it is essential that individuals are informed and explicitly consent to the collection, storage, and use of their biometric data by any organisation or agency. Informed and explicit consent means that individuals are given clear and adequate information about what biometric data is collected, how it is stored, how it is used, who it is shared with, and what are the benefits and risks involved. Informed and explicit consent also means that individuals are given the choice to agree or disagree to each proposed collection, use, and disclosure of their biometric data, and that they can withdraw their consent at any time.

BEST PRACTICES FOR OBTAINING INFORMED AND EXPLICIT CONSENT

According to the Australian Privacy Foundation, some of the best practices for obtaining informed and explicit consent for biometric data usage and privacy are:

- Use plain English and avoid technical jargon or legal terms that may confuse or mislead individuals.
- Provide information in a clear and prominent way, such as through a separate notice or form, rather than buried in a long or complex document.
- Explain the purpose and scope of the biometric data collection, use, and disclosure, and how it relates to the service or benefit that individuals are seeking or receiving.
- Explain the alternatives to biometric data collection, use, and disclosure, such as other forms of identification or authentication, and the consequences of not providing biometric data.
- Explain the security measures that are in place to protect the biometric data from unauthorized access, modification, loss, or breach.

- Explain the retention period and disposal policy for the biometric data, and how individuals can access, correct, or delete their biometric data.
- Explain the rights and remedies that individuals have in case of any violation of their privacy or misuse of their biometric data.
- Provide an opt-out option for each proposed collection, use, and disclosure of biometric data, and make it easy for individuals to opt out (for example, by providing a phone number, email address, or online form).
- Obtain express consent for sensitive biometric data (such as health-related data) or for uses or disclosures that are not directly related to the primary purpose of the service or benefit (such as marketing or research).
- Respect the consent preferences of individuals and do not use or disclose their biometric data for purposes that they have not agreed to.

SECURITY & PROTECTION

Biometric data is any data that relates to the unique physical or behavioural characteristics of a person, such as fingerprints, facial images, voice patterns, or DNA. Biometric data can be used to verify or identify a person's identity, for example, to access a device, a building, or a service. Biometric data can offer many benefits, such as convenience, accuracy, and reliability, but it also raises some privacy and security risks. Here are some best practices to follow when using biometric data in your business or organization.

NOTIFY AND OBTAIN CONSENT FROM INDIVIDUALS

One of the most important steps when using biometric data is to notify and obtain consent from the individuals whose data you are collecting or using.

This means informing them about what biometric data you are collecting, why you are collecting it, how you are using it, who you are sharing it with, how long you are keeping it, and what rights they have over their data.

Provide a clear and easy way to opt out or withdraw their consent at any time. This will help you comply with various biometric privacy laws that exist in some states and countries, such as the Illinois Biometric Information Privacy Act (BIPA) or the EU General Data Protection Regulation (GDPR).

CREATE CLEAR POLICIES ON COLLECTION, USE AND RETENTION

Another best practice is to create clear policies on how you collect, use and retain biometric data in your business or organization. These policies should be based on the principles of data minimization, purpose limitation, and security by design.

This means collecting only the biometric data that is necessary for your specific purpose, using it only for that purpose and not for other unrelated purposes, and implementing appropriate technical and organizational measures to protect it from unauthorized access, disclosure, modification, or destruction.

You should also establish a retention policy that specifies how long you will keep the biometric data and when you will delete it or anonymize it.

CONSTANTLY UPDATE YOUR POLICIES AND PRACTICES

Biometric technology is constantly evolving and becoming more advanced and widespread. Therefore, you should regularly review and update your policies and practices on biometric data usage and privacy to keep up with the latest developments and challenges.

Monitor the legal and regulatory landscape for any changes or updates in biometric privacy laws that may affect your business or organization. Additionally, you should conduct regular audits and assessments of your biometric systems to ensure their compliance, effectiveness, and security.

TAKE CARE WITH RELEASE AGREEMENTS

Finally, you should take care when entering into any contracts or agreements that involve the release of biometric data to third parties. You should ensure that the third parties have adequate policies and safeguards in place to protect the biometric data and respect the rights of the individuals.

Ensure that the third parties comply with any applicable biometric privacy laws and regulations. Moreover, you should avoid releasing biometric data to third parties for purposes that are incompatible with the original purpose for which you collected it .

By following these best practices, you can use biometric data in a responsible and ethical way that benefits your business or organization while respecting the privacy and security of the individuals.

ETHICAL HANDLING OF SENSITIVE DATA

Biometric data is any data that can be used to identify a person based on their physical or behavioural characteristics, such as fingerprints, facial recognition, voice patterns, or iris scans. Biometric data is increasingly used for various purposes, such as security, authentication, health care, or marketing.

However, biometric data also poses significant ethical challenges, as it can reveal sensitive information about a person's identity, preferences, health, or emotions. Moreover, biometric data can be misused, stolen, or manipulated by malicious actors, leading to privacy breaches, discrimination, or fraud.

Transparency. You should inform the data subjects about what biometric data you collect, why you collect it, how you use it, who you share it with, and what rights they have over it.

Fairness. You should use biometric data only for legitimate and lawful purposes that are consistent with the data subjects' expectations and consent. You should not use biometric data to discriminate, harm, or exploit the data subjects or others.

Respect. You should respect the data subjects' dignity, autonomy, and privacy. You should give them control over their biometric data and allow them to opt out, access, correct, or delete their data if they wish.

Security. You should protect biometric data from unauthorized access, disclosure, modification, or destruction. You should use appropriate technical and organizational measures to ensure the confidentiality, integrity, and availability of biometric data.

HOW TO APPLY THESE PRINCIPLES IN PRACTICE

Here are some practical steps you can take to apply these principles in your data handling practices:

Conduct a risk assessment. Before collecting or using biometric data, you should assess the potential risks and benefits of your data processing activities. You should consider the sensitivity of the data, the context of the data collection and use, the expectations and consent of the data subjects, and the legal and ethical obligations you must comply with.

Implement a data protection policy. You should have a clear and comprehensive policy that outlines how you handle biometric data in accordance with the principles of transparency, fairness, respect, and security. You should communicate this policy to your staff, partners, and customers and ensure that they follow it.

Use data minimization techniques. You should collect only the biometric data that is necessary for your specific purpose and delete it when it is no longer needed. You should also use techniques such as anonymization or pseudonymization to reduce the identifiability of the data subjects.

Apply encryption and authentication methods. You should encrypt biometric data at rest and in transit to prevent unauthorized access or disclosure. You should also use strong authentication methods to verify the identity of the data subjects and the authorized users of the biometric data.

Monitor and audit your data processing activities. You should regularly monitor and audit your biometric data processing activities to ensure that they are compliant with your policy and the applicable laws and regulations. You should also report any incidents or breaches that may affect the security or privacy of biometric data.

ACCOUNTABILITY

Biometric data is any data that relates to the unique physical or behavioural characteristics of a person, such as fingerprints, facial images, voice patterns, or gait. Biometric data can be used to verify or identify a person's identity, for example, to access a device, a building, or a service. Biometric data can offer convenience, security, and efficiency, but it also raises privacy concerns.

WHY IS BIOMETRIC DATA PRIVACY IMPORTANT?

Biometric data is sensitive and personal information that can reveal a lot about a person, such as their health, ethnicity, religion, or lifestyle. Biometric data can also be used to track or monitor a person's movements, activities, or preferences. Unlike passwords or tokens, biometric data cannot be easily changed or replaced if it is compromised or misused. Therefore, biometric data privacy is important to protect a person's dignity, autonomy, and human rights.

WHAT ARE THE BEST PRACTICES FOR BIOMETRIC DATA PRIVACY?

There is no comprehensive federal law in the United States that regulates biometric data privacy. However, some states and local governments have enacted specific laws to govern the collection and use of biometric data, such as Illinois, Texas, California, New York City, and Portland. These laws vary in their scope and requirements, but they generally share some common principles:

Obtain informed consent from the person before collecting or using their biometric data.

Provide clear notice and disclosure about the purpose, method, and duration of biometric data collection and use.

Limit the collection and use of biometric data to what is necessary and relevant for the intended purpose.

Implement reasonable security measures to protect biometric data from unauthorized access, disclosure, or destruction.

Establish retention and disposal policies to delete biometric data when it is no longer needed.

Respect the person's rights to access, correct, or delete their biometric data.

Avoid sharing or selling biometric data to third parties without the person's consent or legal authorization.

These principles are consistent with the general guidelines for commercial use of biometrics issued by the International Biometrics + Identity Association (IBIA), a trade association that represents the biometrics industry. They are also aligned with the Information Privacy Principles (IPPs) under the Privacy and Data Protection Act 2014 (PDP Act) in Victoria, Australia.

HOW TO COMPLY WITH BIOMETRIC DATA PRIVACY LAWS?

If you are a business that collects or uses biometric data, you should follow these steps to comply with biometric data privacy laws:

1. **Outline all areas where biometric data** is collected or used. Make sure you're clear on exactly how your business collects and uses biometric data.
2. **Determine who needs to be notified**. Identify the persons whose biometric data you collect or use, and the jurisdictions where they reside. Check the applicable laws and regulations that apply to your business and your customers.

3. **Create clear policies on collection**, use and retention. Draft and publish transparent and accessible policies that explain how you collect, use, store, and dispose of biometric data. Obtain consent from the persons before collecting or using their biometric data.

4. **Constantly update your policies and practices**. Monitor the changes in technology, law, and public opinion regarding biometric data privacy. Review and revise your policies and practices regularly to ensure they are up-to-date and compliant.

5. **Take care with release agreements**. If you need to share or sell biometric data to third parties, make sure you have valid and enforceable release agreements that protect your business from liability and respect the persons' rights.

9.3. DATA LOCALIZATION & SOVEREIGNTY

Data localization and sovereignty are two related concepts that affect how data is stored and processed across borders. Data localization policies require businesses to store and process data within the country or region where it was created, while data sovereignty laws give countries or regions the authority to regulate data within their borders.

These policies and laws are often driven by the fear that a nation's sovereignty will be threatened by their inability to exert full control over data stored outside their borders, especially by dominant players like the US. However, data localization and sovereignty also have implications for privacy, security, innovation, trade and human rights.

PERSONAL PRIVACY VS NATIONAL INTEREST

Recognize the complexity and diversity of data localization and sovereignty requirements across the globe. There is no one-size-fits-all solution for complying with these requirements, as they vary depending on the type, source and destination of data, as well as the legal and regulatory frameworks of different countries or regions.

Assess the risks and benefits of storing and processing data locally versus globally. Data localization may offer some advantages in terms of data protection, access and control, but it also comes with costs in terms of infrastructure, performance, scalability, interoperability and innovation. Data localization may also limit the ability to leverage global data sources and services for analytics, artificial intelligence and cloud computing.

Adopt a data-centric approach to security and privacy. Rather than relying on physical location as the main criterion for data security and privacy, focus on implementing robust data encryption, anonymization, pseudonymization and access control mechanisms that protect data regardless of where it is stored or processed. Use industry standards and frameworks to demonstrate compliance with data protection principles and regulations.

Engage in dialogue and collaboration with stakeholders across borders. Data localization and sovereignty are not only technical issues, but also political, economic and social ones. Therefore, it is important to communicate and cooperate with governments, regulators, customers, partners and civil society groups to understand their perspectives, concerns and expectations regarding data flows and governance. Seek to balance the interests of different parties while respecting their values and rights.

Advocate for multilateral agreements and norms on data governance. Data localization and sovereignty are often driven by mistrust and conflict between countries or regions over data access and use. To reduce these tensions and foster more cooperation and harmony, it is desirable to promote multilateral agreements and norms that establish common rules and standards for data governance that respect privacy, security, the rule of law and human rights.

BALANCING PRIVACY VS NATIONAL INTERESTS

Privacy is the right of individuals to control their personal information and how it is shared with others. Privacy is important for human dignity, autonomy, and freedom of expression. Privacy also protects individuals from discrimination, harassment, and identity theft.

National interests are the goals and objectives of a country in relation to its security, economy, and values. National interests may include defending against threats, promoting trade and innovation, and advancing human rights and democracy. National interests may require access to data for law enforcement, intelligence, or public health purposes.

The boundaries between privacy and national interests are not clear-cut, as they may conflict or overlap in different situations. For example, data localization may enhance privacy by preventing foreign surveillance or hacking, but it may also limit national interests by restricting cross-border data flows and cooperation. Data sovereignty may protect national interests by allowing the country to enforce its own laws and standards on data, but it may also undermine privacy by enabling censorship or repression.

The challenge is to find a balance between privacy and national interests that respects both individual rights and collective needs. This balance may depend on various factors, such as the type and sensitivity of data, the purpose and legitimacy of data use, the level of trust and transparency between actors, and the legal and ethical frameworks that govern data. There is no one-size-fits-all solution, but some possible approaches are:

- Developing global or regional norms and agreements on data governance that reflect common values and principles.
- Establishing clear and consistent rules and procedures for data access and sharing that ensure accountability and oversight.
- Implementing technical and organizational measures to protect data security and privacy, such as encryption, anonymization, or consent mechanisms.
- Promoting dialogue and cooperation among stakeholders, such as governments, businesses, civil society, and users, to address challenges and opportunities of data localization and sovereignty.

DATA LOCALIZATION

Data localization is the practice of storing and processing data in the same country where you originally collected it. Data localization is based on the concept of data sovereignty, which states that data is subject to laws and governance rules of the nation or region where they were collected.

Why Data Localization Matters

There are several reasons why data localization matters for governments, businesses, and individuals. Some of the main reasons include:

Data security. Data localization can enhance the security of data by keeping it within the borders of a particular country, where it is less vulnerable to cyberattacks, theft, or unauthorized access by foreign entities.

Data privacy. Data localization can help to ensure that data is subject to specific privacy laws and regulations that protect the rights and interests of data subjects. For example, the European Union's General Data Protection Regulation (GDPR) requires that personal data of EU citizens be stored and processed in a way that ensures appropriate protection of their privacy.

Economic considerations. Data localization can boost the domestic economy by requiring companies to store and process data within their borders. This can create local jobs, stimulate economic growth, and foster innovation and competitiveness.

National sovereignty. Data localization can assert the national sovereignty and control of a country over its citizens' data. It can also prevent foreign interference or influence over domestic affairs, policies, or decisions.

IMPLEMENTING DATA LOCALIZATION EFFECTIVELY

Implementing data localization effectively can be challenging, especially for organizations that operate across multiple jurisdictions or rely on cloud computing services. Here are some tips on how to implement data localization effectively:

Understand the legal requirements. Different countries have different laws and regulations regarding data localization. It is important to understand the legal requirements of each jurisdiction where you collect, store, or process data, and comply with them accordingly. For example, some countries may require that certain types of data, such as personal data or financial data, be stored locally, while others may allow cross-border transfers under certain conditions or safeguards.

Choose the right service providers. If you use cloud computing services or third-party data processors, you need to choose service providers that can meet your data localization needs. You should look for service providers that have local data centers or servers in the countries where you operate, or that can guarantee that your data will not be transferred outside those countries without your consent or authorization.

Implement appropriate safeguards. Even if you store and process your data locally, you still need to implement appropriate safeguards to protect your data from unauthorized access, use, disclosure, modification, or deletion. You should use encryption, authentication, access control, backup, audit, and monitoring tools to ensure the security and integrity of your data.

Educate your stakeholders. Data localization involves not only technical aspects but also organizational and cultural aspects. You need to educate your stakeholders, such as employees, customers, partners, and regulators, about the importance and benefits of data localization, and how it affects their roles and responsibilities. You should also communicate clearly about your data localization policies and practices and provide transparency and accountability for your data processing activities.

USERS' DATA PRIVACY

Data localization and sovereignty are two concepts that are increasingly affecting how businesses store and process data across borders. Data localization requires that all data generated within a country's borders remain within those borders, while data sovereignty refers to the laws and regulations that govern the data at that location. These requirements are driven by the fear that a nation's sovereignty will be threatened by their inability to exert full control over data stored outside their borders.

Here are some of my best advice on how to respect users' data privacy in the context of data localization and sovereignty, based on research and best practice:

Understand the local laws and regulations that apply to your data. Different countries or regions may have different rules on how data can be collected, used, shared, transferred, or deleted. For example, the European Union's General Data Protection Regulation (GDPR) gives individuals the right to access, correct, erase, or restrict the processing of their personal data. You should comply with these rules and inform your users about them clearly and transparently.

Implement privacy and security frameworks by industry to ensure that your data is protected from unauthorized access, use, or disclosure. You should follow the standards and best practices that are relevant to your industry and the type of data you handle. For example, if you deal with health data, you may want to adopt the Health Insurance Portability and Accountability Act (HIPAA) or the Health Information Trust Alliance (HITRUST) frameworks. You should also invest in cybersecurity measures to prevent data breaches or attacks.

Seek consent from your users before collecting, using, or transferring their data. You should respect your users' choices and preferences regarding their data and give them the option to opt-in or opt-out of certain data practices. You should also inform your users about the purpose, scope, duration, and destination of your data processing activities and obtain their explicit consent before transferring their data across borders.

Collaborate with your allies and partners to develop norms and standards around data use that align with your values and principles. You should work with other countries or regions that share your vision of data as a force for good and a driver of innovation. You should also participate in multilateral agreements or initiatives that facilitate data flows while respecting data sovereignty and localization requirements. For example, the US has signed bilateral agreements under the Clarifying Lawful Overseas Use of Data (CLOUD) Act with several countries to enable cross-border access to electronic evidence for law enforcement purposes.

ETHICAL DILEMMAS

Data localization and sovereignty are two related concepts that refer to the control and regulation of data within a specific geographic area. Data localization policies impose obligations on businesses to store and process data locally, rather than in servers located overseas. Data sovereignty is the principle that data is subject to the laws and governance of the country where it is collected or stored.

WHY HAVE DATA LOCALIZATION AND SOVEREIGNTY POLICIES?

The adoption of data localization and sovereignty policies has been increasing, driven by various motivations, such as:

- Protecting national security and intelligence interests by preventing foreign access or interference with sensitive data.
- Enhancing digital sovereignty and asserting greater control over the domestic digital domain.
- Promoting local economic development and innovation by creating a level playing field for domestic companies and reducing dependence on foreign providers.
- Safeguarding data privacy and human rights by ensuring compliance with local laws and standards.
- What are the challenges and ethical dilemmas of data localization and sovereignty policies?

Data localization and sovereignty policies pose several challenges and ethical dilemmas for different stakeholders, such as:

- Restricting the free flow of data across borders, which can hamper global trade, cooperation, and innovation.
- Increasing the costs and complexity of data management, storage, and compliance for businesses, especially for small and medium enterprises (SMEs) that lack the resources and expertise to operate in multiple jurisdictions.

- Reducing the quality and security of data services, as local providers may not offer the same level of reliability, performance, or protection as foreign ones.
- Undermining human rights, privacy, and the rule of law, as some countries may use data localization and sovereignty policies to justify censorship, surveillance, or repression of dissenting voices.

How can we address the challenges and ethical dilemmas of data localization and sovereignty policies?

There is no one-size-fits-all solution for the future of data localization and sovereignty policies. However, some possible ways to address the challenges and ethical dilemmas include:

Developing a federal national privacy law in the US to reduce the fears that foreign nations have about the power of US tech companies and their access to personal data.

Mandating privacy and security frameworks by industry in the US to demonstrate the importance that US industry places on privacy and security, recognizing it as fundamental to their business success.

Increasing investment in cybersecurity in the US to ensure that in a competitive market, the US has the best offering in both customer experience and security assurance.

Expanding multi-lateral agreements under the CLOUD Act to help alleviate the concerns that data stored by US companies will be inaccessible to foreign governments in cases relevant to a criminal investigation.

Taking a collaborative approach to technology innovation with key allies, working together to facilitate technology development in a way that is safe, effective, and in line with liberal and democratic values.

Developing norms and standards around data use in collaboration with allies, particularly as they relate to privacy, security, the rule of law, and human rights.

Making public and explicit commitments to criticize neo-colonialism with respect to data to give developing countries, or those with less technological capabilities, confidence that the US does not condone data exploitation.

LEGAL MANDATES

Data localization and sovereignty are two related concepts that affect how organizations store, process and transfer data across borders. Data localization refers to the requirement that data must be stored within a certain jurisdiction, while data sovereignty refers to the legal authority that a country has over the data within its territory. Both concepts pose challenges and opportunities for organizations that operate in multiple countries or regions.

WHAT ARE THE BENEFITS AND RISKS OF DATA LOCALIZATION AND SOVEREIGNTY?

Data localization and sovereignty can have both positive and negative impacts for organizations, depending on their context and objectives. Some of the potential benefits include:

- Enhancing data protection and privacy by complying with local laws and regulations
- Improving data quality and accuracy by reducing latency and errors
- Increasing customer trust and loyalty by respecting their preferences and expectations
- Supporting local economic development and innovation by creating jobs and opportunities

Some of the potential risks include:

- Increasing operational costs and complexity by requiring multiple data centers and systems
- Reducing data availability and accessibility by creating barriers and bottlenecks
- Limiting data interoperability and integration by creating fragmentation and inconsistency
- Exposing data to legal conflicts and disputes by involving multiple jurisdictions and authorities

NEGOTIATING THE LEGAL MANDATES IN DATA LOCALIZATION AND SOVEREIGNTY

Given the benefits and risks of data localization and sovereignty, organizations need to adopt a strategic approach to navigate the legal mandates in this area. Some of the key steps include:

- Conducting a comprehensive assessment of the data flows and requirements across the organization.
- Identifying the relevant laws and regulations in each country or region where the organization operates or serves customers.
- Evaluating the costs and benefits of complying with or challenging the legal mandates in each case.
- Developing a data localization and sovereignty policy that aligns with the organization's vision, mission, values and goals.
- Implementing the policy with appropriate technical, organizational and contractual measures.
- Monitoring and reviewing the policy regularly to ensure its effectiveness and compliance.

9.4. IOT ETHICS & TRANSPARENCY

TRUST IN THE AGE OF CONNECTED DEVICES

The Internet of Things (IoT) is the network of devices that can communicate with each other and the internet, such as smart watches, thermostats, cars, and appliances. The IoT has the potential to transform our lives and work, but it also poses significant challenges for privacy, security, and trust.

WHY PRIVACY AND SECURITY MATTER FOR IOT

As more devices collect and share data about our behaviours, preferences, health, location, and activities, we face the risk of losing control over our personal information. Data breaches, cyberattacks, unauthorized access, and misuse of data can harm our privacy, identity, reputation, and safety. For example, hackers could access our cameras, microphones, or GPS trackers and spy on us or blackmail us. Or they could manipulate our devices to cause physical damage or harm, such as turning off our heating system or crashing our car.

According to a survey by Consumers International and the Internet Society, 63% of people find connected devices "creepy" in the way they collect data about people and their behaviours. Half of the people distrust their devices to protect their privacy and handle their information in a respectful manner. And 75% of people are concerned about their data being used by other organizations without their permission.

BUILDING TRUST IN IOT

To build trust in IoT, we need to ensure that the devices and services we use are ethical and transparent. This means that they respect our rights, choices, and values, and that they are accountable for their actions and impacts. Here are some principles and practices that can help achieve this goal:

Informed consent. We should be able to understand what data is collected by our devices, why, how, where, and with whom it is shared, and what benefits or risks it entails. We should also be able to opt-in or opt-out of data collection and sharing at any time.

Data minimization. Our devices should collect only the data that is necessary for their functionality and purpose, and delete it when it is no longer needed.

Data protection. Our devices should use encryption, authentication, and other security measures to prevent unauthorized access or misuse of our data. They should also notify us of any breaches or incidents that affect our data.

Data ownership. We should have the right to access, correct, delete, or transfer our data at any time. We should also have the right to know who owns our data and how it is monetized.

Data governance. Our devices should follow ethical standards and regulations that protect our privacy, security, and human rights. They should also be subject to audits and oversight by independent authorities or organizations.

THE POTENTIAL OF IOT

IOT ETHICS AND TRANSPARENCY

IoT ethics and transparency are the principles and practices that guide the ethical design, development, and deployment of IoT devices and systems. They aim to protect the rights and interests of users, as well as society at large, from the potential harms and risks of IoT.

Some of the key ethical issues that IoT raises are:

Privacy. How can we ensure that IoT devices do not collect, store, or share sensitive or personal data without our consent or knowledge?

Security. How can we prevent IoT devices from being hacked or compromised by malicious actors who could harm us or our data?

Accountability. Who is responsible for the actions and outcomes of IoT devices and systems? How can we hold them accountable for any errors or harms they cause?

Transparency. How can we know what data IoT devices collect, how they use it, and who they share it with? How can we understand how IoT devices and systems work and make decisions?

Fairness: How can we ensure that IoT devices and systems do not discriminate or exclude anyone based on their characteristics or preferences?

To address these ethical issues, I recommend following these best practices:

PRIVACY PROTECTION: ENSURING DATA SECURITY

One of the most pressing concerns when it comes to IoT is privacy protection. As devices become increasingly connected, they gather more and more data about our lives. This data can be incredibly sensitive, and it's crucial that it's handled in a responsible and secure way.

To ensure privacy protection, IoT developers must implement strong encryption and other security measures to prevent unauthorized access to sensitive data. Additionally, they must provide clear and transparent information about what data is being collected, how it's being used, and who has access to it. This allows users to make informed decisions about their data and gives them greater control over their privacy.

DATA SECURITY

Data security is also a key concern when it comes to IoT. As more devices become connected, the risk of data breaches and cyberattacks increases. To mitigate this risk, IoT developers must design secure devices that are resistant to hacking attempts. This includes implementing strong authentication and access controls, as well as regularly updating devices with security patches and fixes. Additionally, developers must conduct regular security testing to identify and address vulnerabilities before they can be exploited by attackers.

By prioritizing data security, IoT developers can help ensure the safety and wellbeing of users and their data.

TRANSPARENCY & INFORMED CONSENT

Another ethical consideration when it comes to IoT is transparency and informed consent. IoT developers must fully inform users about the data being collected, how it's being used, and who has access to it. Additionally, users must be given the opportunity to consent to the collection and use of their data or opt-out completely.

This requires IoT developers to provide clear and accessible information about their data practices, as well as easy-to-use controls that allow users to manage their data preferences.

ACCOUNTABILITY

Accountability is also an important ethical principle when it comes to IoT. Accountability means taking responsibility for the actions and outcomes of IoT devices and systems. This includes ensuring that they comply with relevant laws and regulations, as well as ethical standards and norms.

To ensure accountability, IoT developers must establish clear roles and responsibilities for all parties involved in the design, development, deployment, and operation of IoT devices and systems. They must also implement mechanisms for monitoring, auditing, reporting, and remedying any issues or harms that may arise from IoT devices and systems.

BEST PRACTICES SECURITY & USABILITY

Adopting a user-centric approach that considers the needs, preferences, expectations, and feedback of users throughout the design process.

Applying the principle of data minimization that collects only the data that is necessary for the intended purpose and deletes it when no longer needed.

Following the principle of privacy by design that embeds privacy protection into every stage of the design process.

Applying the principle of security by design that embeds security features into every stage of the design process.

ETHICAL CONSIDERATIONS IN IOT

The Internet of Things (IoT) is the network of physical devices, sensors, and software that can collect, process, and share data over the internet. IoT has many applications and benefits, such as improving efficiency, convenience, and safety. However, IoT also poses ethical challenges that need to be addressed by researchers, developers, and users.

Some of the ethical issues that arise from IoT are:

Privacy. IoT devices can collect personal and sensitive data, such as location, health, and financial information. This data can be accessed by unauthorized third parties, leading to identity theft, fraud, or discrimination. To protect privacy, IoT devices should have clear and transparent data collection policies, consent mechanisms, and security measures. Users should also have control over their own data and be able to access, delete, or correct it if needed.

Accuracy. IoT devices rely on data to function and make decisions. However, data can be inaccurate, incomplete, or outdated due to human or technical errors. This can lead to faulty or harmful outcomes, such as incorrect diagnosis, miscommunication, or accidents. To ensure accuracy, IoT devices should have quality assurance processes, verification methods, and error correction mechanisms. Users should also be able to verify the source and validity of the data.

Accountability. IoT devices can act autonomously or in collaboration with other devices or humans. However, it may be unclear who is responsible for the actions and consequences of IoT devices, especially when they involve harm or damage. This can create legal and moral dilemmas, such as liability, blame, or compensation. To establish accountability, IoT devices should have clear and transparent governance structures, ethical codes of conduct, and audit trails. Users should also be aware of the risks and benefits of using IoT devices and be able to report or complain if needed.

IoT ethics is a complex and evolving field that requires interdisciplinary and stakeholder collaboration. By following ethical principles and best practices, IoT researchers, developers, and users can ensure that IoT devices are used in a responsible and beneficial way.

TRANSPARENCY AS A PILLAR OF TRUST

Transparency is the quality of being open, honest and accountable in one's actions and decisions. Transparency is especially important in the context of IoT (Internet of Things), which refers to the network of physical devices, sensors, software and data that can communicate and interact with each other. IoT has the potential to bring many benefits to society, such as improving health, safety, efficiency and convenience. However, IoT also poses many challenges to ethics and privacy, such as data collection, processing, sharing and security.

PRINCIPLE 1: INFORM & EMPOWER USERS

Users of IoT devices and services should be informed about what data is collected, how it is used, who it is shared with, and what choices they have. This information should be provided in a clear, concise and accessible way, using plain language and visual aids. Users should also be able to access, correct and delete their data, as well as opt out of data collection or sharing if they wish. Users should be empowered to control their own data and privacy preferences.

PRINCIPLE 2: RESPECT USER CONSENT

User consent is the voluntary agreement of the user to the collection, use and sharing of their data. User consent should be obtained before any data collection or processing takes place, unless there is a legitimate reason or legal obligation to do otherwise. User consent should be specific, informed and freely given, not coerced or manipulated. User consent should also be revocable at any time, without negative consequences for the user.

PRINCIPLE 3: PROTECT USER DATA

User data is the personal or sensitive information that is collected or generated by IoT devices or services. User data should be protected from unauthorized access, use, disclosure or modification. User data should also be stored securely and deleted when no longer needed. User data should only be used for the purposes that the user has agreed to, and not for other purposes that may harm or exploit the user.

PRINCIPLE 4: ENSURE ACCOUNTABILITY

Accountability is the responsibility of the actors involved in IoT to comply with ethical standards and legal regulations. Oversight is the process of monitoring and evaluating the compliance and performance of the actors involved in IoT. Accountability and oversight should be ensured by establishing clear roles and responsibilities, implementing policies and procedures, conducting audits and reviews, reporting breaches and incidents, enforcing sanctions and remedies, and engaging with stakeholders.

By following these principles and strategies, I believe that transparency can be achieved as a pillar of trust in IoT ethics. Transparency can help to build trust between users and providers of IoT devices and services, as well as between society and technology. Transparency can also help to prevent or mitigate potential ethical issues or risks that may arise from IoT.

INFORMED CONSENT

Informed consent is a key principle of ethical research and practice, especially when it involves human data. It means that the participants or users of a service or product are fully aware of what they are agreeing to, how their data will be used, and what benefits and risks are involved. Informed consent also implies that the participants or users have the right to withdraw their consent at any time, without any negative consequences.

In the context of IoT, informed consent becomes more challenging and important, as IoT devices collect, process, and share large amounts of data, often without the user's direct involvement or awareness. IoT devices may also affect the user's environment, behaviour, or health in ways that are not obvious or predictable. Therefore, IoT developers and providers have a responsibility to ensure that their users are informed and empowered to make decisions about their data and privacy.

Some of the best practices for ensuring informed consent in IoT ethics and transparency are:

- Provide clear and concise information about the purpose, scope, and methods of data collection and use, as well as the potential benefits and risks for the user and society.
- Use plain language and avoid technical jargon or legal terms that may confuse or mislead the user.
- Use multiple channels and formats to communicate the information, such as text, audio, video, graphics, or interactive elements.
- Use user-friendly interfaces and design elements to facilitate the user's understanding and engagement, such as icons, colours, buttons, or sliders.
- Provide the user with easy and accessible options to consent or decline, as well as to modify or revoke their consent at any time.
- Respect the user's preferences and choices, and do not coerce or manipulate them into consenting or using the service or product.
- Monitor and evaluate the user's feedback and behaviour and update the information and consent process accordingly.

By following these best practices, IoT developers and providers can enhance the trust and satisfaction of their users, as well as comply with ethical standards and legal regulations. Informed consent is not only a requirement, but also an opportunity to create more transparent, accountable, and responsible IoT systems.

DATA PRIVACY & SECURITY

The Internet of Things (IoT) is a network of devices that can collect, process, and transmit data over the internet. IoT devices can range from smart home appliances and wearable gadgets to industrial sensors and medical devices. IoT devices can offer many benefits, such as convenience, efficiency, and innovation. However, they also pose significant challenges for data privacy and security.

PRIVACY & SECURITY IN IOT

Data privacy and security are important in any context where personal or sensitive data are involved. However, in IoT, the stakes are even higher because:

IoT devices can collect vast amounts of granular data about individuals' daily habits, activities, preferences, health, location, and more. This data can reveal intimate details about a person's identity, behaviour, and personality.

IoT data can be used by various entities, such as companies, governments, hackers, or criminals, to monitor, track, profile, influence, or harm individuals. This can lead to violations of human rights, such as privacy, freedom of expression, and non-discrimination.

IoT devices can be vulnerable to cyberattacks that can compromise their functionality, integrity, or availability. This can result in physical harm, financial loss, or reputational damage for individuals or organizations that rely on them.

PROTECTING DATA PRIVACY AND SECURITY IN IOT?

IT professionals have a key role to play in ensuring that data privacy and security are embedded in the design, development, deployment, and maintenance of IoT devices and systems. Some of the best practices that IT professionals can follow are:

Conduct a data protection impact assessment (DPIA) before launching an IoT project. A DPIA is a systematic process that identifies and evaluates the potential risks and impacts of processing personal data in a specific context. A DPIA can help IT professionals to comply with data protection regulations, such as the EU's General Data Protection Regulation (GDPR), and to implement appropriate measures to mitigate the risks.

Apply the principles of data minimization and purpose limitation. Data minimization means that only the data that are necessary for a specific purpose are collected and processed. Purpose limitation means that the data are not used for other purposes than those for which they were collected. These principles can help IT professionals to reduce the amount of data that are exposed to potential threats and to respect the rights and expectations of the data subjects.

Implement privacy-enhancing techniques (PETs) for IoT data. PETs are methods or tools that aim to protect the privacy of individuals or groups by preventing or limiting the disclosure of personal or sensitive information. Some examples of PETs for IoT data are:

Data anonymization. This technique removes or encrypts identifiers that link an individual to stored data, such as names, addresses, or IP addresses. Data anonymization can prevent re-identification of individuals from aggregated or shared datasets.

Data pseudonymization. This technique replaces identifiers with pseudonyms that do not reveal the identity of the individual but allow for linking data across different sources or domains. Data pseudonymization can enable data analysis or processing without compromising privacy.

Data encryption. This technique transforms data into an unreadable form using a secret key that only authorized parties can access. Data encryption can protect data from unauthorized access or modification during transmission or storage.

Adopt security standards and best practices for IoT devices and systems. Security standards and best practices provide guidelines and recommendations for ensuring the confidentiality, integrity, and availability of IoT devices and systems. Some examples of security standards and best practices for IoT are:

ISO/IEC 27001. This standard specifies the requirements for establishing, implementing, maintaining, and improving an information security management system (ISMS). An ISMS is a framework of policies and procedures that covers all aspects of information security in an organization.

NIST Cybersecurity Framework. This framework provides a set of voluntary standards, guidelines, and best practices for managing cybersecurity risks in critical infrastructure sectors, such as energy, transportation, or health care. The framework consists of five core functions: identify, protect, detect, respond, and recover.

OWASP IoT Top 10. This list identifies the most common and critical security risks for IoT devices and systems. The list also provides guidance on how to prevent or mitigate these risks.

ETHICS OF EMERGING TECHNOLOGIES

Some of the ethical challenges in IoT are:

Privacy. How can we protect the personal data of users and customers from unauthorized access, misuse, or theft? How can we ensure that users have control over their own data and can opt out of data collection or sharing?

Security. How can we prevent cyberattacks, hacking, or sabotage of IoT devices and systems? How can we ensure that IoT devices and systems are reliable, resilient, and safe?

Accountability. How can we assign responsibility and liability for the actions and outcomes of IoT devices and systems? How can we ensure that IoT devices and systems are transparent, explainable, and auditable?

Sustainability. How can we minimize the environmental impact of IoT devices and systems? How can we ensure that IoT devices and systems are energy-efficient, recyclable, and reusable?

Adopt a privacy-by-design approach. Design IoT devices and systems with privacy in mind from the start. Implement data protection measures such as encryption, anonymization, or pseudonymization. Inform users about what data is collected, how it is used, and with whom it is shared. Obtain users' consent before collecting or sharing their data. Respect users' rights to access, correct, or delete their data.

Implement security-by-design principles. Design IoT devices and systems with security in mind from the start. Use secure protocols, standards, and algorithms. Update IoT devices and systems regularly with patches and fixes. Monitor IoT devices and systems for vulnerabilities and threats. Educate users about the risks and benefits of IoT devices and systems.

Establish clear accountability frameworks. Define the roles and responsibilities of all stakeholders involved in IoT devices and systems. Establish clear rules and guidelines for the development, deployment, and use of IoT devices and systems. Ensure that IoT devices and systems are compliant with relevant laws and regulations. Provide mechanisms for reporting, investigating, and resolving ethical issues or disputes.

Promote sustainability goals. Design IoT devices and systems with sustainability in mind from the start. Use renewable or low-carbon energy sources. Reduce waste and emissions. Optimize resource efficiency. Encourage reuse or recycling of IoT devices and systems.

By following these best practices, we can ensure that IoT devices and systems are ethical, trustworthy, and beneficial for society.

CHAPTER 9 WORKSHOP: IOT SECURITY & PRIVACY

The Internet of Things (IoT) is the network of physical devices, sensors, and software that can collect, process, and exchange data over the internet. IoT has many applications and benefits, such as smart homes, health care, agriculture, and transportation. However, IoT also poses significant challenges and risks for security and privacy. In this workshop, we will explore some of these issues and how to address them.

EXERCISE 1: IOT SECURITY & PRIVACY

In this exercise, you will work in groups of four to identify and analyse the security and privacy risks of a given IoT scenario. You will also propose some solutions or best practices to mitigate these risks. You will have 10 minutes to complete this exercise.

Scenario: Smart Home

Alice and Bob have a smart home system that controls their lights, thermostat, security cameras, door locks, and appliances. They can access and control their devices remotely using their smartphones or voice assistants. They also use a cloud service to store and analyse their data.

Questions:

- What are some of the security and privacy risks that Alice and Bob face in their smart home system?
- How could these risks affect them or others?
- What are some possible solutions or best practices to reduce these risks?

EXERCISE 2: BIOMETRIC DATA USAGE & PRIVACY

In this exercise, you will work in pairs to discuss the ethical and legal implications of biometric data usage and privacy. Biometric data is any data that can identify a person based on their physical or behavioural characteristics, such as fingerprints, facial recognition, iris scans, voice recognition, or gait analysis. Biometric data is widely used for authentication, identification, and access control in various domains, such as banking, health care, law enforcement, and education. You will have 10 minutes to complete this exercise.

Questions:

- What are some of the benefits and drawbacks of using biometric data for different purposes?
- What are some of the privacy concerns or risks associated with biometric data collection, storage, and sharing?
- What are some of the ethical principles or values that should guide the use of biometric data?
- What are some of the legal frameworks or regulations that govern the use of biometric data in your country or region?

EXERCISE 3: DATA LOCALIZATION & SOVEREIGNTY

In this exercise, you will work individually to research and present a case study on data localization and sovereignty. Data localization is the requirement that data collected or generated within a certain jurisdiction must be stored or processed within that jurisdiction. Data sovereignty is the concept that data is subject to the laws and regulations of the country or region where it is located. Data localization and sovereignty have implications for cross-border data flows, trade, security, privacy, and human rights. You will have 10 minutes to complete this exercise.

Questions:

- Choose a country or region that has implemented or proposed data localization or sovereignty laws or policies.
- What are the main objectives or motivations behind these laws or policies?
- What are the main challenges or consequences of these laws or policies for different stakeholders, such as businesses, consumers, governments, or civil society?
- How do these laws or policies align or conflict with international norms or agreements on data governance?

EXERCISE 4: IOT ETHICS & TRANSPARENCY

In this exercise, you will work in groups of three to design and evaluate an IoT device or system that incorporates ethical principles and transparency. Ethics is the study of right and wrong conduct in human affairs. Transparency is the quality of being open, honest, and accountable for one's actions and decisions. Ethics and transparency are important for building trust and responsibility in IoT systems. You will have 10 minutes to complete this exercise.

Questions:

1. Choose an IoT device or system that you would like to design or improve.
2. What are some of the ethical issues or dilemmas that your device or system may encounter or create?
3. How would you apply ethical principles or frameworks to guide your design decisions?
4. How would you ensure transparency in your device or system for users and other stakeholders?
5. How would you evaluate the ethical performance and impact of your device or system?

CONCLUDING REMARKS

In this book, we have explored the main concepts, challenges and best practices related to the governance, compliance, security, privacy, ethics and law of information technology (IT) in various contexts and domains.

We also discussed the impact of IT on society, culture, economy and environment, and the ethical responsibilities of IT professionals and users. Key points covered in each chapter:

CHAPTER 1: IT GOVERNANCE FRAMEWORKS

IT governance is the process of aligning IT strategy, objectives and resources with the organization's mission, vision and values.

IT governance frameworks provide guidance and standards for implementing and evaluating IT governance practices, such as COBIT, ITIL and ISO/IEC 38500.

IT compliance and regulatory standards are the rules and requirements that IT systems and processes must follow to ensure quality, security, privacy and accountability, such as GDPR, HIPAA and PCI DSS.

Data retention and deletion are the policies and procedures that determine how long and under what conditions data should be stored or erased from IT systems.

CHAPTER 2: CYBERSECURITY & DATA PROTECTION

Cybersecurity and data protection are the measures and practices that aim to protect IT systems and data from unauthorized access, use, disclosure, modification or destruction.

International data transfers and privacy are the issues and challenges related to the movement of data across borders and jurisdictions, such as data sovereignty, adequacy decisions and cross-border agreements.

Privacy by design and default are the principles and methods that ensure that privacy is embedded into the design and operation of IT systems and processes from the outset.

Surveillance and privacy are the trade-offs and conflicts between the use of IT for monitoring, tracking and controlling individuals or groups, and the respect for their rights and freedoms.

AI accountability and transparency are the concepts and mechanisms that ensure that AI systems are explainable, understandable, fair, reliable and responsible for their actions and outcomes.

Data breach notification and communication are the obligations and strategies that inform relevant parties about a data breach incident, its causes, consequences and remedies.

Cybersecurity training and ethical hacking are the educational and professional activities that aim to raise awareness, skills and knowledge about cybersecurity threats, risks and solutions.

CHAPTER 3: CLOUD COMPUTING & OUTSOURCING

Cloud computing and outsourcing are the models and practices that enable organizations to access IT resources and services from external providers over the internet.

Cloud computing and outsourcing offer benefits such as cost reduction, scalability, flexibility and innovation, but also pose challenges such as security, privacy, reliability, vendor lock-in and legal compliance.

CHAPTER 4: DIGITAL ETHICS & RESPONSIBLE AI

Digital ethics and responsible AI are the fields of study and practice that examine the moral values, principles and norms that guide the development, use and impact of IT in society.

Ethical AI and algorithm bias are the issues and challenges related to the fairness, justice, diversity and inclusion of AI systems and their effects on human dignity, autonomy and well-being.

Emerging technologies and ethical regulation are the opportunities and dilemmas posed by new and disruptive IT innovations, such as blockchain, quantum computing, biotechnology and nanotechnology, and their governance and oversight.

Whistleblower protection and digital ethics are the rights and responsibilities of individuals who expose wrongdoing, misconduct or malpractice in IT domains, such as Edward Snowden, Julian Assange and Chelsea Manning, and their legal and social implications.

Ethical considerations in AI art are the questions and debates about the creativity, originality, authenticity and ownership of AI-generated or AI-assisted artistic works, such as music, painting, poetry and literature.

CHAPTER 5: INTELLECTUAL PROPERTY & COPYRIGHT

Intellectual property and copyright are the legal rights and protections that grant owners or creators of IT-related works, such as software, data, images, videos and sounds, the exclusive control over their use, distribution and modification.

Digital rights management are the technologies and methods that enforce intellectual property rights in digital media, such as encryption, watermarking, licensing and authentication.

Open-source software licensing are the alternative models and practices that allow users to access, modify and share software code freely, such as GNU GPL, Apache License and MIT License.

CHAPTER 6: E-GOV & DIGITAL TRANSFORMATION

E-government and citizen engagement are the applications and initiatives that use IT to improve public services, democracy and participation, such as online voting, e-petitions, open data and civic tech.

Smart cities and ethical urbanization are the concepts and projects that use IT to enhance urban living, sustainability and resilience, such as smart mobility, smart energy, smart environment and smart governance.

Remote work and privacy are the trends and challenges related to the use of IT for working from home or anywhere, such as telecommuting, telework and digital nomads, and their implications for productivity, collaboration, security and work-life balance.

CHAPTER 7: IMPACT OF IT ON SOCIETY

Social media and online behaviour are the platforms and phenomena that enable online communication, interaction and expression, such as Facebook, Twitter, Instagram and TikTok, and their effects on social relationships, identity, culture and politics.

Technology for social good are the uses and contributions of IT for addressing social problems, inequalities and injustices, such as digital humanitarianism, social innovation, digital activism and digital citizenship.

Accessibility and inclusion are the principles and practices that ensure that IT is accessible, usable and beneficial for people with disabilities, special needs or diverse backgrounds, such as web accessibility standards, assistive technologies, universal design and inclusive design.

CHAPTER 8: EMPLOYEE IT USAGE & POLICIES

Employee IT usage and privacy are the rules and expectations that govern the use of IT by employees in the workplace, such as acceptable use policies, monitoring policies, BYOD policies and social media policies, and their impact on employee rights, responsibilities and satisfaction.

CHAPTER 9: IOT SECURITY & PRIVACY

IoT security and privacy are the measures and practices that aim to protect IoT devices, networks and data from unauthorized access, use, disclosure, modification or destruction.

Biometric data usage and privacy are the issues and challenges related to the collection, processing, storage and sharing of biometric data, such as fingerprints, facial recognition, iris scans and voice recognition, and their implications for identity, security and human rights.

Data localization and sovereignty are the policies and regulations that require data to be stored or processed within a specific geographic location or jurisdiction, such as China, Russia and India, and their motivations and consequences for global data flows, trade and innovation.

IoT ethics and transparency are the concepts and mechanisms that ensure that IoT systems are ethical, trustworthy, accountable and transparent for their users and stakeholders, such as ethical IoT frameworks, IoT certification schemes and IoT user rights.

We hope that this book has provided you with a comprehensive overview of the main topics and issues in IT Governance, Policy, Ethics and Law. We also hope that it has inspired you to think critically and creatively about the ethical and legal implications of IT in your personal and professional lives. We encourage you to keep learning and exploring this fascinating and dynamic field, as IT continues to evolve and transform our world.

EXPANDED CONTENTS LIST